**Neoclassical and 19th Century Archit**

Robin Middleton / David Watkin

# Neoclassical and 19th Century Architecture/1

## The Enlightenment in France and in England

Electa / Rizzoli New York

*Photographs: Bruno Balestrini*
*Drawings: Studio Lodolo-Süss*
*Layout: Arturo Anzani*

**Library of Congress Cataloging-in-Publication Data**

Middleton, Robin.
Neoclassical and 19th century architecture.
(History of world architecture)
Translation of Architettura moderna.
Bibliography: p.
Includes index.
Contents: v. 1. The enlightenment in France and in England—v. 2. The diffusion and development of classicism and the Gothic revival.
1. Neoclassicism (Architecture) 2. Architecture, Modern—17th-18th centuries. 3. Architecture, Modern—19th century. I. Watkin, David, 1941— II. Title. III. Title: Neoclassical and nineteenth century architecture. IV series.
NA600.M513 1987 724 87-42631
ISBN 0-8478-0850-5 (pbk.: v. 1)
ISBN 0-8478-0851-3 (pbk.: v. 2)

Reprinted, 1993


Paperback edition first published
in the United States of America in 1987
by Rizzoli International Publications, Inc.
300 Park Avenue South, New York, NY 10010



This volume is the redesigned paperback
of the original Italian edition published in 1977
by Electa S.p.A., Milan,
and the English edition published in 1980
by Harry N. Abrams, Inc., New York

Printed in Italy

TABLE OF CONTENTS

*The chronological span of this book is 1750 to 1870. We have avoided reliance on the misleading descriptive term* neoclassicism *and have emphasized the importance of both the rationalist theory developed in France and the Picturesque movement in England. The book is primarily a history of architecture and thus does not cover many of the important developments that took place during the years in question in town planning, transport, and engineering. We also felt it impossible, in a single volume, to give equal attention to each period and country. Thus, the reader will find less on England than on France, for English architecture has been examined by such historians as John Summerson, Henry-Russell Hitchcock, and Nikolaus Pevsner, whereas French architecture—particularly of the nineteenth century—has been much less extensively investigated. Architecture rests on intellectual as well as material foundations, and we hope that fresh light will be shed on the period by our emphasis on the theories and ideas that so often lay behind the new movements.*

Robin Middleton
David Watkin

Chapter One
# THE RATIONAL TRADITION IN FRANCE

The architecture of the eighteenth and nineteenth centuries was conditioned largely by two traditions of thought, the French rationalist tradition emerging from a Cartesian delight in clarity and mathematical certainty, and the English or rather British Empirical tradition that was to suggest another system of ordering, ultimately to be popularized as the Picturesque. The two phenomena were quite distinct and were independently developed, though by the late eighteenth century their particular qualities were clear enough for them to be taken up and adapted to new situations. The impact of Marc-Antoine Laugier's somewhat simplistic rationale of architecture, the primitive hut, was felt throughout Europe, in England no less than in Italy and Germany, while that particular expression of the Picturesque, the *jardin anglais,* was to taken up not only in Italy and Germany and the outer states of Europe but in the home of rational enlightenment itself—not that the French ever understood the subtleties of Picturesque composition or grappled long with the problems. Likewise, the geometrical ordering principles evolved by Jean-Nicolas-Louis Durand at the turn of the century were to be adopted by architects throughout Europe, but in England with noticeably less enthusiasm and effect than anywhere else. But the rational interpretation of Gothic that the French had evolved from the sixteenth century onward was to be introduced into England in the early nineteenth century by A. W. N. Pugin with the most profound and dramatic results. Even John Ruskin, that man of sensitivity and feeling who cared little enough for the way in which a building was organized or the techniques of its construction, was conditioned to the deepest respect for the rigidly deterministic analyses of Gothic made by the Frenchman Eugène-Emmanuel Viollet-le-Duc.

There was thus much exchange of thought and opinion and no little interaction of opposed ideas, but the main development of the two traditions of thought remained separate and distinct, and they are best dealt with independently.

The French rationalist ideal demands the first attention, for it provided the framework of thought for the whole of the Enlightenment. The beginnings, for our purposes, lie in the works of Claude Perrault (1613-1688), a doctor, anatomist, and experimenter in all kinds of devices, mostly mechanical, who turned unaccountably to architecture when he was already over fifty. His chief architectural works were the Observatoire in the Faubourg Saint-Jacques, Paris, a decidedly gaunt and singular building, dating from 1667 to 1672; the east facade of the Louvre, begun in the same year and more or less completed by 1674; and a triumphal arch for the Porte Saint-Antoine, also in Paris, designed in 1668 (started at once, mocked up in lath and plaster, which deteriorated, it was torn down in 1716). The key work is the Louvre facade, which may or may not be Perrault's own composition. It was the outcome of a combined effort by a committee composed of Louis Le Vau, *Premier Architecte du Roi;* Charles Le Brun, *Premier Peintre du Roi;* Perrault himself; and his brother, Charles, who acted as secretary and stand-in for his master, Jean Baptiste Colbert, the king's chief adviser. Claude Perrault's contribution has often been called in question, first by Nicolas Boileau soon after his death, but those who saw the relevant documents and drawings before they were destroyed in the fire at the Hôtel de Ville in 1870 found no evidence to dispute his claim to authorship.

The whole enterprise was an occasion, almost, of national importance. Le Vau had done the first project, but this was little admired by Colbert, who submitted it to the judgment of an array of Italian architects, among them the great Bernini, who was induced to journey to Paris to undertake the design himself. The pope's release of his favorite architect was a triumph for French diplomacy. But having gotten Bernini to Paris, they feared that national prestige might suffer should an Italian complete the royal palace. Bernini's robust, grandiose designs were not, in any case, to French taste. He was sent home, richly rewarded with gold but enraged. Instead, the committee set up by Colbert built the majestic, calm, and rhythmical facade that stands today and that has been regarded always as a model of excellence by architects and connoisseurs of French architecture. Le Corbusier himself found it in him to admire it. Its particular qualities may seem to us negative rather than positive, but they have nonetheless been potent influences. There is very little emphasis in the facade. The traditional French composition of a central feature with outlying pavilions is still in evidence, but there is scarcely a break in the plan, scarcely a break in the outline. The composition is neat and rectangular. The pediment in the center is low and unobtrusive. The essence of the architecture seems to reside in the rows of coupled freestanding columns that link the main elements, a curious paradox but one that evidently embodied Perrault's intentions. He aimed that the column should resume its antique role as a supporting element, thus constituting the architecture and no longer appearing as an applied decorative device. This clear and honest expression of the role and the form of the main elements in the architecture was a quality he thought to discern not only in ancient Greek temples but also, it may be surprising to learn, in Gothic cathedrals. He defended his arrangement of columns on the Louvre facade with reference to the clustered shafts of Notre-Dame in Paris.

In consciously renewing the French tradition by a return to sources, he referred thus to both classical and national prototypes. But he pleaded for no simpleminded return to the past. He was trained as a doctor and a scientist and took it for granted that the contemporary endeavor would be in advance of that of the past. He looked to the past only as a point of departure in the establishment of principles. His most earnest achievement in this respect was the translation of the ten books of architecture ascribed to Vitruvius, the only architectural treatise to survive from antiquity. This was another venture abetted by Colbert. Jean Martin and Jean Goujon had published a French translation in 1547, but the text was unsatisfactory and the plates were culled for the most part from earlier Italian editions. Perrault's professional grounding in Latin and Greek stood him in good

*1. Claude Perrault, Observatoire, Paris, 1667-72*

stead. In 1673 he issued the first edition of his scholarly and altogether competent text. It was not an antiquarian exercise but rather a polemical work. It was illustrated with magnificent plates—the finest by Sébastien Le Clerc, who was later to attempt an architectural treatise on his own account—featuring all of Perrault's own works and an array of suggested reconstructions of antique buildings intended to set a new standard for contemporary architecture. The forms are precisely defined and rectangular; freestanding columns are in evidence everywhere. A revised edition appeared in 1684 with a great many footnotes that make more clear Perrault's theoretical standpoint, though this had been expressed clearly enough the year before in his *Ordonnance des cinq espèces de colonnes selon la méthode des anciens.* This was, as the name implies, largely concerned with the orders. But in it Perrault was to introduce his theory of beauty that served to shatter the Renaissance and post-Renaissance belief in the transcendental role of the orders. There were, Perrault declared, two types of beauty in architecture, positive and arbitrary. Positive beauty was based quite simply on the quality of materials, on precision and neatness of execution, on size, on sheer magnificence, and on symmetry—values that must have seemed obvious enough in the reign of Louis XIV. Arbitrary beauty resided in such qualities as proportional relationships, form, and shape. It was in his ability to manipulate these and compose his designs that the real talent of the architect rested. For there were no sure guides, no fixed rules, only custom. Perrault rejected quite rudely the idea that there was an absolute criterion for architectural proportions. The architectural proportions derived from the orders, he said, were not related to the scale of musical harmonies as was commonly thought; they were in no sense a feature of a divine or universal order; they were simply a matter of custom. The cultivated eye had grown used to certain proportions and was thus shocked by any departure from the norm. Perrault himself respected the norm—like Descartes and even Pascal he upheld an ideal of "médiocrité." He thus determined to investigate the welter of proportional systems that had been proposed by theorists from the Renaissance onward and to find a workable mean. Antoine Desgodets's carefully measured drawings of forty-nine buildings in Rome, to be published in 1682 as *Les édifices antiques de Rome,* confirmed his belief that there was no consistency in antique proportions. His own system was based on a single module, readily applicable to all parts of each of the five orders.

Perrault does not appear to have been a member of the Académie Royale d'Architecture that Colbert established in 1671—one year after Le Vau's death—but he nonetheless attended some of its meetings and proposed that the Académie take up his system of proportioning and adopt it as its own. The members were shocked by his rude disregard for the Renaissance system of belief and were confused, moreover, by his suggestion that a new set of rules be substituted for the old. They did not grasp clearly his determination, like that of Colbert in all his undertakings, to establish a

*2. Claude Perrault and others, east facade of the Louvre, Paris, 1667-74*

*3. Frontispiece of Claude Perrault's translation of Vitruvius, 1673. Represented are three of Perrault's works; in the background, the Observatoire; in the middleground, the east facade of the Louvre, to the left, the triumphal arch for the Porte Sainte-Antoine (now the Place de la Nation)*

common and sensible working standard. To what extent Perrault's system was adopted is impossible to judge until the buildings of the period have been measured. We can be sure, though, that his published works were widely read. He was staunchly upheld during the eighteenth century by that most respected, and indeed academic, of teachers, Jacques-François Blondel (1705-1774). In England his architectural works had been translated and issued by the end of the first decade of the century, and, perhaps more significant, they were embodied in Isaac Ware's *Complete Body of Architecture* in 1756.

Though he offered a more reticent and rational architecture as a model and radically reinterpreted and reassessed accepted assumptions, it is clear that Perrault did not provide a coherent body of theory. His commonsensical approach, however, was to be followed up and rendered more useful in two small books published early in the eighteenth century, Michel de Frémin's *Mémoires critiques d'architecture,* of 1702, and Jean-Louis de Cordemoy's *Nouveau traité de toute l'architecture; ou, l'art de bastir: utile aux entrepreneurs et aux ouvriers,* of 1706. Neither if these men was an architect. Frémin appears to have been a tax collector; Cordemoy (1631-1713) was settled in the church, a cousin, or brother even, of Gerauld de Cordemoy, upholder of Descartes, author of that pioneering study of language the *Discours physique de la parole,* of 1668. Frémin's book is a plea for a reasoned approach to design, expressing a concern for the restrictions imposed by the site, the qualities of materials, the cost, and the needs of the client. The orders and the classical measures were of no real importance in architecture, he said, and in demonstrating his convictions he compared St.-Eustache and Le Vau's church of St.-Sulpice with Notre-Dame and the Ste.-Chapelle and concluded forcefully that the Gothic buildings were more rationally designed and thus preferable as architecture. This sympathy for Gothic arrangements and, in particular, structural manipulations is a feature also of Cordemoy's treatise, though the latter was intent to show that the qualities he admired in Gothic architecture could be interpreted in classical terms. Cordemoy required an architecture that was made up of rectangular forms, largely unadorned, with plain masonry walls or series of columns supporting lintels. He disliked arches and all acute angles, including those of the classical pediment. The ancien, he said, would have preferred the mansard roof to the pitched roof, had they known it, because it more nearly approximated to the rectangle. He proposed a model church with freestanding columns between the nave and aisles, supporting horizontal entablatures (absolutely not arches, he insisted) and, above, a barrel vault. For the west front he suggested a portico of columns with a balustrade over them, not unlike that built many years before by Inigo Jones at St. Paul's in London. He was consciously emulating both Gothic and, he fancied, Early Christian and Greek models. The structural supports, indeed, the whole structural system, were to be expressed and made evident so as to constitute the architecture, as in pre-Renaissance times. He wanted a trabeated architecture. Michelangelo's

*4. Claude Perrault and others, east facade of the Louvre, Paris, detail of the colonnade, 1667-74*

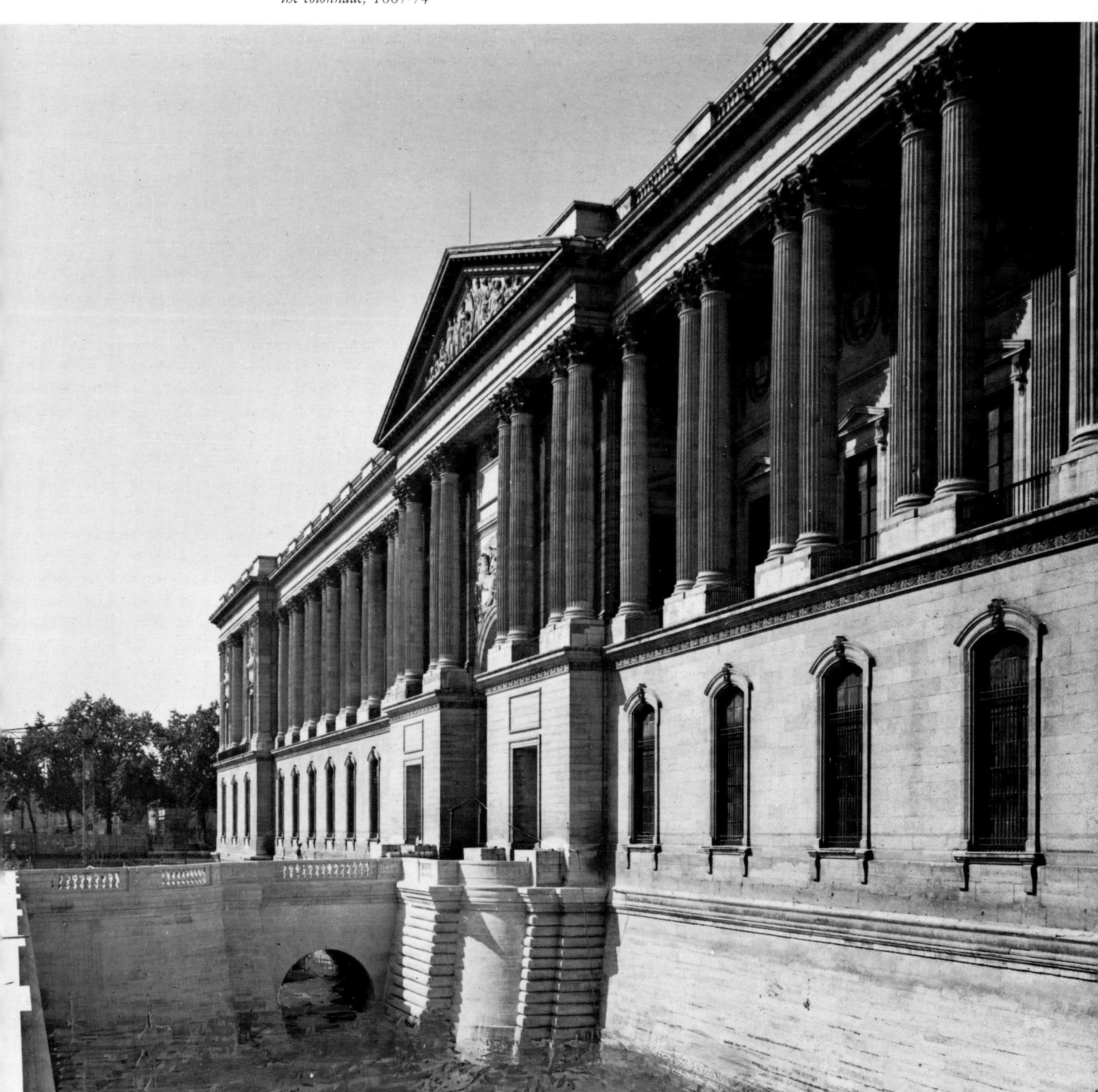

5. *Philibert de l'Orme, structural frame of a Gothic vault illustrated in his* Architecture, *1567*

150 VITRUVE

La hauteur des Colonnes des Basiliques sera égale à la largeur, des Portiques, & cette largeur sera de la troisiéme partie de l'espace du milieu. Les colonnes d'enhaut doivent être

portion des Basiliques de la ville de Chalcis : mais la construction du texte ne peut souffrir cette interpretation.

Comme je ne trouve aucune de toutes ces interpretations differentes qui me satisfasse, j'en forme une nouvelle, que je fonde sur les autoritez des plus anciens Interpretes de ce mot : & estant assuré par le témoignage d'Ausone, que *chalcidica* estoit un lieu élevé que nous appellons un premier étage, & par le témoignage d'Arnobe, que *chalcidica* estoit un lieu ample & magnifique, j'estime que ces Chalcidiques estoient de grandes & magnifiques salles où on rendoit la justice, situées aux bouts des Basiliques de plain-pié avec les galleries par lesquelles on alloit d'une salle à l'autre, & où les Plaideurs se promenoient, car ces Galleries hautes sans ces Salles semblent estre inutiles. Suivant cette interpretation, lorsque Vitruve dit que s'il y a assez de place pour faire une Basilique fort longue, on fera des Chalcidiques aux deux bouts, il faut entendre que si elle est courte, on ne fera qu'une Salle à un des bouts, ou que si l'on en fait à chaque bout, elles seront trop petites pour pouvoir estre appellées Chalcidiques, dont le nom signifie une grandeur & une magnificence extraordinaire. Palladio semble l'avoir entendu autrement, parce que dans la figure qu'il a faite de la Basilique, il luy a donné beaucoup moins de longueur que le double de sa largeur, peut-estre parce que n'ayant pû se determiner à ce qu'il devoit entendre par Chalcidique, & par cette raison n'en voulant point faire aux bouts de sa Basilique, il l'a faite plus courte, pour faire entendre qu'il croyoit que les Basiliques qui estoient sans Chalcidiques n'avoient pas la proportion que Vitruve leur donne en general.

7 DES PORTIQUES. Il faut entendre par Portiques les ailes qui sont aux costez de la grande voute du milieu, & que l'on appelle bas costez dans les Eglises.

6. *Interior perspective of a basilica, illustrated in Claude Perrault's translation of Vitruvius, 1673. Engraved by Sébastian Le Clerc.*

plus petites que celles C
d'embas, comme il a esté dit.[8] La cloison qui est entre les colonnes d'enhaut ne doit avoir de hauteur que les trois quarts de ces mesmes colonnes, afin que ceux qui se promenent sur cette

8. La cloison. Vitruve met icy *Pluteum* pour *Pluteus*, ainsi qu'il fait en plusieurs autres endroits. Philander & Barbaro ont pris ce *Pluteum* ou *Pluteus* pour l'espace qui est entre les colonnes d'embas & celles d'enhaut, & ils ont crû que Vitruve ayant dit *Spatium quod est inter superiores columnas*, il falloit suppléer *& inferiores*, mais il n'est parlé dans le texte que de la *cloison qui est entre les colomnes d'enhaut*, ce qui peut avoir un fort bon sens, pourveu qu'on entende que Vitruve a conçû que cette cloison qui étoit comme un piedestail continu sous toutes les colonnes d'enhaut, ne devoit passer pour cloison qu'à l'endroit qui répondoit entre les colonnes : parce que l'endroit de ce piedestail continu qui estoit immediatement sous les colonnes, devoit estre pris pour leur piedestail. Il est plus amplement prouvé sur le 7. chapitre de ce Livre, que *Pluteus* ne sçauroit signifier icy que Cloison, Balustrade ou Appuy.

## EXPLICATION DE LA PLANCHE XXXVIII.

*Cette Planche contient l'élevation perspective de la Basilique. Il faut entendre que de mesme que l'on a fait servir un seul Plan pour les deux étages de la Basilique ; on n'a aussi mis icy qu'une partie de son élevation, supposant que l'on comprendra aisément que ce qui est icy ne represente qu'environ un quart de tout l'Edifice, representé dans le plan par ce qui est renfermé dans des lignes ponctuées.*

*7. Claude and Charles Perrault, project for Ste.-Geneviève, Paris, c. 1680*

work at St. Peter's, Rome, was to be dismissed in the second edition of the *Nouveau traité,* published in 1714, though Bernini's colonnade on the piazza was to be admired. The real source of inspiration for Cordemoy's model church, however, was a design made about 1680 by Claude and Charles Perrault for the new church of Ste.-Geneviève in Paris. Freestanding columns line the long nave, carrying a horizontal entablature with a curved vault above. There was at that time no church like this, though the genesis of the arrangement can be traced back to the plan of an entranceway in Fra Giocondo's edition of Vitruvius, of 1511, and then to the work of Raphael and his pupils on the entrance of the Palazzo Farnese and its imitation in France by Le Vau, on the south side of the Louvre. An antique precedent was concocted also at this time by the engraver Jean Marot, who inaccurately illustrated the interior of the Temple of Bacchus at Baalbek in this form, perhaps at the behest of the Perraults. It was Charles Perrault who, as Colbert's secretary, was responsible for issuing instructions and payments to travelers to the east who went in search, for the most part, of manuscripts for Colbert's collections. Claude Perrault himself acknowledged the use of some drawings done by one such traveler, M. de Monceaux, who was to visit Baalbek in 1668; however, it is possible that the reconstruction was based on the observations of Balthasar de Monconys, who was there in 1647.

But even as Cordemoy was writing, a church was being put up in France that embodied some of the qualities he demanded—the royal chapel at Versailles. Once again, Claude Perrault appears to have been involved in the early design, though the building begun in 1698 is generally attributed to Jules Hardouin Mansart, with Robert de Cotte responsible for its completion. The lower level of the chapel has heavy piers and arcades between the nave and aisles, but at the upper level, from which the king was to follow the service, there are majestic, widely spaced Corinthian columns with a horizontal entablature and vault above. The details are all classical, but the effect is of the spacious Gothic kind, with flying buttresses outside to confirm the hybrid basis of the inspiration.

The play of Gothic that is so curious a part of the architectural theory of Perrault, Frémin, and Cordemoy requires, perhaps, further explanation. It was not an isolated and idiosyncratic excursion into thought, but part of a long-standing French tradition, upheld, as a rule, by adventurous thinkers. Gilles Corrozet, a humanist scholar, translator of the works of Leon Battista Alberti and Trissino (Palladio's patron), and author of one of the first guidebooks to Paris, issued first in 1532, chose, surprisingly, to study Gothic buildings and to praise their manner of construction. His lead was taken up, in the years that followed, by other such authors, many of them associated with the Benedictine congregation of St.-Maur, the founders of French historical study. Terms such as "hardiesse," "légèreté," and "délicatesse" are invariably encountered in descriptions of Gothic buildings in these popular guidebooks or histories—of which there were many. In the more restricted field of architectural theory there was a similar emphasis on the structural finesse of Gothic architecture. Philibert de l'Orme, who thought of himself as the first architect to introduce classical refinements into France, nevertheless described and illustrated the construction of a Gothic vault in his *Architecture,* of 1567. And it is evident that he thought of the columns and ribs as an independent and clearly expressed structural scaffold supporting the webs of the vault above. This separation of the structural features from the enclosing elements was to assume great importance in the years to come. François Derand, the Jesuit mathematician and architect, author of *L'architecture des voûtes; ou, l'art des traits et coupe des voûtes,* a standard work on building construction published first in 1643, but issued again in 1743 and yet again in 1755, emphasized not only the structural elegance of the Gothic columns and ribs but also the role of the flying buttress and the outer buttress. He saw Gothic architecture as the solution to a problem in equilibrium.

*8. Jean Marot, reconstruction of the Temple of Bacchus at Baalbek, c. 1680, based on plans made at the site by either M. de Monceaux or Balthasar de Monconys*

*9, 10. Jules Hardouin Mansart and Robert de Cotte, Royal Chapel, Versailles, interior, 1698–1710*

A great deal more evidence could be adduced to show the vitality of this tradition of thought in France, in particular, the works of Amédée-François Frézier (1682-1773), who, in a lively exchange of letters in the *Mémoires de Trévoux* early in the eighteenth century, was to disparage Cordemoy's conception of a trabeated architecture, noting correctly that with the small stones available in France it was sounder to put arches rather than lintels over columns. Frézier attacked Cordemoy on many other points, but he proved himself equally sympathetic as an interpreter of Gothic, and far more knowledgeable than his predecessors. In his *Théorie et pratique de la coupe des pierres et des bois pour la construction des voûtes...; ou, traité de stéréotomie à l'usage de l'architecture,* published first between 1738 and 1739, he described Gothic architecture as a precisely calculated affair, dependent on a carefully worked out system of vaulting. And he extended the usual structural analysis to show that the webs of the vaults were particularly light and strong because they were slightly concave. His analysis was more subtle and penetrating than any yet made. He was not, however, an admirer of Gothic architecture. Like most interested Frenchmen he intended to analyze Gothic architecture and to infuse its principles of organization and construction, not its forms, into contemporary building. The detailed study of Gothic in France was thus in no way a preliminary to a revival of the style, though it is noteworthy that the Benedictines of the congregation of St.-Maur did uphold the Gothic style as such: St.-Wandrille, for example, was constructed in the Gothic manner between 1636 and 1656, and at their center, St.-Germain-des-Prés, in Paris, the Benedictines introduced Gothic vaults of stone over the nave and transepts, in 1644. When they came to build the west front of St.-Pierre at Corbie, in the first decade of the eighteenth century, they substituted a design in the Gothic mode for the proposed classical facade that was submitted earlier, a decision parallel to that made at the same time for the west front of Orléans cathedral, where the king, possibly under the influence of the Maurist scholar Bernard de Montfaucon, demanded that "l'ordre gothique" be adhered to. These, though, may all be interpreted as examples of Gothic survival.

More problematical and far more challenging was the design prepared in 1718 by the master mason of Orléans cathedral, Guillaume Hénault, for a Maurist chapel in the same town. For the interior he adapted the chapel at Versailles, for the exterior he provided a Gothic pastiche, complete with pointed windows, finials, and flying buttresses. This was not built. And nothing like it was to be designed in France until the end of the century, when the introduction of a playful Gothic mode in garden architecture resulted in something of a Gothic revival. But this was an English intrusion.

Cordemoy's ideas were not to be taken up immediately in France; the columnar screen around the forecourt of Pierre-Alexis Delamair's Hôtel de Soubise, of 1705-9, may owe something to his suggestions, as may the columnar episodes that appear so frequently in Germain Boffrand's early works, but only the chapel that Boffrand designed for the château at

Slavia

*11. St.-Pierre, Corbie, west facade, begun, c. 1706*

*12. Guillaume Hénault, design for Notre-Dame-de-Bonne-Nouvelle, Orléans, 1718, a chapel for a Benedictine Congregation of St.-Maur, 1718*

Lunéville in 1709—to be completed several years later—demonstrably fulfilled Cordemoy's program. The first architect to develop Cordemoy's ideas with any real consistency was the Parisian Pierre Contant d'Ivry (1698-1777), who designed the church of St.-Vasnon at Condé-sur-l'Escaut, in 1751, and that of St.-Vaast at Arras a year or two later, both with freestanding columns supporting horizontal lintels of stone and, above, barrel vaults. But by then another propagandist and interpreter of the ideas of both Perrault and Cordemoy had emerged, the Abbé Marc-Antoine Laugier (1713-1769). His starting manifesto, the *Essai sur l'architecture,* was first issued anonymously in 1753.

Laugier dutifully paid his respects to Perrault, praising highly the Louvre facade—though he noted that it would have been improved if the central pediment had not broken the line of the balustrade—and was careful to acknowledge his debt to Cordemoy, but he was more radical than either of his predecessors. In his determination to purge and invigorate the tradition of architecture by a return to sources, he was led to entertain the idea that the basis of all architecture should be envisaged as the rustic hut, a hut stark and almost natural in its forms. It consisted of four tree trunks, still growing, as supports, with logs as lintels, and smaller branches above making up a pitched roof. This was to be illustrated as the frontispiece in the second edition of the *Essai,* in 1755. The concept was not new. Commentators of Vitruvius, including Perrault, had illustrated the origins of architecture in the guise of the rustic hut, but none had proposed that it be taken as the model of excellence in architecture. The essential elements in architecture, in Laugier's analogy, were, thus, the freestanding column, acting as a support, the attendant lintel, as a beam, and the pediment, as an expression of the pitched roof. Everything else was to be regarded as secondary. The rich heritage of Renaissance forms and ornamentation was to be disregarded. Inevitably, for practical design purposes, walls were to be provided, doors and windows accepted. But there was to be nothing superfluous to necessity.

Laugier's ideal, as may be imagined, was best adapted to the design of churches, and, like Cordemoy, he proposed one made up with single or coupled freestanding columns in one or two tiers along the aisles, all supporting horizontal entablatures without cornices, and a barrel vault above. As before, the arrangement was related to both the temples of ancient Greece and the cathedrals of Gothic France. But Laugier's moving descriptions of the interior of Notre-Dame show that new emotions, new feelings, had come into play. He admired the lightness and the structural strength of Gothic architecture and hoped to incorporate these qualities into contemporary design in the most rational way possible. But he was susceptible also to those more intangible qualities of mystery and sublime grandeur of the Gothic. That he was influenced by these tastes beyond the bounds of restraint usually accepted in France was particularly evident in 1765, when he published his *Observations sur l'architecture.* Therein he

*13. Frontispiece of the second edition of Marc-Antoine Laugier's* Essai sur l'architecture, *1755. The muse points to the primitive hut, the foundation of all architectural form*

proposed churches no longer based on Latin- or Greek-cross plans, but of a variety of shapes, ordered internally with soaring columns bursting at their tops into formalized palm fronds and an array of richly decorated vaults. Gone were the lintels and entablatures, gone were the classical measures, though for the exterior, he insisted, classical forms were to be retained. But for domestic architecture, he suggested, Gothic effects might be conjured up externally by introducing turrets and broken roof lines. In compensation, perhaps, the ideal system of proportioning that he proposed in the *Observations* was more limited and restrictive than ever before. The ideal ratio was 1:1; the best figure the square; the best volume the cube. Not surprisingly, his second book was regarded as quirky and highly idiosyncratic. His first book, however, was acclaimed and eagerly read throughout Europe; it was considered a revolutionary tract.

The first major building that might be seen as an illustration of Laugier's ideal, and one that Laugier himself was to praise as "le premier modèle de la perfaite architecture, le véritable chef-d'oeuvre de l'architecture française" ("Discours sur le rétablissement de l'architecture antique," Lyons, Académie des Sciences, MS 194), was the church of Ste.-Geneviève, now known as the Panthéon. The architect was Jacques-Germain Soufflot (1713-1780). Soufflot had been to Rome as a young man and had spent seven years there, from 1731 to 1738, during which time he measured St. Peter's and other Italian churches, including the Milan cathedral. He then returned to his native Burgundy, settling in Lyons, where he was to build the great Hôtel-Dieu, a grand if unlovely building, stretching over two hundred fifty meters (eight hundred twenty feet) along the banks of the Rhône. The prestige it brought him prompted Mme. de Pompadour to select him as companion to her brother, soon to become the Marquis de Vandières (later the Marquis de Marigny), on his grand tour of Italy, in preparation for the young man's assumption of the position of *Directeur Général des Bâtiments.* Their journey was begun in December 1749; by February 1751 Soufflot was back in Lyons. But in the following year he was installed in an apartment in the Louvre and in January 1755 was made *Contrôleur des Bâtiments du Roi au Département de Paris* and commissioned to design the church of Ste.-Geneviève. This was intended to initiate a new departure in architecture. The plan was a Greek cross, to which Soufflot was forced by the clergy to add two bays and flanking towers at the east end, making the geometry less pure. Inside, the nave and aisles were divided by rows of giant Corinthian columns, supporting a continuous entablature from which sprang an array of lightly constructed and cut-away vaults and domes. The spatial elegance of the whole was extraordinary. But even more extraordinary was the structural finesse of the whole undertaking. "Le principal objet de M. Soufflot en bâtissant son église," his pupil Maximilien Brebion wrote later, "a été de réunir, sous une des plus belles formes, la légèreté de la construction des églises gothiques avec la pureté et la magnificence de l'architecture grecque" (Brebion to Ch. Cl. de Flahaut de la Billarderie, Comte d'Angiviller, October 20, 1780, Paris, Archives Nationales, O[1] 1694-[43]).

During the long period of construction, Soufflot and his friends the engineer Jean-Rodolphe Perronet (1708-1794), *Inspecteur Général des Ponts et Chaussées,* and founder in 1747 of the École des Ponts et Chaussées, and his pupil Émiliand-Marie Gauthey (1732-1808), scoured France for stones, building machines to test their compressive strengths in a laboratory set up in the Louvre, coordinating and interpreting their results, and arriving at formulas and equations that they applied to the design of Ste.-Geneviève. They continued to refine the structure and whittle away the masonry mass but were forced to justify their procedures to the members of the Académie, particularly when the main piers were found to be cracking. They might be said to have mounted a campaign, presenting drawings of a whole range of lightly constructed churches for inspection: S. Agostino in Piacenza, the Cappella della SS. Sindone in Turin, S. Maria della Salute in Venice, and a number of French Gothic churches. The Gothic parallel remained of paramount importance in the justification of Ste.-Geneviève. Soufflot's pupil Jallier sent painstaking measured drawings of Notre-Dame in Dijon, in 1762, the first such drawings of a Gothic church to be made. Soufflot himself read a paper on Gothic architecture, chiefly on the proportional system involved, that he had delivered first to the Académie des Sciences in Lyons in 1741, when it was probably heard—or heard of—by Laugier, then at the Jesuit college there.

The discussion occasioned by the building of Ste.-Geneviève was of the highest importance in furthering theories of construction in France. Soufflot and his associates stressed the development of abstract theories based on experiment and mathematical calculation; their adversaries, chief among them the architect Pierre Patte (1723-1814), relied rather on empirical knowledge alone. But even Patte was to extend greatly the common understanding of structure, especially Gothic structure. He planned a treatise on this subject that he was never to finish, but when that great pedagogue Jacques-François Blondel died in 1774, Patte took over and completed the last two volumes of Blondel's *Cours d'architecture,* devoted to building materials and construction. These were issued in 1777. Blondel's *Cours d'architecture,* the issue of a lifetime's teaching—first at an independent school that he started in 1743, then from 1762 onward as an authorized professor of the Académie—served to consolidate and disseminate French doctrine at its most sound and most sensible. His judgements were always cautious and carefully explained. He could scarcely be thought intolerant, though he was not too adventurous. Tradition and reason conditioned all his attitudes. He did, however, take up the idea of designing churches with freestanding columns along their naves—but with arches above, as Frézier had shown that they were more sensible in France—and was fully aware of the Gothic sympathies thus involved, defending them in terms that were to be taken up by A. W. N. Pugin and the Ecclesiologists in nineteenth-

*14. Pierre Contant d'Ivry, St.-Vasnon, Condé-sur-l'Escaut, interior, 1751*

*15. Jacques-Germain Soufflot, Hôtel-Dieu, Lyons, facade and central feature, 1741–48*

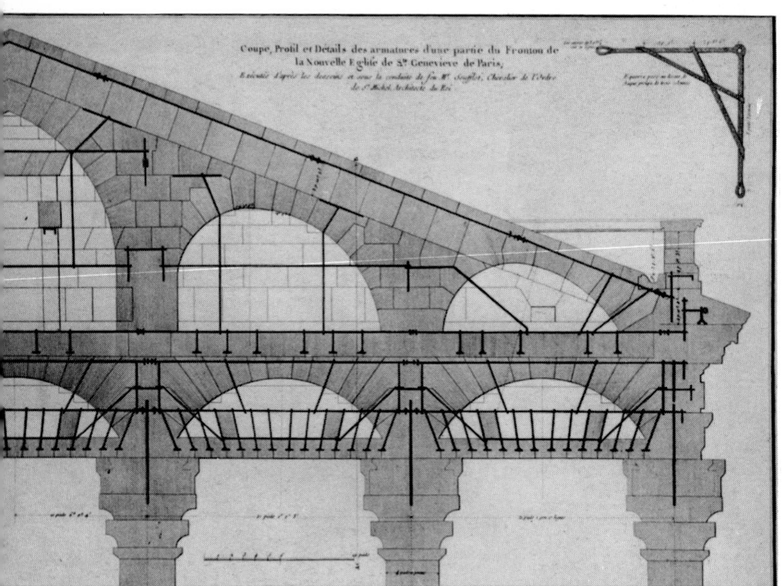


16. *Jacques-Germain Soufflot, Ste.-Geneviève, Paris, detail of the internal iron framework proposed for the pediment*

17. *Jacques-Germain Soufflot, final plan of Ste.-Geneviève, Paris. Engraved by F. N. Selliers*

18. *Jacques-Germain Soufflot, final design for Ste-Geneviève, Paris, after 1770. Engraved by G.-P. Dumont*

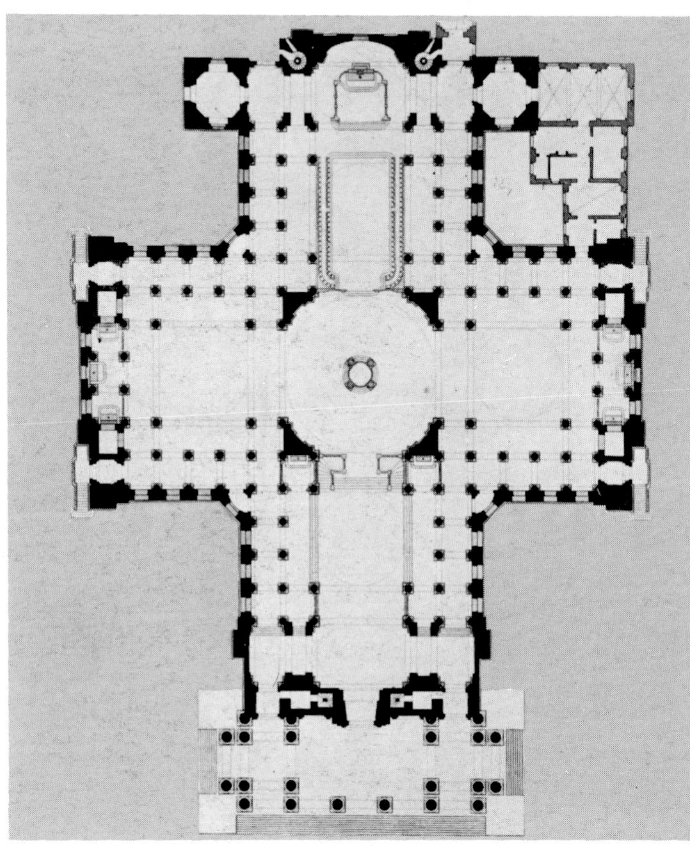

century England, on the grounds of religious tradition.

Blondel was in no sense a connoisseur of construction. "La magie de l'art," he wrote, "veut des bornes; trop de hardiesse étonne plus qu'elle ne satisfait" (*Cour,* vol. 4, p. 315). He lagged in completing the last two volumes of the *Cours* through lack of vital interest. But Patte had a long-sustained and inquisitive concern with the techniques of building. He had already written several memoirs on the subject, and he returned in the *Cours* to his attack on Soufflot's great church and to the intricacies of Gothic engineering.

To illustrate his text, Patte chose drawings of Notre-Dame in Dijon that Jallier had prepared for Soufflot, and, in analyzing the section, he showed that not only were the ribs of the vaults, the flying buttresses, and the outer buttresses essential structural features—nothing more—but so also were the finials, which acted as counterthrusts to the forces directed through the flying buttresses. He thought that even the timber trusses over the aisles were designed as buttresses. His ingenuity in isolating what he recognized as the Gothic principle never deserted him. He discerned it even in the Augustinian church at Lille, where iron tie-rods rather than buttresses were used to restrain the thrust of the vaults. Whatever their basic disagreements, like Soufflot he sought an architecture that was altogether economical and honest in its expression.

Something of this spirit, it should be noted, was developed independently in Venice, during the first half of the eighteenth century, by Carlo Lodoli (1690-1761). Lodoli was not an architect; he was a brilliant, radical polymath, a Franciscan friar, who started a small academy about 1720 for the sons of Venetian noblemen, teaching them languages, mathematics, law, and statesmanship for a few hours each day. He also taught them something of architecture, his favorite subject. He evolved no fully worked-out theory of architecture but some highly original notions, based in part on the experiments and mathematical theories of a succession of Scottish engineers active in Padua, among them James Gregory and James Stirling. Lodoli's ideas were to be recorded by two of his disciples, the fashionable gadabout Francesco Algarotti (1712-1764), whose ironical commentary, the *Saggio sopra l'architettura,* was to be published in 1757, and the more staid but dreadfully muddled Andrea Memmo (1729-1793), who did not start to write his account until 1784. It was published in two parts: the first, *Elementi dell'architettura Lodoliana; ossia, l'arte del fabbricare con solidità scientifica e con eleganza non capricciosa,* in 1786, reprinted together with the second in 1833 and 1834. It was once thought that Laugier—who published the *Histoire de la République de Venise* between 1759 and 1768, and is known to have been in Venice in 1757, and perhaps in 1752, to collect material for this work—was directly influenced by Lodoli when he came to write the *Essai sur l'architecture.* But this has been disproved. To judge by the references made to French architects and ideas in both Algarotti's and Memmo's accounts, the Venetian was strongly influenced rather by the works of

*19. Jacques-German Soufflot, Ste.-Geneviève, Paris, 1756–90.*

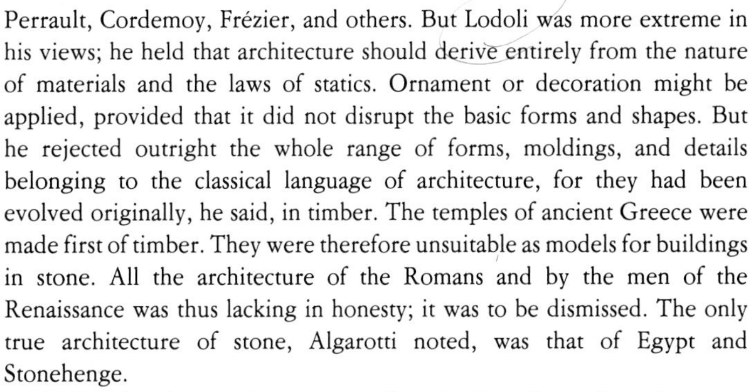

Perrault, Cordemoy, Frézier, and others. But Lodoli was more extreme in his views; he held that architecture should derive entirely from the nature of materials and the laws of statics. Ornament or decoration might be applied, provided that it did not disrupt the basic forms and shapes. But he rejected outright the whole range of forms, moldings, and details belonging to the classical language of architecture, for they had been evolved originally, he said, in timber. The temples of ancient Greece were made first of timber. They were therefore unsuitable as models for buildings in stone. All the architecture of the Romans and by the men of the Renaissance was thus lacking in honesty; it was to be dismissed. The only true architecture of stone, Algarotti noted, was that of Egypt and Stonehenge.

Neither the niceties of argument offered by Lodoli nor the refinements of structure proposed by Soufflot and his friends were to be greatly favored in late eighteenth-century France. Architects were no longer interested in structural elegance and lightness of form: they had learned by then to appreciate the strong sculptural qualities of the architecture of antiquity, Greek no less than Roman, and had begun to cherish in their own work large and simplified mass. Those uncomplicated proportional relationships that Laugier had so much admired had come into their own. The square and the cube had passed into favor, and with them the sphere. But whatever the mathematical certainties relied upon to produce this purified geometry, there was a delight in large-scale elementary forms for their visual effects alone. Explanations offered were often, as we shall see, of a sophisticated kind. Étienne-Louis Boullée (1728-1799), the greatest of the visionary architects, who had intended at first to pursue a career as a painter, saw embodied in the sphere all manner of marvelous qualities.

The irrational, emotive streak that appears in architectural theory in the late eighteenth century was no doubt conditioned by the complete break in building activity during the French Revolution, so that the practicalities of architecture could be set aside for a time in favor of the production of grand and ever more vast imaginative projects. But this tendency was evident even before 1789, when the less restrictive, sensational English attitudes toward beauty—and, in particular, Edmund Burke's concept of the Sublime—were introduced into France in the form of Picturesque gardening theory. The first significant book on the subject to appear in France was the translation and extension of Thomas Whately's *Observations on Modern Gardening,* itself the first coherent attempt to systematize Picturesque theory. This was issued in 1771, only a year after its publication in England. The translator was François de Paule Latapie, a protégé of Montesquieu, who is often credited with having laid out the earliest *jardin anglais* in France, at his estate at La Brède, soon after his return from England in 1750. No record or trace of this survives. A better-known and certainly more influential exemplar of the natural garden in something of an English manner was that begun soon after 1754 at Moulin-Joli near Bézons, by

20. *Jacques-Germain Soufflot, Ste.-Geneviève, Paris, detail of the vaults, 1756–90*

21. *Jacques-Germain Soufflot, Ste.-Geneviève, Paris, interior, 1756–90*

Claude-Henri Watelet, who was to record his experiences and all his intentions in his *Essai sur les jardins,* of 1774. This was intended as only a part of a general treatise on taste and beauty. Its influence was considerable. The fashion for Picturesque gardens in France dates from its publication. More important, it introduced a whole new range of ideas and notions into artistic theory. *Le génie de l'architecture; ou, l'analogie de cet art avec nos sensations,* issued in 1780 by Nicolas Le Camus de Mézières (1721-1789)—the architect of the great circular Halle aux Blés in Paris, who was to dedicate his work to Watelet—marks a new departure in French architectural thought. For the first time, a major part of an architectural treatise was devoted to the idea that architecture should be pleasing to the senses and that it should, in addition, induce elevating impressions on the spirit and soul. This heady, speculative venture was to be balanced in the second part of the book by a detailed discussion of the matter-of-fact problems of planning. In the following year Le Camus was to publish an even more practical manual on building construction, *Le guide de ceux qui veulent bâtir.* But it was his more rarefied notions that were to appeal to such architects as Boullée. Boullée virtually gave up building at this time and turned instead to that sublime abstract architecture of monuments without practical function, for which he is famous, and to the composition of his *Essai sur l'art.* A measure of how far he had moved from any acceptance of the standard French criteria for architectural excellence is evident in his opening lines: "Qu'est-ce que l'architecture? La définirai-je avec Vitruve l'art de bâtir? Non. Il y a dans cette définition une erreur grossière. Vitruve prend l'effet pour la cause. Il faut concevoir pour effectuer. Nos premiers pères n'ont bâti leurs cabanes qu'après en avoir conçu l'image. C'est cette production de l'esprit, c'est cette création qui constitue l'architecture, que nous pouvons, en conséquence, définir l'art de produire et de porter à la perfection tout édifice quelconque. L'art de bâtir n'est donc qu'un art secondaire, qu'il nous paraît convenable de nominer la partie scientifique de l'architecture" (J. M. Pérouse de Montclos, ed., *E. L. Boullée: Architecture, essai sur l'art,* 1968, p. 49).

There is nothing in his essay on that scientific aspect of architecture, nothing on those practical, rational notions that had occupied architectural theorists in France from Perrault onward, though there was a great deal on Perrault's proposition that beauty be regarded as both positive and arbitrary, with interest directed in particular to the arbitrary, fantastical forms. Not that Boullée's architecture was ever wayward or disorderly. Though he and most of his contemporaries were sympathetic to the theories that sustained the Picturesque movement, they were intent to interpret them always in compositions of a rigid symmetry and pure geometrical form. Clear-cut geometry for the French (Jean-Jacques Lequeu apart) remained all. The legacy of eighteenth-century architectural thought in France was to be contained and summed up in two books, the *Traité théorique et pratique de l'art de bâtir,* issued between 1802 and 1803, and the *Précis des leçons*

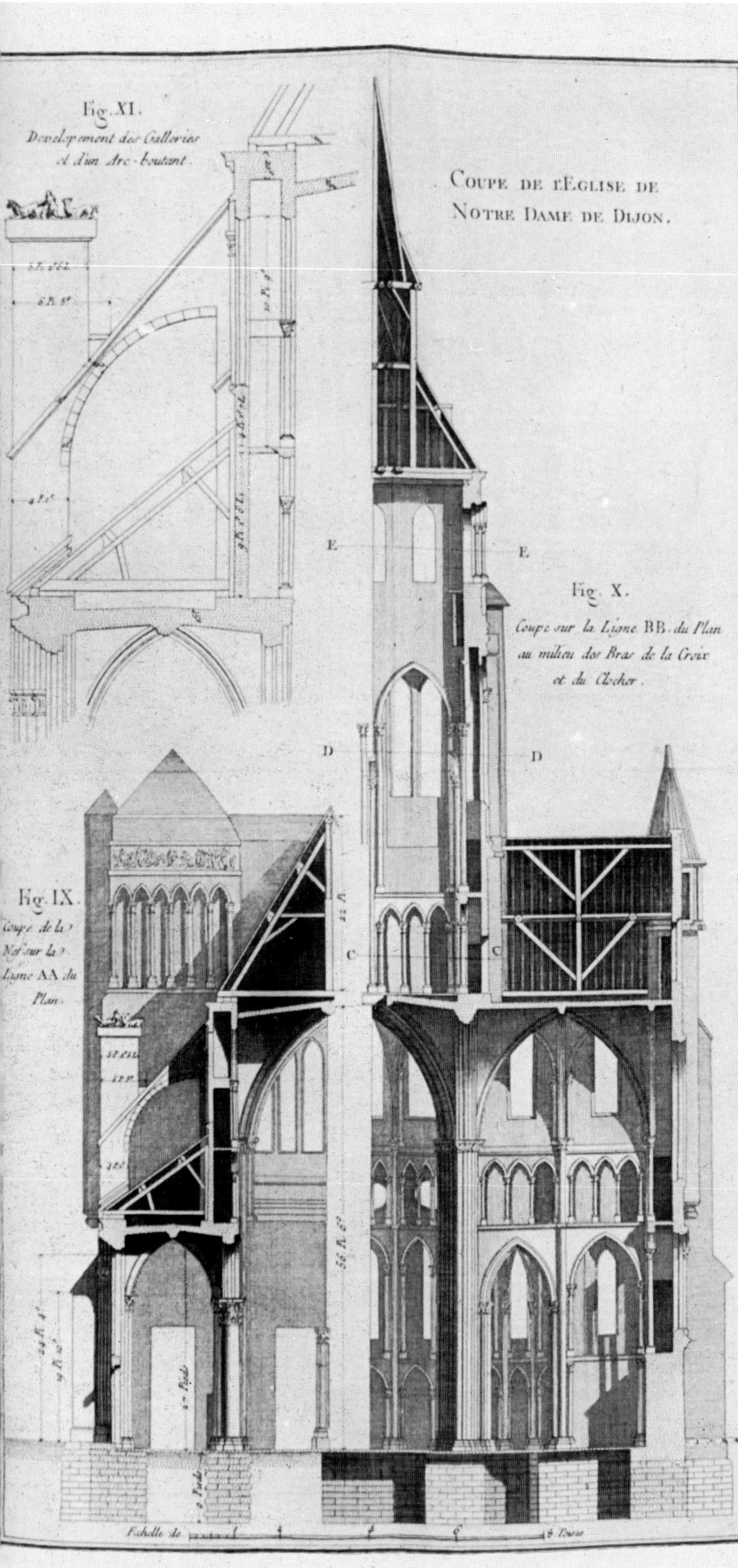


*22. Drawings by Jallier of Notre-Dame, Dijon, 1762, illustrated in Jacques-François Blondel's and Pierre Patte's* Cours d'architecture, *1777*

*d'architecture données à l'École royale polytechnique,* published between 1802 and 1805. They were to remain standard texts for fifty years and more. The first was written by Jean-Baptiste Rondelet (1734-1829), a pupil of Soufflot, who had been responsible for the completion of Ste.-Geneviève and had later reinforced the main piers with inestimable tact and skill when they were found, for the second time, to be collapsing. Rondelet's knowledge of building construction was unsurpassed. The second book was the work of Boullée's favorite pupil, Jean-Nicolas-Louis Durand (1760-1834), who was made professor of architecture at the École Polytechnique in 1795 and was to teach there for the rest of his life, mainly instructing surveyors and engineers. The only architects of note who passed through the school were Hubert Rohault de Fleury and his son Charles and Émile-Jacques Gilbert. But Durand exerted his enormous influence on architects through the medium of books. In addition to the *Précis,* he wrote the *Recueil et parallèle des édifices de tout genre anciens et modernes,* of 1800, and an appendix to the *Précis,* the *Partie graphique des cours d'architecture faits à l'École royale polytechnique,* of 1821. His works propounded the strictest standards of formal geometry and design.

Rondelet's book is probably unique among architectural treatises in that it contains almost no general discussion of architecture, apart from a few pages at the beginning (published twice, separately) that make it clear nonetheless that his treatise was to be regarded as a comprehensive foundation for the study and practice of architecture. Architecture was constituted entirely in "l'art de bâtir." "La théorie," he wrote, "est une science qui dirige toutes les opérations de la pratique. Cette science est le résultat de l'expérience et du raisonnement fondé sur les principes de mathématique et de physique appliquées aux différentes operations de l'art. C'est par le moyen de la théorie qu'un habile constructeur parvient à déterminer les formes et les justes dimensions qu'il faut donner à chaque partie d'un édifice en raison de sa situation et des efforts qu'elle peut avoirà soutenir, pour qu'il résulte perfection, solidité et économie" (vol. 1, p. v.).

Architecture, Rondelet insisted, was not an imaginative art but a science, controlled by need and necessity. The five volumes of his treatise were therefore devoted to lengthy accounts of building materials, their properties and their strengths, the techniques of all manners of building, and the most efficient means of estimating and calculating costs. There was much challenging reinterpretation of Gothic construction, as one might expect from a pupil of Soufflot, and much more up-to-date information on the latest experiments in building in iron, once again reflecting an interest of Soufflot. Most of the new bridges in iron in both England and France were illustrated, with suggestions as to how their design might have been improved. French theorists, whether they looked to the architecture of the past or the present, sought always to refashion it in terms of their own ideals.

Durand took as part of the frontispiece of his *Recueil et parallèle* that view of the Propylaea in Athens that had first appeared in Julien-David Le Roy's

*Ruines des plus beaux monuments de la Grèce* (1758) in which all the elements are rearranged in axial symmetry around a monumental flight of stairs. Throughout, Durand redrew the buildings in the illustrations so that they might appear more neat and orderly, for though he selected his examples from all periods of history—from Egyptian, Greek, Roman, Gothic, or Renaissance times—he was intent to disregard their oddities and stylistic characteristics and to present them all drawn to the same scale and arranged for comparison, as particular building types. Temples are grouped together on one page, churches on another, theaters on yet another, and so on. Once again the initial idea can be traced back to Le Roy, who illustrated a set of plans thus in the second edition of his book on Greek architecture, though the idea was initiated by Soufflot's pupil Gabriel-Pierre-Martin Dumont (1720-1791), who issued two such plates illustrating theaters in 1764 or 1765.

Durand's theoretical approach to architecture is contained in the *Précis* and the *Partie graphique.* He refused to consider Laugier's rustic cabin as the model for all architecture; it was no more, he said, than a rude beginning. Architecture was a reasoned affair, a considered and evolving solution to practical problems. "Soit que l'on consulte la raison," he wrote, "soit que l'on examine les monuments, il est évident que plaire n'a jamais pu être son objet. L'utilité publique et particulière, le bonheur et la conservation des individus et de la société, tel est le but de l'architecture" (*Précis,* vol. 1, p. 18).

Such high-minded sentiments, however, cannot be taken as grounds for considering Durand as a strict utilitarian; his language is only an aspect of post-Revolutionary cant. Though he proposed that architecture be conditioned by social demands, convenience, and economy, his criteria in designing were symmetry—at best, true symmetry—and a simplified geometry, which happened to be his aesthetic preferences. He developed his themes with logic, but it is a logic not free from naivety. He argued that symmetry and regularity resulted in economy of means and were thus ideals. The circle and the sphere were the finest figures because they enclosed the maximum area—or volume, in the case of the sphere—for the minimum circumference or surface area. He accepted, though, that these figures might be impractical in building design and chose, therefore, as the next best, the square and the cube. To learn to be an architect, he said, one had only to learn to divide a square into a regular grid. Architecture, he claimed, was a graphic formula. His method of composition was to start with the plan (almost invariably a square), to transform this into a grid, to draw on the main and subsidiary axes required to link the rooms, and then to impose upon this grid what he recognized to be the elements of architecture: the walls and columnar supports, together with such "negative" elements as doors and window openings. To arrive at the section and form of the building, the established grid was projected vertically. Durand had no feeling for form and volume. Even his plans were altogether unsatisfactory from the point of view of human requirements, though as geometrical

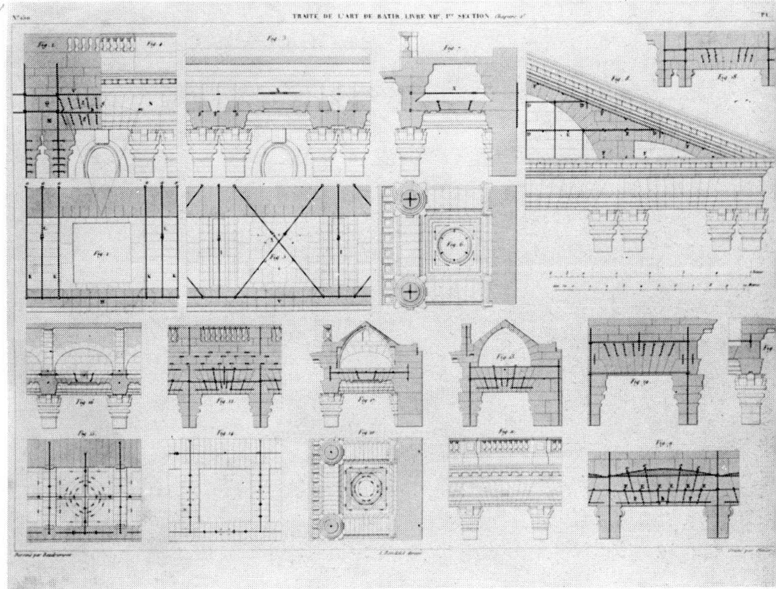

*23. Plate from Jean-Baptiste Rondelet's* Traité théorique et pratique de l'art de bâtir, *1802-3*

*24. Julien-David Le Roy, reconstruction of the Propylaea, Athens, from his* Ruines des plus beaux monuments de la Grèce, *1758*

*25, 26. Plate from Jean-Nicolas-Louis Durand's* Précis des leçons d'architecture, *1802-5, illustrating his theories of architectural design*

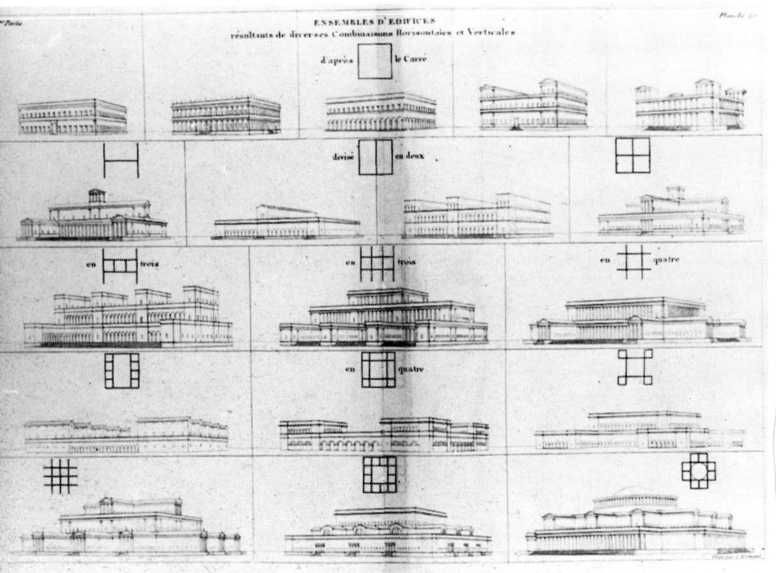


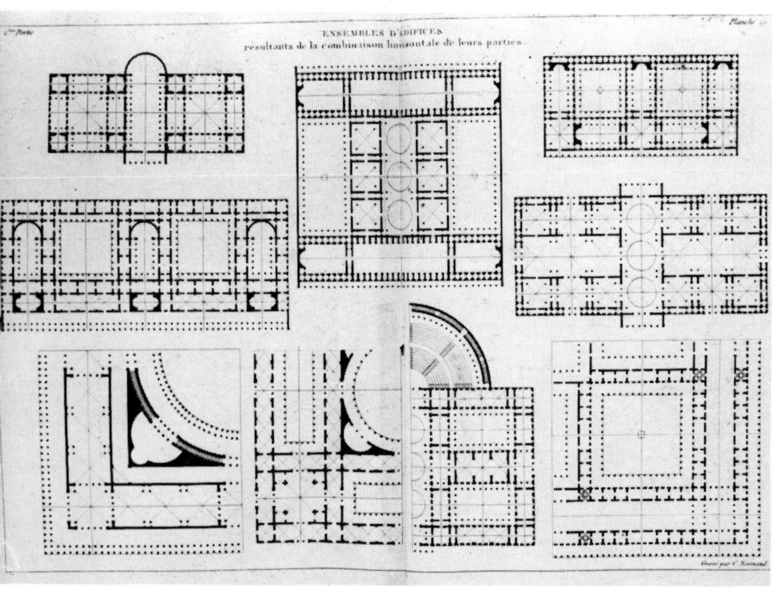


patterns they are undeniably impressive. Certainly they were to impress architects throughout Europe, and in Germany in particular. It is of some significance, perhaps, that the one building he was to approve without restraint, the vast circular Hôpital Ste.-Anne in Paris, begun in 1788 by Bernard Poyet (1742-1824), was stopped soon after on grounds of inefficient planning and inordinate cost. But there was more to Durand's theory than grid planning; he wished to do away with all unnecessary extravagance and decoration in architecture (the normally accepted forms of expression), and he proposed therefore that the style of a building be the visible expression of its functioning parts. The walls were to appear as plain masonry surfaces. The independent supports were to be in the form of piers or columns, equally spaced and made of materials that were demonstrably stronger than those used for the rest of the structure. There was to be a minimum of adornment and molding, and what there was had to present a palpable argument to the spectator of the role of the form to which it was applied. For richness or variety architects were to turn to plants, and many of Durand's stark and barren buildings were relieved with vines and creepers.

Rondelet and Durand together reduced architecture to two of its component parts, structure and formal geometry, and though Rondelet cared little for formal planning and Durand knew next to nothing of the art of construction (he had relegated it to a few notes at the back of the *Précis,* he was to explain in a later edition, lest it disrupt the thread of his argument), their books were by no means opposed in spirit; indeed, most architects regard them as complementary studies summarizing and reformulating the chief interests of the architects of the eighteenth century. Architecture entered a period of doctrinaire orthodoxy in the early years of the nineteenth century, and these books were to provide suitable formulas for building countless *mairies, palais de justice,* hospitals, prisons, and barracks throughout France. Émile-Jacques Gilbert, Durand's most enlightened pupil, was to make a sustained and serious attempt to reinvigorate architecture by introducing into it those humanitarian and social concerns of the early penal and health reformers, and later the ideas of Claude-Henri, Comte de Saint-Simon himself. Gilbert devoted his life to building no more than a prison, an asylum, a hospital, and a police barracks—and also, one might note, a morgue—yet he reflected faithfully in all his work and in all his teachings the ideals of Durand and Rondelet. The only other attempt to disrupt the torpor of architecture in France in the early decades of the century was the desperate bid by Jacques-Ignace Hittorff (1792-1867)—born in Cologne, but trained in France under François-Joseph Bélanger—to justify the application of riotous surface coloring to architecture. He fought bitterly to prove that the ancient temples of Greece had been richly colored. He recorded and publicized the murals and decorations of Pompeii and Herculaneum and even Raphael's grotesques. He sought to decorate his own buildings with enameled plaques, but such was not the means to renew

27. *Eugène-Emmanuel Viollet-le-Duc, house built between 1860 and 1863 in the valley below the Château de Pierrefonds (now École Secondaire d'Agriculture du Prieuré)*

architecture. Yet there can be no doubt that Gilbert and Hittorff prepared the way for those riformers of the middle years of the century Guillaume-Abel Blouet, Félix-Jacques Duban, Pierre-François-Henri Labrouste, Louis-Joseph Duc, and Léon Vaudoyer. Only the eldest of these, Blouet, was to attempt a full-scale exposition of his theory, and it is scarcely surprising to find that as his architectural activity was close in its range to that of Gilbert (he designed prisons and built a penal colony), his ideas were no more than an extension of those expounded many years before by Rondelet. Indeed, Blouet's treatise took the form of a *Supplément à la traité théorique et pratique de l'art de bâtir de Jean Rondelet,* issued in two volumes in 1847 and 1848.

This is essentially a catalogue of nineteenth-century engineering achievements, though there is a clear enough exposition of the theoretical underpinnings of such structures. Blouet's arguments are based on two tenets, which are worth quoting at length, for they served to reaffirm and reestablish the rationalist position worked out half a century before.

1°—à concevoir ce qu'il faut, rien de plus, et à le réaliser le plus simplement possible, ce qui ne peût être obtenu qu'en subordonnant d'abord ses conceptions, qui doivent devenir des réalités, aux moyens d'exécution et aux propriétés des materiaux dont on dispose.

2°—à n'employer la décoration que pour compléter l'expression en ébauché dans la disposition et la construction, accentuer les parties en raison de leurs fonctions relatives et déterminer par suite, avec plus de précision, le caractère de l'édifice à l'aide des moyens qui favorisent les matériaux auxquels ils sont appliqués, de moyens, en un mot, rendant sensible à la fois le but de l'édifice et sa construction, tant sous le rapport du mode de l'exécution que sous celui de la nature des matières employées (vol. 2, pp. ix, 227).

There is scarcely any need to comment on this program, though it is worth noting that it served from 1846 until 1853, when Blouet was *Professeur de Théorie* at the École des Beaux-Arts, as the official doctrine. At the École Polytechnique itself, oddly enough, a rationalist doctrine of considerably less intellectual rigor and restrictiveness was being propounded from 1837 onward by François-Léonce Reynaud (1803-1880), the engineer, who was to publish his *Traité d'architecture* in two volumes in 1850 and 1858. This is devoted largely to building materials, methods of construction, and various building types, but the seventeen pages of theoretical text and the introduction make the guiding principles disarmingly clear. The aim of architecture, Reynaud declared, was beauty, not utility, though practical requirements must always be carefully fulfilled. Taste was to be the ultimate arbiter of architectural harmony and expression. Ornament and decorative forms, though certainly not to be regarded as essential, were vital to such expression and might give value to architecture. But in other respects Reynaud was far less lax and tolerant than Blouet; whereas Blouet extolled the economy of Gothic construction and was even prepared to set up programs for his students for churches in the Gothic style, Reynaud disliked all aspects of the Gothic and dreaded lest there be a Gothic revival. "L'art du moyen âge est mort," he wrote, "aussi bien que son esprit et ses institutions, et leur résurrection est impossible. On peut galvaniser un cadavre, mais non le rappeler à la vie" (vol. 2, p. 270).

It was precisely those men of Gothic inclination who were to take up the rationalist doctrine of Blouet and his circle—in particular, that transmitted by Henri Labrouste—and who were to demonstrate that, by a renewed and more thorough analysis of Gothic architecture, more stringent principles yet might be adduced that could even lead to an architecture with style, but one that owed nothing to any styles of the past. Eugène-Emmanuel Viollett-le-Duc (1814-1879) was the chief exponent of this brand of rationalism. He was the bugbear of the École des Beaux-Arts. And it is not without irony that Jean-Louis-Charles Garnier, architect of the Paris Opéra—who was to destroy, almost, the intellectual tradition of architecture in France, and to show that by conjuring up a whole medley of styles, forms, and motifs a vigorous architecture could be produced—should have been asked, as a student, to swear "Haine à Viollet-le-Duc" on the "Grand Durand," the *Recueil et parallèle des édifices de tout genre anciens et modernes.*

The Gothic movement in nineteenth-century France sprang from romantic beginnings, from Alexandre Lenoir's atmospheric museum in the Couvent des Petits Augustins, later to become part of the École des Beaux-Arts, where fragments from the past were reassembled after the Revolution and imbued with an aura of poetry and mystery. Chateaubriand's

*28. Eugène-Emmanuel Viollet-le-Duc, project for a* hôtel de ville *with cast-iron struts, from his twelfth* Entretien sur l'architecture, *c. 1866*

Gothic leanings were first nurtured there; so also were those of the historian Jules Michelet. But though Michelet's brilliant *Introduction à l'histoire universelle,* of 1831, and the six volumes on French medieval history that followed were to arouse a popular passion for the Gothic past—particularly in Catholic circles—he was to find that his ideal image had little relation to reality and he was to become the leader of an anticlerical coterie of historians who despised the Middle Ages. The Catholic national credo and the manifesto for the restoration, if not the revival, of Gothic architecture was, in fact, a novel, Victor Hugo's *Notre-Dame de Paris,* issued first in February 1831, but republished in the following year with three additional chapters that made quite explicit Hugo's aims: "Inspirons," he wrote, "s'il est possible à la nation l'amour de l'architecture nationale. C'est là, l'auteur le déclare, un des buts principaux de ce livre; c'est là un des buts principaux de sa vie" (1832 ed., preface).

Viollet-le-Duc was inspired by such works, and he was to retain always a romantic, emotional sympathy for the Gothic, but it was rather those self-sure Protestant historians of the Middle Ages grouped around François-Pierre-Guillaume Guizot—and, in particular, Guizot himself—who were to supply his knowledge of the national past and to give him the opportunity to devolop his inclinations. When Guizot assumed political power, he at once established the Commission des Monuments Historiques and began to provide money for the restoration of historical buildings. Viollet-le-Duc was drawn early into this orbit by Prosper Mérimée, *Inspecteur Général des Monuments Historiques.* In 1840, at the age of twenty-six, he was appointed to restore Ste.-Madeleine at Vézelay; later in the same year he joined Labrouste's pupil Jean-Baptiste-Antoine Lassus (1807-1857) on the restoration of the Ste.-Chapelle; and in another four years they began the restoration of Notre-Dame. His career was to be largely concerned with restoration. This was the source of his immense knowledge and understanding of Gothic architecture and the basis of those two great works for which he is famous, the *Dictionnaire raisonné de l'architecture française du XI^e^ au XVI^e^ siècle,* published between 1854 and 1868, and the *Dictionnaire raisonné du mobilier français de l'époque carlovingienne à la renaissance,* issued from 1858 to 1875.

In his early years Viollet-le-Duc's energies were directed not only to the restoration of Gothic architecture but also to a revival of the style itself. Lassus, together with a group of Gothic enthusiasts and archaeologists, chief among them Adolphe-Napoléon Didron, was then busy restoring the church of St.-Germain-l'Auxerrois, and was showing both there and at the Ste.-Chapelle that an image of the Middle Ages could conjured up that was quite as colorful and rich as that proposed at the same time by Hittorff for Greek architecture. They all propagated their ideas in Didron's *Annales archéologiques,* begun in 1844. But from Lassus Viollet-le-Duc also learned something of that rationalist doctrine of the Gothic that was contained in the works of Rondelet and that had been transmitted by Lassus's master,

*29. Eugène-Emmanuel Viollet-le-Duc and Félix Narjoux, gallery in the Château de Pregny, near Geneva, 1875*

Labrouste. Already, in his first major series of articles, "De la construction des édifices religieux en France depuis le commencement du Christianisme jusqu'au XVIe siècle," published in the *Annales* between 1844 and 1847, Viollet-le-Duc indicated that he had absorbed all that his predecessors could teach him on the structure and the rational nature of the Gothic. Soon after, he was to reject the idea of a revival of the style and to turn his attention instead to the most rigorous analysis of every form, every detail, of Gothic, to arrive at a set of principles for design that he hoped might be applicable to the nineteenth century. The architecture of the nineteenth century was thus to be analogous to, though distinct from, that of the thirteenth century; it was to be the visible expression in contemporary terms, using contemporary materials such as iron, of a system evolved in the thirteenth century. In the *Dictionnaire raisonné de l'architecture française* he illustrated a section through the aisle and nave of a church showing how timber props might be substituted for the stone of the flying buttresses, and cast-iron columns used in place of the piers of the nave; this, in its most elementary form, was the way in which he thought Gothic structural principles might begin to be reinterpreted. His analyses were to become far more complex and subtle than this, for he was led to believe that every feature, every molding, of a Gothic building could be interpreted as a functional device, whether as part of a supporting system or to throw off rainwater. He was convinced that architecture was a clear expression of function, a function that embodied political and social aspirations, material limitations and needs. His analyses of medieval social organizations were marvelously distorted so that they might accord with his architectural theories.

Later, he assaulted the citadel of classical rationalism, the École des Beaux-Arts itself, first, in 1857, by opening an independent *atelier* of his own in the Rue Bonaparte, taking over some of Labrouste's students, and then, in 1863, by intriguing with Prosper Mérimée, a long-standing friend of the Empress Eugénie, to have himself appointed *Professeur d'Histoire de l'Art et Esthétique* at that venerable institution. He retired soon after, rudely rebuffed by the students. He had attempted to show that the rational theories he had evolved in relation to the Gothic style were applicable also to all great architecture—among which he ranked Greek and Byzantine architecture, with some reservations as to the quality of Roman buildings. Roman structure was sound enough, he thought, but the decorative overlay adopted had been evolved in relation to Greek architectural forms and was altogether inappropriate. His exposition of these ideas took the form of the *Entretiens sur l'architecture,* appearing in chapters from 1858 onward; the first volume was completed in 1863, the second in 1872. The second volume reveals Viollet-le-Duc at his most adventurous. He was a dogged theoretician who argued his way through even the knottiest problems with determination and an air of success, but he was never able to give convincing form to his ideas. His restorations apart, he designed almost one hundred buildings on his own account (often credited to his students and associates), but he never once built anything that accords successfully with his theories. His buildings, individual houses for the most part, are lackluster and commonplace, conceived in a range of styles from Gothic to late Renaissance. The ultimate disappointment was his gallery, of 1875 in the Château de Pregny, on the outskirts of Geneva—built in 1860-64 for the Baron de Rothschild by none other than Sir Joseph Paxton, designer of the Crystal Palace of 1851. The gallery is a fussily decorated period pastiche.

Yet in a handful of plates in the twelfth *Entretien,* issued about 1867, he showed that with dogged determination he could produce a visual embodiment of his theories that was to be almost as memorable to twentieth-century architects as the Crystal Palace itself. Viollet-le-Duc's designs are awkward and ungainly, but the system of angled iron struts that he indicated first for a town hall, then in increasing complexity for a series of large covered spaces, and finally for a concert hall for three thousand people, provided just that liberating stimulus required by architects trained in a rational functionalist ideal but encumbered always by a range of historical styles. Viollet-le-Duc suggested how they might abandon these and evolve a new style for the future. This not only was to be an expression of a solution to a problem in structure but was to embody also an absolute geometrical ideal based on the form of the equilateral triangle. Viollet-le-Duc's giant concert hall is an illustration of his belief that everything in nature, indeed the whole universe, was built up of polyhedra based on the equilateral triangle. This was, to him, the essence of style.

## Chapter Two
# THE PICTURESQUE TRADITION IN ENGLAND

Perhaps the most striking architectural impact of the Picturesque was the new emphasis it placed on architecture as part of an environment. We may interpret the word *environment,* so fashionable today, in a rather broad way so as to refer not merely to the physical setting, whether rural or urban, but also to the historical setting. Architecture, in other words, came to be regarded as possessing evocative narrative or literary powers. This emphasis on architecture as part of something else, as an incident in history or in a landscape, encouraged the concept of growth, of flexibility, in architecture; thus, buildings were thought to have a special merit if one could read in them the process of their alteration during the years or even centuries of their existence.

One of the clearest ways in which this new approach to architecture was expressed in the eighteenth century was, perhaps ironically, in the obsession with the ruin. Admiration for ruins is an obvious indication of a belief that there are more important aspects to a building than the functional and visual roles its designer intended it to fulfill. Thus some architects, at once frustrated and excited by this implied shift in their role, began to imagine what their own buildings would look like when change and decay had reduced them to ruin. Perhaps the first English design that is clearly part of the international neoclassicism developed in Franco-Italian circles in the 1740s is the one for a mausoleum for the Prince of Wales, of 1751-52, by Sir William Chambers. Yet its monumental neoclassicism, doubtless derived from designs by such architects as Louis-Joseph Le Lorrain for the Festa della Chinea in Rome, is dissolved by Chambers's unexpectedly Romantic decision to show the mausoleum not merely in a landscaped setting but also as it would appear when ruined. Few went so far as Racine de Monville, who, with help from the architect François Barbier, in 1780 built a house for himself in the form of a ruined column, at the Désert de Retz, not far from Paris. The essentially pictorial character of this enterprise is emphasized by the fact that the *jardin anglais* that surrounded this bizarre dwelling was designed with assistance from the painter Hubert Robert. The continual dissolution of neoclassicism by the Picturesque is a particularly English phenomenon, and it reached a climax with Sir John Soane (1753-1837), who commissioned Joseph Michael Gandy (1771-1843) to depict his vast rotunda at the Bank of England, London, at a point when it could be said to possess the status of a Piranesian ruin.

*30. Sir William Chambers, project for the mausoleum of Frederick, Prince of Wales, 1751–52.*

Sir John Vanbrugh's memorandum of June 11,1709, arguing for the preservation of the ruins of Woodstock Manor in the park at Blenheim is a key document in the history of eighteenth-century ruin mania. Vanbrugh (1664-1726) urged the upkeep of buildings of distant times because "they move [inspire] more lively and pleasing Reflections (than History without their aid can do) on the Persons who have inhabited them; on the remarkable things which have been transacted in them, or the extraordinary occasions of erecting them." Vanbrugh went on to argue that because the park at Blenheim "has little variety of objects" it "stands in need of all the helps that can be given... Buildings and Plantations." These, in his opinion, "rightly dispos'd will indeed supply all the wants of Nature in that place. And the most agreeable disposition is to mix them in which this old Manour gives so happy an occasion for; that were the enclosure filled with Trees (principally fine Yews and Hollys) promiscuously set not grow up in a wild thicket, so that all the buildings left might appear in two risings amongst'em, it would make one of the most agreeable objects that the best of Landskip painters can invent" (*The Complete Works of Sir John Vanbrugh,* ed. B. Dobrée and G. Webb, 4 vols., 1928, vol. 4, pp. 29-30). This quotation encapsulates the Picturesque tendency to dethrone architecture, to replace the traditional Renaissance architect with historians, Romantics, painters—people who see a building as an incident in an environment, whether natural or historical. We can usefully tabulate the three principal points of Vanbrugh's thesis as follows: "1. Buildings can bring the past to life more vividly than written history; 2. Buildings can be composed as an integral part of a landscape; 3. In mingling buildings and trees in a designed landscape we should take seventeenth-century landscape paintings as a model if we want the result to be authentically 'Picturesque.'"

From Vanbrugh in the early eighteenth century to Edwin Lutyens in the early twentieth we can trace the development of the ideas contained in these three points. An intense emphasis on architecture as part of a landscape or of a natural setting, which was so much to characterize the work of John Nash, led in time to an emphasis on local materials and local techniques, which marks the work of Philip Webb and Lutyens.

Vanbrugh lost his battle with the forceful duchess of Marlborough over the preservation of Woodstock Manor, but the victory was ultimately his since his ideas were adopted later in the eighteenth and nineteenth centuries. Thus the ruins of medieval houses or castles were preserved as Picturesque objects in the landscaped parks of many new houses: in the 1760s, at Tabley house, Cheshire, by John Carr (1723-1807); in the 1770s, at Wardour Castle, Wiltshire, by James Paine; in 1807, at Belsay Castle, Northumberland, by Sir Charles Monck; and, most strikingly of all, in 1835, at Scotney Castle, Kent, by Edward Hussey, Anthony Salvin (1799-1881), and William Sawrey Gilpin. At Scotney, Salvin's new house is, in a sense, a mere window placed to catch a view of the Picturesque ruins of the moated castle in the valley below. Hussey and Salvin made these ruins even more "Picturesque" by eliminating most of the additions made to them in the seventeenth century. With further help from the landscape gardener Gilpin, son of the celebrated Picturesque theorist, the castle was linked visually to the house by a landscaped garden of dreamlike quality and intense beauty. At Peckforton Castle, Cheshire, Salvin provided a different interpretation to a similar theme. Here, from 1844 to 1850, he created a vast new castle on a hill adjacent to the thirteenth-century Beeston Castle. As at Scotney, the principal rooms commanded views of the nearby ruins, but the parallel ends there since Beeston Castle plays only a very minor role in the whole composition. It is the expansive new castle of Peckforton and not the landscape or the ruins that is the center of attention.

The story of the Picturesque begins not with architecture but with gardens. The Romantic "natural" garden, or park, developed in England in the eighteenth century, had undoubtedly been anticipated in Renaissance Italy. So far, research into either the Italian gardens themselves or English knowledge of them has been insufficient to enable us to assess the measure of their influence. The groves, grottoes, nymphaea, and irregular areas of Italian gardens were as rich with antique literary and mythological symbolism as Stourhead was to be in the eighteenth century. In the Vatican gardens, the early sixteenth-century Fontana dello Scoglio was a cross between a grotto and a ruin that would have delighted the poet Alexander Pope, while the largest of the four sections of the grounds of the Villa Borghese was laid out as a park at the beginning of the seventeenth century in a way that might similarly have pleased the designer William Kent (1685-1748). A description of the Villa Borghese written in 1700 claims that the inspiration for this part of the garden was antique and that it "seems irregular but art and industry have so well regulated it that it alternates from hill to plain and from wild to domesticated valleys" (see G. Masson, *Italian Gardens,* 1961, p. 154).

Among the first English landscaped parks and gardens were Pope's own at Twickenham, Middlesex (begun 1719), with its little wilderness, shell temple, and grotto. The new movement had strong literary and philosophical overtones, not only in the writings of Pope but in those of the first earl of Shaftesbury and Joseph Addison as well. The gardens of Stephen Switzer and the writings of Batty Langley (*New Principles of Gardening,* 1728) lent support to a movement that reached a climax in William Kent's garden at Rousham, Oxfordshire, in the 1730s. The second phase in the history of the Picturesque is represented by Lancelot "Capability" Brown (1716-1783), whose work from about 1750 to about 1780 is an extension and popularization not so much of what Kent had achieved at Rousham—which is still essentially a *garden*—but of the bigger, barer *parks* he had projected at Euston and Holkham Hall. Reaction quickly set in to Brown's rather bland landscapes, thus producing the third phase of the Picturesque, associated with the writings of Sir Uvedale Price (1747-1829) and Richard Payne Knight (1750-1824) in the 1790s. For our purposes at the moment this third phase is the most significant, since it had more impact on architectural design than the other two phases. Nonetheless, we should look at some of the great landscaped parks of the mid-eighteenth century with their pictorial treatment of nature and architecture.

A contemporary described the Elysian Fields at Stowe, Buckinghamshire, as "the painting part" of the gardens. In this "sacred landscape," with its complex mythological and political iconography, Kent designed the circular Temple of Ancient Virtue (1734), based on Palladio's drawing of the Temple of Vesta at Tivoli. The antique source makes both the building and

*I. Jules Hardouin Mansart and Robert de Cotte, Versailles, Royal Chapel, interior, 1698-1710*

*II. Jacques-Germain Soufflot, Ste.-Geneviève, Paris, interior, 1756-90*

*31. Joseph Michael Gandy,* The Bank of England, *c. 1830*

*32. Plan of the garden at Alexander Pope's villa at Twickenham, Middlesex, begun 1719*

*33. Anthony Salvin, Scotney Castle, Kent, 1835–43*

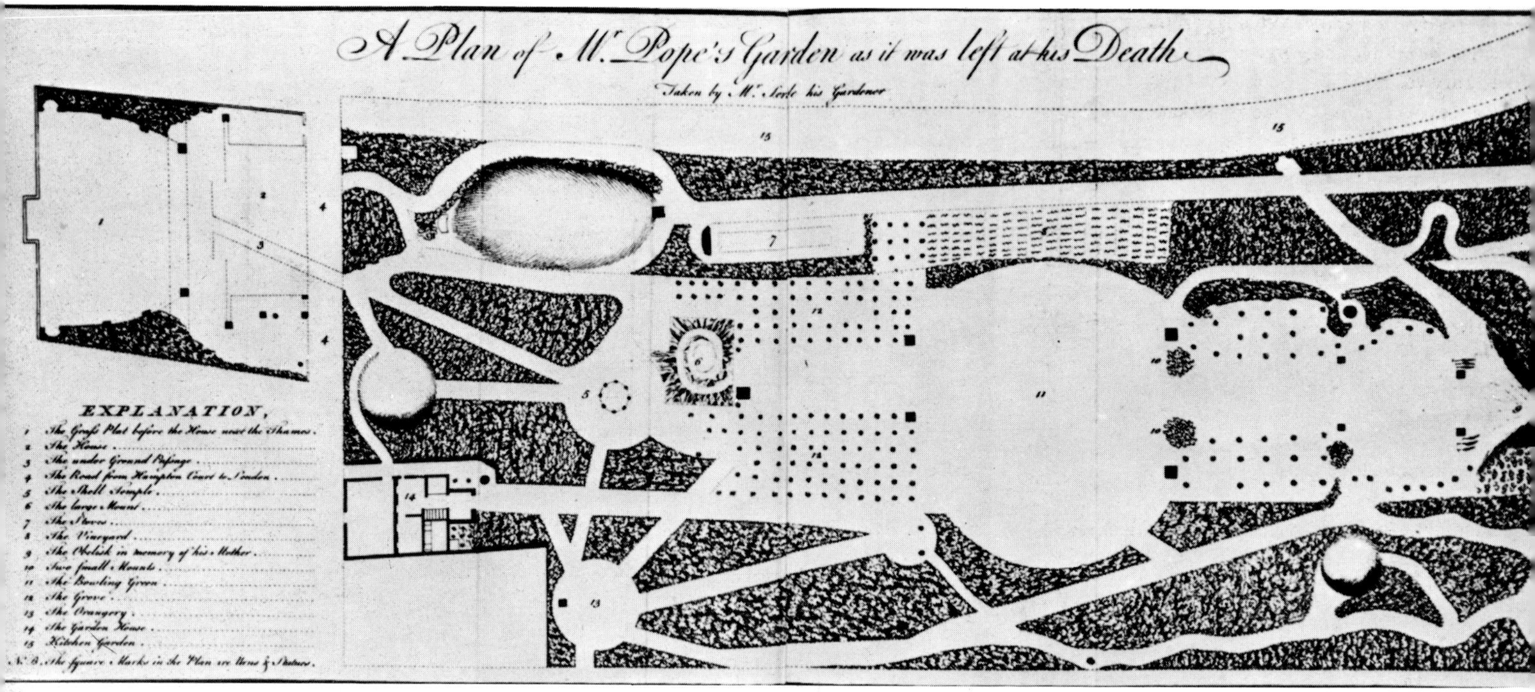

A Plan of Mr. Pope's Garden as it was left at his Death

Taken by Mr. Serle his Gardener

EXPLANATION,

1 The Grass Plat before the House next the Thames.
2 The House
3 The under Ground Passage
4 The Road from Hampton Court to London
5 The Shell Temple
6 The large Mount
7 The Stoves
8 The Vineyard
9 The Obelisk in memory of his Mother
10 Two small Mounts
11 The Bowling Green
12 The Grove
13 The Orangery
14 The Garden House
15 Kitchen Garden

N. B. The square Marks in the Plan are Urns & Statues.

34. *William Kent, Temple of British Worthies, Stowe, Buckinghamshire, 1734, detail.*

the pastoral scene of which it is part important in the history of neoclassicism since the temple and gorge at Tivoli are the only Roman "sacred landscape" to survive. However, Kent was equally susceptible to Italian Renaissance sources, as is shown in the remarkable Temple of British Worthies on the other side of the Elysian Fields. This may have been inspired by the exedra, or circus, on the grounds of the Villa Mattei in Rome. Thus it is probably not quite accurate to say that Kent was attempting to re-create paintings by Claude Lorrain or Poussin, though such an attempt may be seen in the Grecian Valley, which extends from the upper end of the Elysian Fields. Laid out in the 1740s—probably from designs by Lord Cobham, after Kent had left Stowe—and dominated by the imposing Temple of Concord and Victory, designed by Cobham's nephew, Lord Grenville, about 1748, it is a landmark in the history of British neoclassicism. On another part of the grounds, Kent had designed a temple perhaps as early as 1731 that is also unique for its time in Europe. This is the Temple of Venus, in which a Palladian quadrant theme is handled with a neoclassical austerity. The open screen of columns before a coffered apse was to recur more than thirty years later in the work of Robert Adam and Claude-Nicolas Ledoux. At Rousham, Oxfordshire, in the 1730s, Kent laid out a garden that had much in common with the Elysian Fields at Stowe but that was at once more varied and more unified. It is approached from a remarkable balustraded terrace called the Praeneste, which may have been based on the pedimented arcades of the Roman Baths as illustrated by Palladio in the *Fabbriche antiche disegnate da Andrea Palladio Vicentino,* published by Lord Burlington in 1730. The source of the Praeneste itself is the Roman Temple of Virtue; with its ramped terraces commanding distant views, it is itself the prototype of continental garden design from the Villa d'Este to Versailles. From the Praeneste a path leads to the small valley originally laid out by Charles Bridgeman as a wilderness with tortuous paths. This was opened out by Kent so as to become Venus's vale, with "the opening and retiring shades" admired by Horace Walpole. Kent remodeled Bridgeman's uncompromisingly square pool into an octagon, which, though perhaps softer on the eye than the square, was still a long way from the dreamy undulations of Capability Brown. The pool is flanked by an Upper and Lower Cascade in the form of grottoes, perhaps based on the Fontana Rustica at the Villa Aldobrandini, Frascati.

The type of garden represented by the development from Twickenham to Rousham was popularized much later in France as the *jardin anglais.* Characteristic examples, crowded with naive architectural incident, are the gardens at Ermenonville (1766-76) and Louis Carrogis de Carmontelle's Jardin de Monceau, Paris (1773-78).

Stowe and Rousham are essential preliminaries to an appreciation of the work carried out at Stourhead, Wiltshire, in the 1740s and 1750s. At Stourhead, more than anywhere else in Europe, one can admire the way in which poetry, painting, gardening, architecture, travel, the study of antiquity, and topography blend to form the single art of Picturesque

*35. William Kent, Temple of Ancient Virtue, Stowe, Buckinghamshire, 1734*

landscape. Both the house and its contents—pictures, books, and furniture—and the grounds and their contents—trees, water, and temples—merge to form an idyllic, narrative, cultural picture dominated by a profound sense of place. That sense of place, that *genius loci,* was perhaps the particular legacy to Europe of the English Picturesque movement. What Alexander Pope had written in his "Epistle to Lord Burlington on the Use of Riches," in the 1730s, sums up the spirit that created Stourhead:

> "Consult the Genius of the Place in all
> That tells the Waters or to rise or fall
> Or helps th'ambitious Hill the heav'n to scale,
> Or Scoops in circling theatres the vale,
> Calls in the Country, catches opening glades,
> Joins willing woods, and carries shades from shades,
> Now breaks or now directs th'intending Lines,
> Paints as you plant, and, as you work, designs."

Stourhead lies at the center of a historic and beautiful part of English geography and history, at the point between Salisbury Plain and Glastonbury where myth and history have been intertwined for centuries. There, at the remote meeting point of three counties—Somerset, Dorset, and Wiltshire—Henry Hoare, a rich city banker, built a large, bleak Palladian villa, designed by Colen Campbell (1676–1729), in 1718. Situated on a height, the house faces east across the bare plain. But just three hundred yards to the west, the ground drops sharply into a lush, almost tropical, hidden valley, long known as "Paradise," which contains the tiny village of Stourton. In 1743 Hoare's son, also Henry, began to plan a Picturesque circuit tour around the sides of the valley, in the manner of Stowe and Rousham. In August 1744, in a letter to Henry Hoare, Henry Flitcroft (1697–1769), who was completing the interiors of the house, referred to his designs for a "Circular Open Temple of the Ionic order, Antique." He also sent "a sketch of how I conceive the head of the lake should be formed. Twill make a most

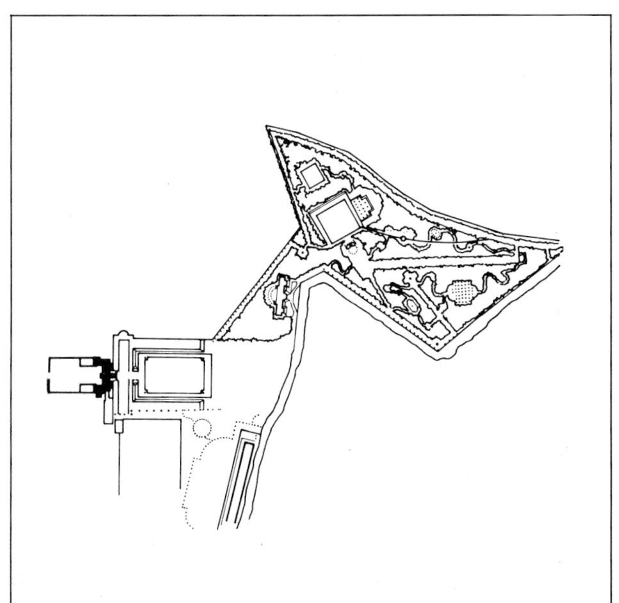

*36. Charles Bridgeman plan of the gardens at Rousham, Oxfordshire, before William Kent's alterations, 1715-20*

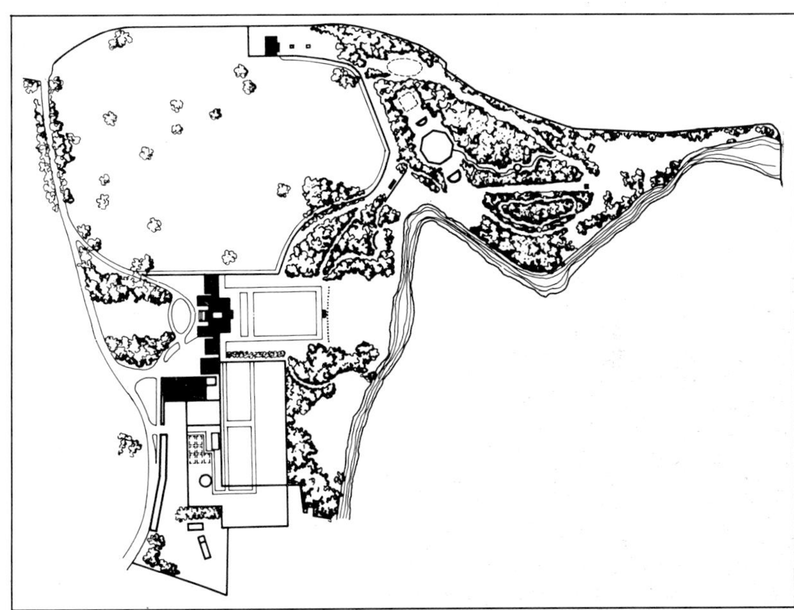

*37. William Kent, plan of the gardens at Rousham, Oxfordshire, 1730 and later*

*38. William Kent, Venus's Vale, Rousham, Oxfordshire, after 1730*

39. *Stourhead, Wiltshire, view toward the Pantheon, completed 1756*

40. *Stourhead, Wiltshire, plan, 1743 and later*

agreeable scene with the solemn shade about it and the variety of other agreeable circumstances." The letter establishes that as early as 1744 Hoare envisaged uniting his garden buildings within the valley by means of a lake. In fact, the dam that made the lake possible was not formed until ten years later. Flitcroft's Temple of Ceres (or Flora) contains altars designed by Flitcroft as well as an inscription over the door from the sixth book of Virgil's *Aeneid:* "Procul, o procul este profani" ("Begone all you who are uninitiated"). The lakeside Virgilian overtones were thus established from the first, though it is possible that in creating his lake landscape—which is what distinguishes Stourhead from Stowe and Rousham—Hoare may also have had in mind Pliny's description of the Source of the Clitumnus (*Letters,* book 8, chapter 8).

On the other side of the lake from the Temple of Flora an elaborate grotto was created, in 1748, containing a statue of the Nymph of the Grot carved in white lead by John Cheere, after the antique. The grotto is very much in the style of Italian Mannerist gardens and would have appealed to Pope. Indeed, a suitable quotation from Pope is carved in the marble bath within

*41. Henry Flitcroft, Temple of the Sun, Stourhead, Wiltshire, 1765*

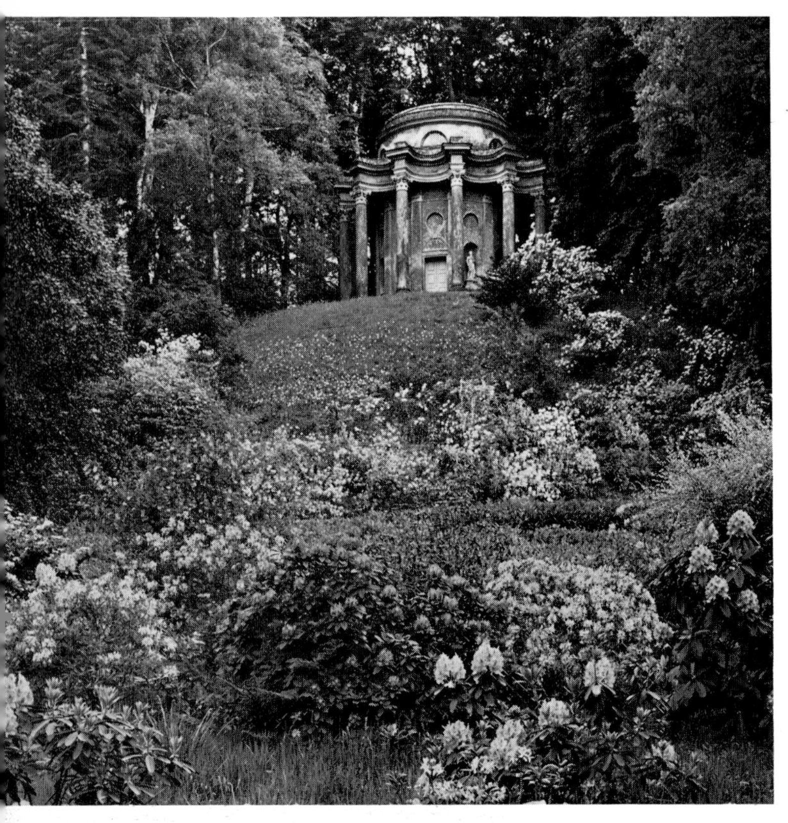

the grotto. Hoare wrote in 1765: "I have made the passage up from the souterrain serpentine & will make it easier of access *facilis descensus Averno,"* thus confirming the notion that the path around the lake is an allegory of Aeneas's journey through the underworld.

From the grotto we reach the Claudian and Virgilian Pantheon, a remarkable neoclassical building completed in 1756 from designs by Flitcroft. Its impressively austere interior contains statues of Hercules and Flora by John Rysbrack, and an antique marble figure of Livia Augusta as Ceres, brought from Herculaneum. Here the analogy with landscape painting, adumbrated by Vanbrugh, becomes more relevant than ever, for the form, position, and iconographical significance of the Pantheon seem to have been inspired by Claude's *Coast View of Delos with Aeneas.* We know that Hoare owned a version by Andrea Locatelli of Claude's *View of Delphi with a Procession,* which contains just such a pantheon temple. Higher up on the other side of the lake is a companion piece to Flitcroft's Pantheon, another "antique" temple, which was completed in 1765. Flitcroft took its design from the late Roman Temple of Venus at Baalbek, which had been included in Robert Wood's *The Ruins of Balbec,* published in 1757. This wholesale incorporation of antique monuments into a landscaped scene is significant enough, but the deliberate inclusion of views of the village of Stourton into the composition is equally worthy of comment. Whereas at Stowe the medieval parish church was deliberately planted out, at Stourhead one of the great composed vistas is of the medieval church tower rising above cottage roofs and a village cross. This incorporation of the quintessence of the English rural scene into the Picturesque elegiac idyll is, of course, a make-believe in every possible way. The village cross is not the village cross but a sophisticated urban market cross of 1373 brought to Stourton from Bristol High Street in 1768. Moreover, it is not even in the village at all—though it appears to be, from the Pantheon—and the triangle of grass behind it, which looks like the village green, is also within the park boundary. The Picturesque make-believe is exposed in a letter written by Hoare to his daughter, in 1762, about the bridge that he constructed in front of the cross: "I took it from Palladio's Bridge at Vicenza, 5 arches, & when you stand at the Pantheon the Water will be seen thro the arches & it will look as if the River came down thro the Village & that this was the Village Bridge for the Public use; the view of the Bridge, Village and Church altogether will be a charming Gaspard view at the end of that Water". Hoare's words remind one forcibly of Vanbrugh's claim half a century earlier that if architecture and trees were combined at Woodstock Manor "so that all the buildings left might appear in two risings amongst'em, it would make one of the most agreeable objects that the best of Landskip painters can invent."

Robert Adam's Culzean Castle, Ayrshire (1777 onward), towering dramatically above the rocky coastline, is a realization in stone of the imaginary landscape architecture Adam (1728–1792) spent so much of his spare time painting. A celebrated example of an architect's deliberately designing a building that appears to have strayed from a painting by Claude is Nash's Cronkhill, Shropshire (c. 1802). The undoubted source for this round-towered villa is the buildings that appear in the backgrounds of such paintings as Claude's *Landscape with the Ponte Molle.* Moreover, the Ponte Molle is very close in form to the bridge at Stourhead. A curious example of the pictorial approach to architecture and landscape is afforded by an aquatint of the front door of Sezincote House, Gloucestershire, of 1810, by John Martin, showing the Picturesque park reflected in the glass. As soon as this remarkable Indian-style country house was completed, its owner commissioned the aquatints from Martin—which suggests that a house that came into being as a realization in architecture of Picturesque drawings and views of India could only be fully appreciated once it had been translated back into pictorial imagery.

Even an architect so imbued with classical archaeology as Charles Robert Cockerell (1788–1863) found it impossible to look at William Wilkins's

42. *Henry Flitcroft, the Pantheon, Stourhead, Wiltshire, interior, 1754–56*

Grange Park, Hampshire (1809), without immediately recalling landscape paintings by Claude and Poussin. It is not clear whether Wilkins (1778–1839) had such analogies in mind when designing the great temple-like house, but to Cockerell, in a now-celebrated passage in his diary for 1823, "nothing [could] be finer, more classical or like the finest Poussin. It realises the most fanciful representations of the painters pencil or the poets description . . . there is nothing like it on this side of Arcadia." More surprisingly, it occurred to Cockerell only *after* he had designed the Hanover Chapel in Regent Street, in 1821, that its source lay in a painting by Claude. Looking at some of Claude's seaport scenes in the collection of J. J. Angerstein, in 1823, Cockerell noted in his diary: "much flattered at Claude's pictures & finding in 2 of the 5 pictures in this collection the idea of the two turrets at the entrance of a building as in my chapel. I have little doubt that the idea of this adoption arose in my mind from having seen these pictures and engravings. In these wonderful pictures one feels the balmy rosy atmosphere of the Mediterranean, that agreeable air . . . which I so well remember in those parts." Rather unexpectedly, Cockerell also found that his twin-towered chapel reminded him of Vanbrugh's Morpeth Town Hall, Northumberland (1716). After passing through Morpeth, in July 1822, he noted in his diary that the town hall was "picturesque *like my chapel.*"

There can be no doubt that the heroic romance of Vanbrugh's buildings, of his "Castle style" in particular, was a source of inspiration to his successors from Adam to Cockerell, even though they worked in a style different from his. Adam's eulogy of Vanbrugh in the preface to his *Works in Architecture of Robert and James Adam, Esquires* (1773) is well known, but as a central and beautiful text in eighteenth-century aesthetics it must be quoted here. He begins by describing the revolution his own architecture had achieved in defeating neo-Palladianism: "The massive entablature, the ponderous compartment ceiling, the heavy frames . . . are now universally exploded." In their place he had established what he called "movement," a quality he defined as follows: "*Movement* is meant to express, the rise and fall, the advance and recess, with other diversity of form, in the different parts of a building, so as to add greatly to the picturesque of the composition. For the rising and falling, advancing and receding, with the convexity and concavity, and other forms of the great parts, have the same effect in architecture, that hill and dale, fore-ground and distance, swelling and sinking have in landscape: That is, they serve to produce an agreeable and diversified contour, that groups and contrasts like a picture, and creates a variety of light and shade, which gives great spirit, beauty and effect to the composition . . .

We cannot however allow ourselves to close this note without doing justice to the memory of a great man, whose reputation as an architect has been long carried down the stream by a torrent of undistinguishing prejudice and abuse.

*43. Robert Adam, Culzean Castle, Ayrshire, aerial view, 1777–90*

Sir John Vanbrugh's genius was of the first class; and, in point of movement, novelty and ingenuity, his works have not been exceeded by anything in modern times (*The Works in Architecture of Robert and James Adam, Esquires,* vol. 1, 1773, p. [4]).

How far Adam achieved this movement in his own architecture is a matter for debate. One distinctly Vanbrughian building by him is his last work, Seton Castle, East Lothian (1789–91), which seems to have been inspired by Vanbrugh's own house at Greenwich, Vanbrugh Castle (1718, with later additions). The combination at Vanbrugh Castle of symmetrical with consciously asymmetrical forms in the disposition of both the house and its linked outbuildings was fraught with consequences for the future. However, it was not this aspect of Vanbrugh's work that, on the whole, was to influence Adam. It was in the subtle variety of the volumes of his rooms and in his internal planning that Adam sought to recapture the "movement" that had marked Vanbrugh's handling of exterior forms. A characteristically beautiful example of this is Adam's Syon House, Middlesex (1762–69), of which he claimed, in 1773, that "the inequality of the levels has been managed in such a manner as to increase the scenery and add to the movement so that an apparent defect has been converted into a real beauty" (ibid., p. 9). Here, another central tenet of Picturesque theory is stated: that the architect should make use of, not ignore or conceal, natural accidents.

A quintessentially Picturesque environment was created at Strawberry Hill, Middlesex, from 1749 onward, by Horace Walpole (1717–1797). The slow growth of his villa was emphasized, not concealed, so that one could follow its development northward from the simple cottage he found on the site. Strawberry Hill was consciously asymmetrical, and the architect's choice of the Gothic style consciously associational. Its principles were further elaborated upon in a brilliant, asymmetrical house created by the greatest theorist of the Picturesque movement, Richard Payne Knight. Knight's own house, Downton Castle, Herefordshire (1772–78), superbly sited above the deep valley of the Teme River, with views to the Welsh hills beyond, is the first and most influential of those houses that rely for their effect on painterly and asymmetrical massing and grouping. Fortunately, Knight gave a clear account of his intentions at Downton in his distinguished and stimulating book, *An Analytical Inquiry into the Principles of Taste* (1805): "It is now more than thirty years since the author of this inquiry ventured to build a house, ornamented with what are called Gothic towers and battlements without, and with Grecian ceilings, columns, and entablatures within . . . It has, however, the advantage of being capable of receiving alterations and additions in almost any direction, without any injury to its genuine and original character.

The best style of architecture for irregular and picturesque houses, which can not be adopted, is that mixed style, which characterizes the buildings of Claude and the Poussins: for as it is taken from models, which were built piece-meal, during many successive ages, and by several different nations;

*44. Robert Adam, Seton Castle, East Lothian, 1789–91*

*45. John Nash, Cronkhill, Shropshire, c. 1802*

it is distinguished by no particular manner of execution, or class of ornaments; but admits of all promiscuously, from a plain wall or buttress, of the roughest masonry, to the most highly wrought Corinthian capital . . .

In choosing a situation for a house of this kind, which is to be a principal feature of a place, more consideration ought to be had of the views towards it, than of those fromwards it: for, consistently with comfort, which ought to be the first object in every dwelling, it very rarely happens that a perfect composition of landscape scenery can be obtained from a door or window; nor does it appear to me particularly desirable that it should be: for few persons ever look for such compositions, or pay much attention to them, while within doors. It is in walks or rides through parks, gardens or pleasure grounds that they are attended to and examined, and become subjects of conversation . . .

Sir John Vanbrugh is the only architect, I know of, who has either planned or placed his houses according to the principle here recommended; and, in his two chief works, Blenheim and Castle Howard . . . The views from the principal fronts of both are bad . . . but the situations of both, as objects to the surrounding scenery, are the best that could have been chosen" (4th ed., 1808, pp. 225–27).

This passage makes clear the revolutionary way in which the Picturesque dissolved the compositional techniques that were traditional in Palladian and Baroque architecture in favor of an architecture of growth and change, designed pictorially so as to be absorbed into its landscape setting. In emphasizing this point Knight found it necessary to censure the great Capability Brown, whose landscaped parks, which seem so beautiful to us today, were too smoothly artificial for Knight's tastes, and whose designs for country houses were for the most part conventionally Palladian. Less fairly, Knight associated Humphry Repton (1752–1818) with his attacks on Capability Brown. Yet it is the executed work of Repton and his partner John Nash (1752–1835) that most closely approximates the ideals laid down by Knight, Uvedale Price, and William Gilpin. It was Gilpin (1724–1804) who had first popularized the term Picturesque in a book called *Observations Relative Chiefly to Picturesque Beauty* (1789). This was quickly followed by three important publications, of 1794: his own *Three Essays on Picturesque Beauty*, Knight's *The Landscape, a Didactic Poem* (dedicated to Uvedale Price), and Price's *Essay on the Picturesque*. In 1795 Humphry Repton produced his own contribution to the corpus of Picturesque theory, *Sketches and Hints on Landscape Gardening*, which was, of course, more practical and less theoretical than the work of Price and Knight. Indeed, in the next year, 1796, Repton formed an alliance with John Nash, a practicing architect, to show how architecture and landscape could be designed according to the same principles.

Perhaps the principal achievement of the partnership between Repton and Nash was Luscombe Castle, Devon (1799–1804), built for Charles Hoare, great-nephew of Henry Hoare of Stourhead. The *Red Book* in which Repton

*III. Sir William Chambers, Project for the Mausoleum of Frederick, Prince of Wales, section, 1751–52*

*IV. Stourhead, Wiltshire, view toward the Pantheon, completed 1765*

46. Horace Walpole, Strawberry Hill, Middlesex, north and west fronts, 1749–92

47. Horace Walpole, Strawberry Hill, Middlesex, plan, 1749–92

presented his proposals to Mrs. Hoare contains a view of Luscombe as developed according to Capability Brown's ideas, contrasted with a view showing Nash's and Repton's proposals for a more dramatic and Picturesque scheme in accordance with the ideas of Price and Knight. Derived from the asymmetrical composition of Downton Castle, the smaller Luscombe pivots on an octagonal tower containing a drawing room leading into a large conservatory. Varied, compact, and practical, with all the groundfloor windows coming down to floor level so as to make the most of the views across the park and valley to the sea, the plan is totally original. Such planning anticipates the "organic" sophistication of Frank Lloyd Wright's so-called Prairie Houses. Certainly no other European country could produce plans as revolutionary as this as early as 1799.

Other architects adopted Nash's daring and delectable asymmetry, notably Sir Jeffry Wyatville (1766–1840), who, at Endsleigh, Devon (1810–11), created one of the most striking houses of the nineteenth century. With a view to the erection of a large cottage orné, the duke of Bedford had selected a superb site in the wooded hills above the Tamar River already occupied by a simple cottage. Repton was called in to landscape the grounds while Wyatville provided a long, low house of astonishing freedom of plan in a mixed vernacular style, the whole anticipating the Shingle style of later nineteenth-century America. With the strange diagonal articulation of its plan, the rustic verandas and bay windows, Endsleigh, like Salvin's Scotney, is a perfect visual expression of the essential Picturesque idea so clearly stated by Uvedale Price: "If the owner of such a spot, instead of making a regular front and sides were to insist on having the windows turned towards the points where objects were most happily arranged, the architect would be forced into inventing a number of picturesque forms and combinations which otherwise might never have occurred to him; and would be obliged to do what has so seldom been done—accommodate his building to the scenery, not make that give way to the building" (*Essays on the Picturesque,* 2d ed., vol. 11, 1810, p. 268).

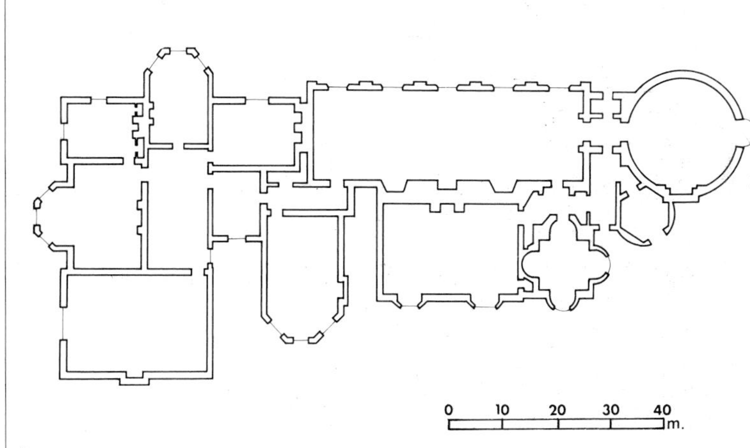


Another Picturesque extravaganza, with a plan as bizarre and unprecedented as that of Endsleigh, is Highcliffe Castle, Hampshire (1830–34), by W. J. Donthorn (1799–1859). The first Lord Stuart de Rothesay employed Donthorn to blend the transported fragments of an early sixteenth-century French Flamboyant Gothic mansion into a sympathetic modern re-creation. The deliberate blurring of the visual boundary between what twentieth-century man would call "original," on the one hand, and "fake," on the other, must be regarded as characteristic of neoclassical and Picturesque taste. Lord Stuart's daughter complained that Donthorn "was ambitious of his own fame and wanted to emulate Fonthill and Ashridge"—and certainly the astonishing composition of Highcliffe, with its aspiring verticality and its tangential wings thrusting forward along the cliff top, owes much to the planning revolution effected by the practitioners of the Picturesque in late eighteenth-century England. Highcliffe was also Picturesque in the literal

*48. Richard Payne Knight, Downton Castle, Herefordshire, entrance facade, 1772–78*

sense in that, in reconstructing this Normandy château, Donthorn relied on views of it *in situ,* by J. S. Cotman, made before Lord Stuart de Rothesay brought the house to England in 1830.

A very different house built at about the same time as Endsleigh shows that an irregular building could be designed in a style other than Gothic or Tudor and still fit appropriately into a dramatic or Picturesque landscape. This is Dunglass, Haddingtonshire, executed from 1807 to 1813 for the architectural historian Sir James Hall (1761–1832), from designs by Richard Crichton (1771–1817). Pivoting on a tower perched at the head of a rocky glen, Dunglass has some stylistic affinities with the Vanbrugh/Nicholas Hawksmoor approach and recalls the enthusiasm for Vanbrugh shared by Price and Knight. Hall went so far in following Price's recommendations as to employ the services of a landscape painter, Alexander Nasmyth, to settle the site of the house, before calling in the architects.

Another rather later Picturesque house which seems to owe something to Vanbrughian composition is Beaufront Castle, Northumberland (1836–42), by John Dobson (1787–1865). A prolific north-country architect, Dobson is today best remembered for his austere, late neoclassical country houses, but the pictorial massing of Beaufront reminds us that he had been a pupil of the watercolorist John Varley, and that one of his first commissions had beed to carry out alterations at Vanbrugh's powerfully romantic Seaton Delaval, also in Northumberland.

Dodington Park, Gloucestershire (1798–1808), by James Wyatt (1746–1813), and Sezincote House, Gloucestershire (c. 1805), by Samuel Pepys Cockerell (1753–1827)—though one is neoclassical and the other neo-Mogul—are among the most successful examples of pictorially composed houses, blending nature and architecture by means of long quadrant greenhouses. Equally significant, though now demolished, was Thomas Hope's remarkable country house, The Deepdene, near Dorking, in Surrey. This was a late eighteenth-century house that Hope (1769–1831) bought in 1807 and to which he made a series of irregular Picturesque additions in 1818–19 and 1823. First of all came a new entrance front and private wing, with exteriors ranging stylistically from Gothic to Pompeian and culminating in an asymmetrically placed, loggia-topped tower of Lombard or Tuscan origin. With this striking object Hope had created, at a stroke, the language in which so many Italianate villas of the first half of the nineteenth century—by such architects as Sir Charles Barry (1795–1860) and Thomas Cubitt (1788–1855), and their many followers—were to be composed. In April 1819 Hope's friend, the novelist Maria Edgeworth, recorded in a letter that the house appeared "grotesque and confused among trees in no one particular taste." Had she been more familiar with the writings of Knight she might have welcomed the blending of styles as a realization of his recommendations concerning "that mixed style, which characterizes the buildings of Claude and the Poussins." The irregular skyline of The Deepdene, the tower and the detached group of kitchen

*49. John Nash, Luscombe Castle, Devon, plan, 1799–1804*

*50. John Nash, Luscombe Castle, Devon, south front, 1799–1804; chapel by Sir George Gilbert Scott, 1862*

*51. Sir Jeffry Wyatville, Endsleigh, Devon, detail, 1810–11*

*52. Sir Jeffry Wyatville, Endsleigh, Devon, plan, 1810–11*

*53. William Wilkins, Grange Park, Hampshire, 1809; conservatory wing by Charles Robert Cockerell, 1823*

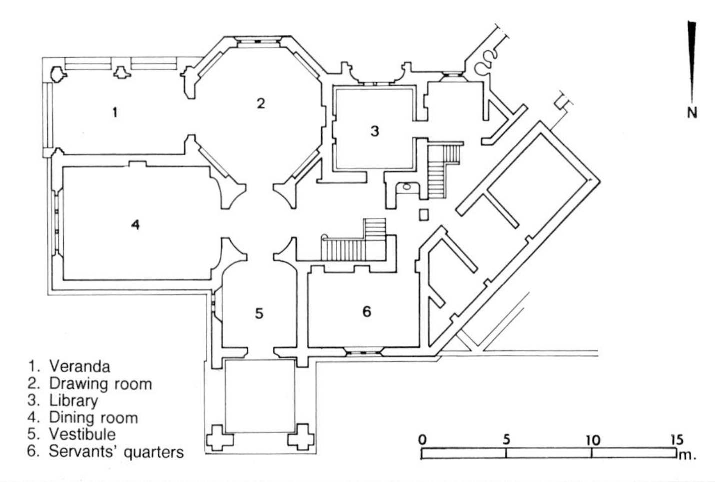

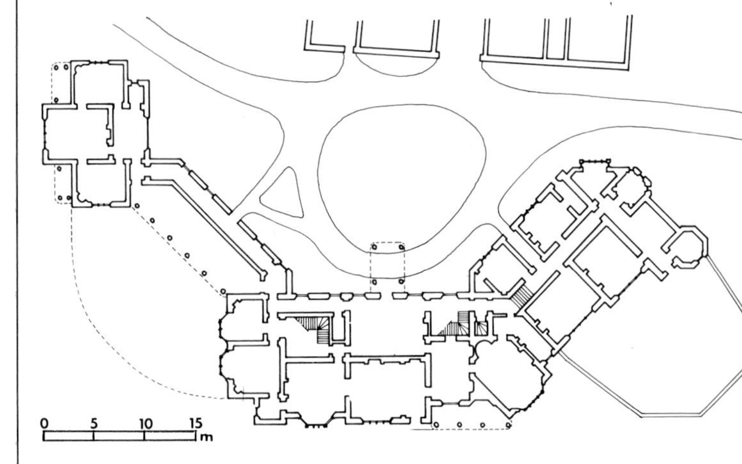

offices placed among trees on sloping ground and sporting a belvedere and spire, similarly followed advice given by Sir Uvedale Price.

Thomas Hope was, of course, himself a Picturesque theorist. In 1808 he published an article "On the Art of Gardening," which was reprinted in Mrs. Hofland's *A Descriptive Account of . . . White-Knights* (1819). Here Hope developed further the occasional expressions of regret made by Price and Knight at the way in which Capability Brown swept away all survivals of formal gardens, terraces, and balustrades, so as to bring his shaven lawns right up to the house. Thus Hope felt able to speak warmly of "the suspended gardens within Genoa, and of the splendid villas about Rome . . . those striking oppositions of the rarest marbles to the richest verdure; those mixtures of statues, and vases, and balustrades, with cypresses, and pinasters, and bays; those distant hills seen through the converging lines of lengthened colonnades . . ." (pp. 11–13).

By developing ideas outlined by Price and Knight, Hope anticipated, as with his loggia-topped tower, later nineteenth-century practice: in this case the vast, formal Italianate gardens laid out by Barry and William Eden Nesfield (1835–1888). In the same essay he wrote of the new Picturesque architecture; he wished to establish that "the cluster of highly adorned and sheltered apartments that form the mansion . . . should shoot out, as it were, into . . . ramifications of arcades, porticos, terraces, parterres, treillages, avenues. . . ." He gave a striking demonstration of this in the additions he made to The Deepdene, in 1823: a bizarre complex of conservatories, sculpture galleries, and orangeries from the house down the hill at an angle of about forty-five degrees. This represented the height of the Picturesque ambition to break down the barriers between nature and architecture. In general, this ambition was, in these years, a particularly English one—indeed, it was England's gift to Europe and North America—but we can also find it clearly stated in the work of the German Karl Friedrich Schinkel (1781–1841).

In 1824 work began on Schloss Glienicke, a villa near Berlin, by the side of the Potsdam Bridge over the Havel River. Schinkel built it for the twenty-five-year-old Prince Karl, one of the sons of King Friedrich Wilhelm III of Prussia. The house is simple, asymmetrical, and low-spreading and pivots around a tower. It forms a courtyard of simplified Italianate architecture on the walls of which are displayed antique Roman sculpture and casts acquired by Prince Karl in Italy. The small, undulating park, prettily landscaped by P. J. Lenné (1789–1866), contains numerous garden buildings by Schinkel as well as the remarkable Klosterhaus, a small cloister in a rich Byzantine style, built shortly after Schinkel's death in order to house the collection of Byzantine sculptures that the prince brought back from Venice, Padua, and elsewhere. Near the edge of the river are two additional buildings by Schinkel, the gardener's house and the Kasino (1826). With its vine-clad loggias looking out across the water, the elegant Italianate Kasino reminds one how much Berliners must have wished to forget the forbidding Prussian climate and imagine themselves on the shores of Italian

*54. John Dobson, Beaufront Castle, Northumberland, stable courtyard, 1836–42*

*55. James Wyatt, Dodington Park, Gloucestershire, 1798–1813*

*56. Samuel Pepys Cockerell, Sezincote House, Gloucestershire, c. 1805*

lakes. Also from 1826 is the Schloss Charlottenhof at Potsdam, designed by Schinkel on his return from an important visit to England. This was a pleasure pavilion for Prince Karl's brother, the crown prince, an architect manqué to whom the general disposition of the buildings is due. The relationship of the low, Italianate house with its Greek Doric portico to the gardens, loggias, canals, and pavilions, is masterly. In 1829–36 Schinkel and Ludwig Persius (1803–1845) greatly heightened the Picturesque charms of Charlottenhof by laying out a water garden punctuated by irregularly placed buildings such as the court gardener's house, the Tea House, and Roman Bath. The subtle and delectable blending of nature and architecture, though developed from hints in the writings of J.-N.-L. Durand, J. K. Krafft, and Pierre-Nicolas Ransonnette, closely parallels both what Thomas Hope had achieved at The Deepdene from 1818 to 1823, and the remarkable village of Clisson in the Vendée, built from 1805 to 1820 in an Italianate vernacular style.

For yet another of King Friedrich Wilhelm's sons, Prince Wilhelm, Schinkel designed the extensive Schloss Babelsberg near Potsdam (1833) in Nash's castellated style; its turrets can be glimpsed through the trees from Schloss Glienicke. The crown prince certainly had a hand in selecting the style of Schloss Babelsberg, which is so closely based on such castles by Nash as Luscombe, Caerhayes, and East Cowes that it must be one of the most English buildings in Germany.

So far, we have spoken as though the Picturesque could be realized only in the country, but John Nash showed brilliantly its suitability for urban design. In 1811 his Blaise Hamlet near Bristol, curiously similar to Richard Mique's *hameau* at Versailles, of 1778–82, was a foretaste of subsequent garden suburbs from Richard Norman Shaw's Bedford Park onward, but it is Nash's redevelopment of central London, also initiated in 1811, to which we should now turn our attention.

John Fordyce, Surveyor-General of the Office of Woods and Forests, was a great believer in comprehensive town planning. Seeing that the king's largely rural Marylebone estate, which was leased to the duke of Portland, was to revert to the Crown in 1811, Fordyce argued for the creation of a new major road leading to the estate from Charing Cross. In 1806 he appointed Nash as one of the two architects in the Office of Woods and Forests, and in October 1810 the department commissioned two alternative schemes for the development of the Marylebone estate and the new road. The architects invited to submit designs were Thomas Leverton and Thomas Chawner, the department's surveyors, and Nash and James Morgan. When Nash's plans were accepted in July 1811 the Prince of Wales was so pleased with their magnificence that he exclaimed: "It will quite eclipse Napoleon."

If he had in mind such schemes as the Rue de Rivoli by Charles Percier and Pierre-François-Léonard Fontaine he was quite right in supposing that Nash's genius in town planning was of an altogether different order. Instead of covering Marylebone with a grid of streets and squares, as Leverton and

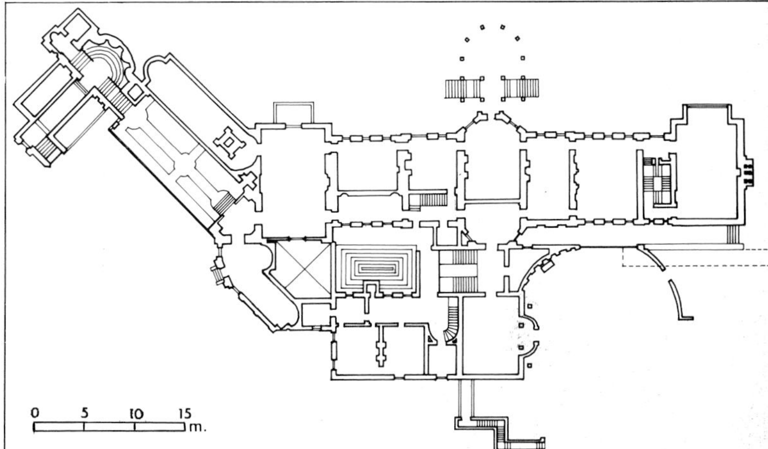


*57. Thomas Hope and William Atkinson, The Deepdene, Surrey, plan, 1818–23*

*58. Thomas Hope and William Atkinson, The Deepdene, Surrey, conservatory wing, 1818–23. British Architectural Library Drawings Collection*

*59. Karl Friedrich Schinkel, Schloss Charlottenhof, Potsdam, 1826*

*60. Karl Friedrich Schinkel and Ludwig Persius, court gardener's house, Schloss Charlottenhof, Potsdam, 1829–36*

Chawner envisaged, Nash realized that since many people living in London would prefer to live in the country, the most popular way of developing the Marylebone estate would be to turn it into a Picturesque rural park dotted with villas and flanked by broken runs of terraced houses glimpsed irregularly through trees. In fact, Nash's first plan of 1811 was rather more stilted than the final proposals. Nevertheless, in 1812 a part of the 1811 plan was begun, the southern half of the circus at the north end of Portland Place, but the builder went bankrupt so that the northern half was never built. The result is more is more in keeping with Nash's eventual proposals since it enables the greenery of the park to be seen from Portland Place. In 1812 Nash also presented his scheme for linking the new buildings in the park with the prince's dwelling at Carlton House, and from there, by implication, to the seat of government at Westminster. Nash saw immediately what no one else had thought of, that the line of his new road should follow that curious division between the sleaziness of Soho to the east and the elegance of Mayfair to the west. Thus he could buy up property fairly cheaply at Soho prices and sell it at Mayfair prices. Henry Holland's impressive colonnaded screen in front of Carlton House provided the visual climax at the southern end of Nash's scheme, but, since Portland Place and the entrance to the Marylebone estate lay to the northwest of this, the new processional route would necessarily have to follow a convoluted course. Here Nash heeded the advice of the Picturesque theorists—to make use of, rather than to conceal, natural accidents. Hence the celebrated Picturesque curve of the Regent Street quadrant, which he justified as "resembling in that respect the High Street at Oxford." Hence also the scenically placed if eccentrically planned All Souls' church, Langham Place, which subtly and seductively directed one's glance around an awkward shift in axis.

Behind the sweeping terraces surrounding Regent's Park, Nash developed a Picturesque enclave of Italianate villas and cottages ornés known as Park Village East and Park Village West. An outgrowth of his Blaise Hamlet theme, these were the prototypes of subsequent garden suburbs.

The strong emphasis that the Picturesque theory of the eighteenth century placed on domestic architecture led, in the nineteenth century, to a not unhealthy preoccupation with the house as a building type. This preoccupation survived the Gothic Revival of the first half of the century and its concern with church building and reemerged in the so-called Queen Anne movement, or Domestic Revival, of the 1870s, which had been created by Nesfield and Shaw in the 1860s. Indeed, there was an almost moral seriousness in the approach to house design after 1850. It became a kind of sacred task. We can sense something of this in the lectures on architecture that Ruskin delivered at Edinburgh in 1853. His lecture on domestic architecture proclaimed a belief in the value of vernacular buildings and the country cottage, which linked him, ironically, with the Picturesque movement and the Regency pattern-books of rural architecture. What

*61. Karl Friedrich Schinkel, Schloss Charlottenhof, Potsdam, 1826*

*62. John Nash, the Regent Street quadrant, London, 1818–20*

*63. John Nash, Regent Street and Regent's Park, London, plan, 1811–30*

*64. John Nash, Chester Terrace, Regent's Park, London, 1820 and later*

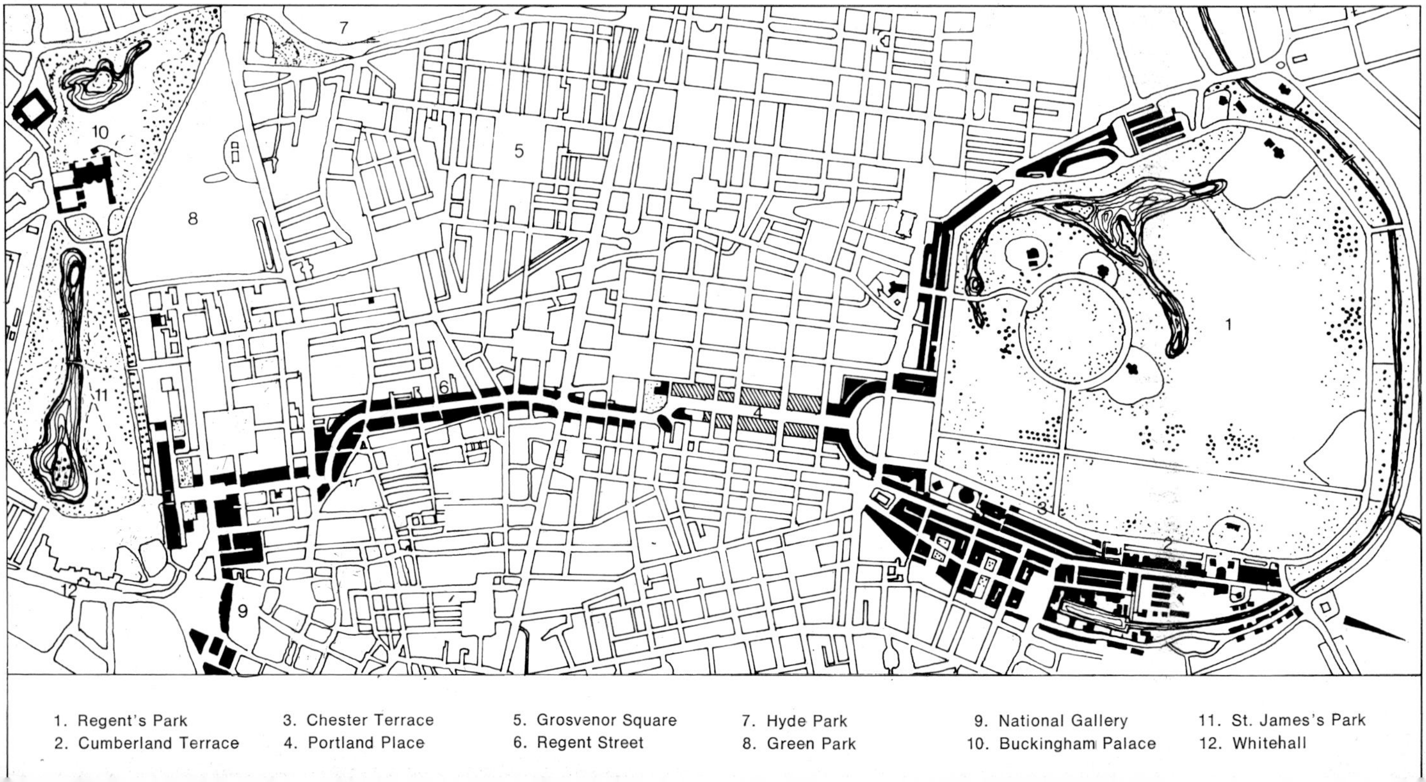

1. Regent's Park
2. Cumberland Terrace
3. Chester Terrace
4. Portland Place
5. Grosvenor Square
6. Regent Street
7. Hyde Park
8. Green Park
9. National Gallery
10. Buckingham Palace
11. St. James's Park
12. Whitehall

CHESTER TERR
ACG 160J

*65, 66. John Nash, cottages at Blaise Hamlet, near Bristol, 1811*

*67. John Nash, Cumberland Terrace, Regent's Park, London, 1820 and later*

*68. George Devey, Betteshanger, Kent, 1856–61*

*69. George Devey, cottages, Penshurst, Kent, 1850*

## Chapter Three
## ARCHAEOLOGY AND THE INFLUENCE OF THE ANTIQUE

distinguished such cottages from the boxlike neoclassicism he so much despised was their roofs. These, he felt, were not merely Picturesque in themselves but deeply expressive of the human need for shelter. He argued that the cottage was "really more roof than anything else." For him, "The very soul of the cottage—the essence and meaning of it—are in its roof; it is that, mainly, wherein consists its shelter; that, wherein it differs most completely from a cleft in rocks or bower in woods. It is in its thick impenetrable coverlid of close thatch that its whole heart and hospitality are concentrated. Consider the difference, in sound, of the expression 'beneath my roof' and 'within my walls.'" Ruskin went on to ask: "Do you suppose that which is so important in a cottage can be of small importance in your own dwelling-house? . . . It is vain to say you take the roof for granted. You may as well say you take a man's kindness for granted." Second only to the roof in architectural and spiritual significance was the bay window: "You surely must all of you feel and admit the delightfulness of a bow-window; I can hardly fancy a room can be perfect without one."

In fact, there were a good many architects who shared Ruskin's fancies and, from George Devey (1820–1886) in the 1850s to Edwin Lutyens (1869–1944) in the 1890s, they put them unceasingly into practice. At Penshurst, Kent, in 1850, Devey designed cottages for Lord de l'Isle that are narrative statements about the Old English rural way of life. They are Picturesque not only for that reason but also because they remind one of both old country cottages and *pictures* of such cottages. Devey had been trained as a watercolorist under J. D. Harding, and Penshurst in the 1840s and 1850s became something of an artists's colony. Devey's patrons at two of his major country houses in Kent, Sir Walter James at Betteshanger and W. O. Hammond at St. Alban's Court, were both keen watercolorists and appreciators of Old English rural traditions. At Betteshanger, from 1856 to 1861 and in 1882, Devey created "instant history" by echoing the enthusiasm of eighteenth-century Picturesque theorists for buildings in which one could read a process of growth and change. The historical and pictorial fantasy which Devey created at Betteshanger is that of a late-medieval house, successively altered, extended, and patched with different materials in the Elizabethan period and in the seventeenth and eighteenth centuries. A lazy, spreading plan of the type pioneered by Wyatville at Endsleigh, in 1810, heightens the impression of informal growth. St. Alban's Court (1874–78) is a more unified design, but even here the lower parts of the walls are of stone, ending in a ragged, uneven line, and the upper parts are of brick, so as to suggest, falsely, the re-use of an earlier house on the site. In fact, the earlier house lay in the valley below, and its remains, suitably restored and romanticized by Devey, form a Picturesque object much as the old Scotney Castle does on the grounds of Salvin's new Scotney.

Greece was described in 1650 by Roland Fréart de Chambray as "the divine country." Claude Perrault declared that he aimed to renew architecture by reverting to the purity of the temples of ancient Greece, and in his translation of Vitruvius's works he illustrated a baseless and fluted Doric column, a concept that had been illustrated also by Renaissance commentators, though never as accurately. But though Greek architecture was long regarded as the basis of all excellence, and though there were attempts to conjure up and explore its visual forms, almost nothing was known about it. It remained, largely, a literary ideal. Not until 1750, when J.-G. Soufflot and his pupil G.-P.-M. Dumont measured the Doric temples of Paestum, were French architects to begin to make any serious inspection of the ruins of Greek antiquity. They were not quick, however, to use this information. Soufflot introduced an engaged version of the Paestum Doric column, with a base and pedestal, into the crypt of Ste.-Geneviève about 1758, but not until 1764 was Dumont to publish the results of their fieldwork in *Suite de plans . . . de trois temples . . . de Paestum,* and even then it was the first publication of its sort. One may wonder at their lack of response. The answer lies in their aesthetic preferences. Not until the late eighteenth century did architects in Europe learn to respond to the bold sculptural qualities of the Doric. They followed their Renaissance predecessors in finding their inspiration rather in the forms of Roman antiquity. When Colbert thought to ensure that his architects might have the correct antique models, he sent Antoine Desgodets to Rome, where he measured no less than forty-nine Roman monuments; engravings of these were published in 1682 in the sumptuous *Les édifices antiques de Rome.* This was to remain the standard reference for two hundred years. Colbert made no attempt to sponsor a similar publication on the monuments of Greece. Yet for twenty years and more, at considerable expense, he sent out agents to the mainland of Greece, to the islands, to Turkey, Palestine, Syria, and even to Persia and beyond to collect manuscripts, medallions, and coins for his extensive collections. And though these agents were instructed by Claude Perrault's brother, Charles, and told to take their copies of Pausanias with them and to visit all possible ancient sites, they can scarcely be said to have enhanced existing knowledge of Greek architecture. Early travelers to Greece—and there were many who went on trade and diplomatic missions—stopped at Athens and penetrated to the Parthenon, then more or less intact, and recorded their wonder. Robert de Dreux, for instance, who was there in 1668, said that it appeared so magnificent that, having seen it, there was no need to look further for architectural perfection.

That most enlightened of early ambassadors, the Marquis de Nointel, explored Athens and several of the islands in 1674 with a carefully chosen and extremely costly retinue, including the author of *Les mille et une nuits,* Antoine Galland, and two artists, Rombaut Faydherbe and Jacques Carrey, who were to record the sculptures of the Parthenon, but they did very little, indeed, to publicize the results of their investigations. Nointel did, however,

*70. Jacob Spon, engraving of the Parthenon, Athens, from his* Voyage d'Italie, de Dalmatie, de Grèce, et du Levant, *1676*

*71. Jacques Carrey (attributed),* The Expedition of the Marquis de Nointel to Athens. *Chartres, Musée des Beaux-Arts*

send back to France some notes and observations made by the Jesuit missionary J.-P. Babin, which were published at once by the scholar and doctor Jacob Spon. Spon himself was inspired to travel to Greece and—financed by Colbert—he set out; in Venice he encountered the English botanist George Wheler, whom he took with him. By 1676 he was back in his native Lyons, where he published his *Voyage d'Italie, de Dalmatie, de Grèce, et du Levant.* This was to remain for almost seventy years the most reliable and, from an architectural standpoint, most illuminating account of the buildings of Athens. It contained a miserable engraving of the Parthenon, showing that the columns were heavily proportioned, fluted, and baseless. Although the illustration was not of the sort to inspire architects, it nonetheless became famous, having been reproduced by Wheler in his plagiarized account of the journey with Spon, published in England in 1682, and in a description of Athens by Cornelio Magni, issued in Italy from 1679 to 1692. When Bernard de Montfaucon published his monumental compilation of all the known artifacts of antiquity, *L'antiquité expliquée,* issued in fifteen folio volumes, from 1719 to 1724, he was still forced to rely on Spon's record of the Doric temple. Similarly, for the temples of Baalbek, the only ones in Palestine that he was able to illustrate, Montfaucon was compelled to turn to seventeenth-century engravings, those made about 1680 by Jean Marot, probably on the basis of drawings, provided by another of Colbert's agents, M. de Monceaux, who visited the site in 1668. The Perrault brothers, as we have seen, may have had a hand in Marot's distorted reconstruction of the Temple of Bacchus at Baalbek, endowing it with a nave and aisles separated by columns, and a coffered barrel vault above. This variant, however incorrect, had its appeal, and soon after its appearance in Montfaucon's work it became the basis for the reconstruction drawings of the temples at Palmyra and Olympia by Johann Fischer von Erlach (1656-1723), author of that first extensively illustrated history of architecture *Entwurff einer historischen Architektur,* issued first in 1721, and then in 1725, 1730, 1737, and 1742. This was a book to which architects could respond; the text was limited to a few lines underneath each engraving.

The plates depicted an extraordinary and breathtaking array of buildings, real and imaginary, including the wonders of the ancient world, the mosques of Constantinople, the palaces and bridges of China, and also a sheaf of Fischer von Erlach's own designs. At the end of the eighteenth century Boullée was basing his pyramids on those reconstructions by Fischer von Erlach, while in the early years of the next century Fischer's naumachia was being adapted for an arena in Milan by Luigi Canonica. Fischer's imagery was to remain potent for almost one hundred years, although there was no great accuracy of observation in his views.

A more informed knowledge of Greek architecture became possible only in the middle years of the eighteenth century when measured drawings of the temples of Athens were included in the third volume of Richard

*72. Johann Fischer von Erlach, plates from his* Entwurff einer historischen Architektur, *1721, showing Chinese buildings, artificial rock mounds and a suspension bridge*

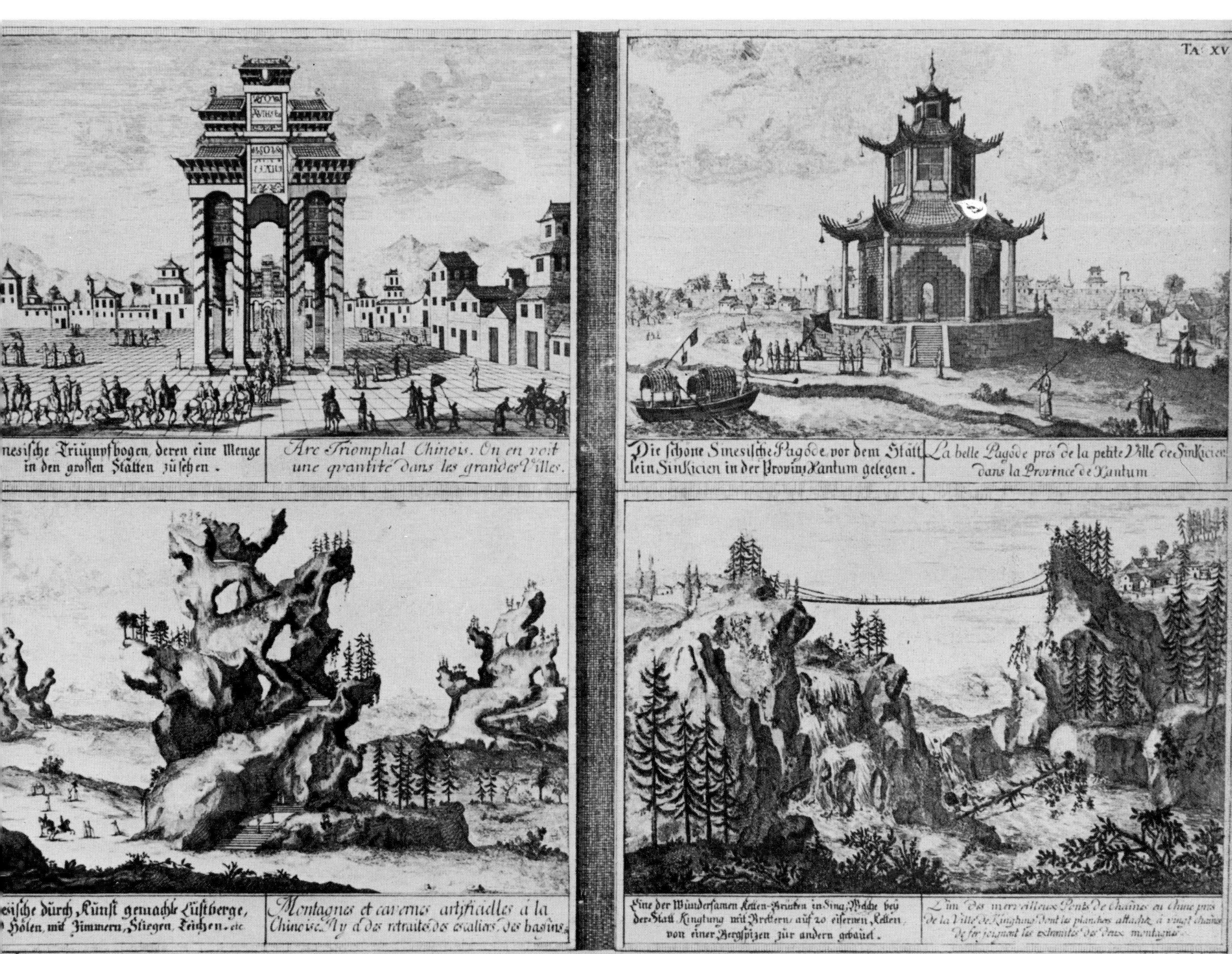

*73. Johann Fischer von Erlach, reconstruction of the Temple of Zeus at Olympia, from his* Entwurff einer historischen Architektur, *1721*

*74. Johann Fischer von Erlach, plates from his* Entwurff einer historischen Architecktur, *1721, showing the Egyptian pyramids*

Pococke's *Description of the East and Some Other Countries,* of 1745, to be followed in 1752 by the work of another Irishman, Richard Dalton's *Antiquities of Greece and Egypt.* Something of the nature of the Doric temples of Sicily was made known also at exactly the same time with the appearance of the second volume of G. M. Pancrazi's *Antichità siciliane.* However, there was nothing either reliable or captivating in these works. Among the first of that succession of scholarly studies that were to open up a real knowledge of antique architecture and provide models for emulation and even imitation were *The Ruins of Palmyra,* of 1753, and *The Ruins of Balbec,* of 1757, the results of an expedition undertaken in 1750 by James Dawkins and Robert Wood (1716–1771) together with John Bouverie and the draftsman Giovanni Battista Borra. These books marked the ascendancy of the British, and in particular the Society of Dilettanti, as patrons and explorers of antiquity. All the important archaelogical publications to follow emanated from the British Isles. In France—Dumont's publication of the temples of Paestum apart (and he was to issue a revised edition in 1769)—only Julien-David Le Roy's *Ruines des plus beaux monuments de la Grèce,* of 1758, may be said to have provided hard archaeological information of the sort required by practicing architects. The information contained there, however, was soon shown to be less hard than might have been expected. In the first volume of their *Antiquities of Athens,* of 1762, Le Roy's rivals James Stuart and Nicholas Revett were to remark that his errors "have most of them been made before, tho'in fewer words by Wheler and Spon" (vol. 1, p. 35). Le Roy's work was, in fact, inspired by Stuart's and Revett's; in 1751 they published two detailed proposals for their work and began their proctracted studies in Greece. By the beginning of 1754 Le Roy was in Greece and, soon after, he published a proposal of his own, based on one of Stuart's and Revett's; by 1758 he had published his own book. This in turn was to be plagiarized when Robert Sayer issued his *Ruins of Athens and Other Valuable Antiquities in Greece,* in 1759. Le Roy's publication, for all its haste and inaccuracy, offered a most seductive array of views and measured drawings of the antiquities of Athens, Attica, and Corinth. Its impact in France, at least, was considerable. When he issued a second edition in 1770, he rearranged all his plates as a rebuke to Stuart and Revett, demonstrating that the monuments included in their first volume—the Temple on the Ilissus, the Choragic Monument of Lysicrates, the Tower of the Winds, and the Stoa at Athens—were all post-Periclean works, and thus somewhat lax in style. And he answered their gibes at his errors by pointing out that he was in no way interested in the minutiae of measurements. He did not wish to provide models for imitation. He was intent to conjure up only the effects and the qualities of architecture. And this statement might be taken as a hint as to why the French, though they continued to visit classical ruins with great eagerness—witness the studies of the French *pensionnaires* (students, usually winners of the Grand Prix, sent to study at the Académie de France in Rome) and the magnificent volumes of the Abbé Richard de Saint-Non's *Voyage*

*75. Julien-David Le Roy, view of the Parthenon, Athens, illustrated in his* Ruines des plus beaux monuments de la Grèce, *1758*

*76, 77. Louis-Joseph Le Lorrain, designs for the first Festa della Chinea, Rome, 1746, 1747*

*pittoresque; ou, description des royaumes de Naples et de Sicile,* issued between 1781 and 1786, Jean-Pierre Houel's *Voyage pittoresque des isles de Sicile, de Malte, et de Lipari,* of 1782 to 1787, and the Comte de Choiseul-Gouffier's *Voyage pittoresque de la Grèce,* of 1782 and 1809—did not at any time instigate a Greek or even a doctrinaire Roman revival. The French were not interested in copying Greek and Roman forms. As with their study of Gothic architecture, they were concerned only to discover principles, methods of grouping and composing, means of handling scale and proportion, and techniques of building. They sought the spirit of antiquity—and also of Gothic architecture—not the detail.

Yet there was something of a minor Greek revival in France in the 1760s known as the *goût grec,* and also a fierce polemic waged against the fiery Piranesi in Rome as to the merits of Greek architecture.

The *goût grec* was the creation of the Comte de Caylus (1692–1765). He had, in fact, set out in 1716 to search for the site of Troy and had spent almost a year wandering in Asia Minor, visiting the Temple of Diana at Ephesus, but he returned home when recalled by his mother without having explored Athens itself. He was to become a connoisseur and antiquarian, and in 1729 he began to form a mixed collection of antiquities similar to that begun by Montfaucon in 1693. This was to become the focus of his salon and to serve as the basis for the seven volumes of his *Recueil d'antiquités* that appeared between 1752 and 1767. There was not much in these on architecture, though the later volumes did include the Gallo-Roman antiquities of southern France. His influence was exerted rather through his friends, the collector and publisher Pierre-Jean Mariette, the critic Abbé Jean-Baptiste Leblanc, and the Abbé Jean-Jacques Barthélemy, and through his personal efforts.

The young painter Louis-Joseph Le Lorrain (1715-1759) was a *pensionnaire* in Rome who had made something of a name for himself with three designs for the Festa della Chinea of 1745, 1746, and 1747 that may be said to have taken up where Perrault left off. He was warmly recommended by Caylus to Ange-Laurent La Live de Jully, master of ceremonies at court, for whom, in 1756, he designed a suite of furniture, in ebony and gilt-bronze, a writing table, cabinet, and clock that were regarded as startlingly Greek in inspiration and form. Each object was decidedly heavier and clumsier than contemporary French furniture, recalling that of Louis XIV's reign, but was in no sense antique. Yet this furniture led, at once, to a wide if ineffectual fashion for things *à la grec*—fans, snuff boxes, occasional chairs or tables, and a handful of houses. Details for the more authentically antique works were taken from such early publications on the ruins of Herculaneum—where excavations had started in 1738—as that produced in 1751 by Soufflot's companion on his voyage C.-N. Cochin. Even in its revised form of 1754, this was not particularly informative. Revelation had to await the appearance of the nine large volumes of the *Antichità d'Ercolano,* which appeared from 1755 until 1792. But the

*78. Louis-Joseph Le Lorrain, writing desk, cabinet, and clock designed for Ange-Laurent La Live de Jully, 1756*

disclosures they contained were taken up by painters rather than by designers and architects. Joseph-Marie Vien, a protégé of Caylus, introduced an authentic-looking antique tripod into his insipid Grecian study *Une prêtresse qui brûle de l'encens sur un trépied,* of 1763 (later to become known as *La vertueuse athénienne).* In Rome, it should be noted, such attempts to depict antique furniture had already been made in 1761 in Gavin Hamilton's *Andromache Bewailing the Death of Hector,* and, in the same year, in Anton Raphael Meng's *Augustus and Cleopatra.* But the French, as we have seen, were not greatly interested in archaeological accuracy.

The Abbé Laugier acclaimed the Hôtel de Chavannes on the Boulevard du Temple, in Paris, built between 1756 and 1758 by Pierre-Louis Moreau-Desproux (1727-1793), as an exemplar of the new Greek mode, but the surviving drawing of the elevation shows that the only features that might connect it to Greek architecture were some bands of fretwork—and they were probably derived from Renaissance buildings—and an unusual largeness of scale conveyed by the use of giant pilasters. The fashion was soon ridiculed both by that spry entertainer Louis Carrogis, known as Carmontelle (1717-1806), in some masquerade costumes, and later, in 1771, in a similar set of costumes designed by Ennemond-Alexandre Petitot (1727–1801), who had been a student in Rome with Le Lorrain but had been sent as architect to the court of Parma in 1753 at the instigation of Caylus himself. On Caylus's recommendation Le Lorrain was employed to tidy up Le Roy's drawings for *Les ruines des plus beaux monuments de la Grèce* and was then given a post in Russia, where he died in 1759.

The *goût grec* was an ephemeral fashion, but it cannot be overlooked. Yet another of Caylus's protégés, the Belgian-born architect and engraver Jean-François de Neufforge (1714–1791), who was to engrave more than half the plates for Le Roy's publication, began to issue his *Recueil élémentaire d'architecture* in 1757. It comprised nine volumes and a total of nine hundred illustrations by 1772. Because these diffused and popularized a coarsened and heavy geometrical style thought to be antique in manner, they may be held to have prepared the ground for the more considered classicism of Louis XVI's reign. The first full-scale example of the new taste was the Hôtel de Varey, in Lyons, designed about 1758 by Toussaint-Noël Loyer (1724–1807), a pupil of Soufflot. There is no feeling for the refinements of classical architecture either in the facades on the Rue Auguste-Comte or on the Place Bellecour, or in the moldings of the salons of this *hôtel,* although they very convincingly reflect the coarsened taste inspired by Caylus and his associates.

Piranesi's quarrel over the merits of Greek architecture, instigated in 1761 with Le Roy and then with Mariette, was prompted more by nationalistic pride and a very real concern for his own livelihood than by any scholarly convictions. Giambattista Piranesi (1720–1778) arrived in Rome at the age of nineteen; he came from Venice, where he had learned etching and may have absorbed some of Carlo Lodoli's radical notions. In Rome he was stunned and then stirred by the sight of the ruins and

*79. Pierre-Louis Moreau-Desproux, project for the Hôtel de Chavannes, Paris, 1756*

*80. Jean-Honoré Fragonard, Temple of the Sibyl at Tivoli. Besançon, Musée des Beaux-Arts*

influenced by a whole range of artists and stage designers such as the Bibienas and the Valeriani brothrs, by the architect Filippo Juvarra, and, in particular, by the painter Gian Paolo Panini, who, in 1711, had himself come south from Piacenza to Rome, where he had established himself as the most prolific painter of scenes of ruins, both real and imaginary. Panini was to teach perspective drawing at the Académie de France and to open the eyes of a whole generation of French architects to the picturesque qualities of ruins—and thus to a more atmospheric view of architecture. He taught them to see architecture in painterly terms. Jean-Laurent Legeay (c. 1710–c. 1788), G.-P.-M. Dumont, Nicolas-Henri Jardin, Charles-Louis Clérisseau, Jérôme-Charles Bellicard (1726–1786), and Petitot, all of whom were in Rome in the 1740s, learned to present their projects in an atmospheric and painterly manner—a manner that conferred more interest on their works than they sometimes merited. Piranesi was in close contact with all these architects, an also with those French painters and sculptors studying in Rome—Jean-Baptiste Lallemand, Le Lorrain, the Challe brothers, Jacques Saly, Claude-Joseph Vernet, Vien, and, later, Hubert Robert. One of the first works to which Piranesi contributed, Fausto Amidei's *Varie vedute di Roma antica e moderna,* issued in 1745, also contained plates by Legeay, and in later editions views of Bellicard were to be added.

But Piranesi soon established himself on his own merit. Already in July 1743, he had published his first suite of etchings, the *Prima parte di architetture e prospettive,* which, though influenced by the works of Fischer von Erlach and the Bibienas, was to influence, in turn, Le Lorrain's designs for the Festa della Chinea of 1746 and 1747. Then in 1748 came the *Antichità romane de tempi della repubblica, e de primi imperatori,* which established his style and his reputation as a recorder of buildings old and new, in and around Rome. Some more idiosyncratic works followed, the four plates of the *Grotteschi,* mysterious rococo confections influenced by his contact with G. B. Tiepolo in 1744, and the fourteen plates of the *Invenzioni capric. de carceri,* the initial version of his theatrical prison designs. All these works were combined and published together in various combinations, for they were not equally successful. What the connoisseurs and cognoscenti who visited Rome wanted, above all, were renderings of the monuments of the city. For four years Piranesi worked feverishly, excavating and measuring ruins, using his imagination for what he could not inspect for himself. In 1756 he began to issue the grandest and most stunning of all his works, the *Antichità romane,* to run eventually to two hundred plates, each two feet across. He had used his wife's dowry to pay for the plates and his strongest influence to secure a tax exemption to cut the cost of the paper. His future was thus tied up in the enterprise. When Le Roy's volume of Grecian antiquities appeared in 1758, with the threat of Stuart's and Revet's to follow, Piranesi determined to shatter all rival claims to originality and magnificence in architecture. With the aid of several local scholars he concocted the long and muddled text and the thirty-eight plates of *Della magnificenza ed*

*81, 82. Ennemond-Alexandre Petitot, Berger et Bergère à la grecque, costumes for a masked ball at the court of Parma, 1771*

*architettura de' Romani,* which appeared in 1761. Refuting both Le Roy's claim that Roman architecture was derived from that of the Greeks—whose architecture was based, in turn, on that of the Egyptians—and a similar historical analysis made in a *Dialogue on Taste,* published as far back as 1755 by the Scottish painter Allan Ramsay, he sought to prove that Roman architecture owed nothing to Greece, that it developed rather from ancient Etruscan architecture, and that if there was not much of that at hand to prove his point, there were at least stupendous engineering works such as the Cloaca Maxima, substructures, aqueducts, and roadways extant. Greek architecture had no such logic and splendor of engineering. Roman architecture, moreover, was richer and far more varied than that of the Greeks, and thus infinitely to be preferred. Reason played small part in Piranesi's propaganda. Caylus's friend Mariette responded succinctly to this outburst in November 1764, in the *Gazette littéraire de l'Europe,* adding to Le Roy's summary history the suggestion that not only was Roman architecture altogether dependent on that of the Greeks, but that it owed whatever finesse it might possess to the labors of Greek slaves. Incensed, Piranesi rushed into print in 1765 his rebuttal of Mariette's arguments, the *Osservazioni . . . sopra la lettre de M. Mariette,* and the related *Parere su l'architettura* with its handful of extraordinary compositions, in which he abandoned all archaeological verisimilitude in favor of original composition. This was followed in 1769 by his equally outrageous, altogether shocking designs for the *Diverse maniere d'adornare i camini.* "Je pense absolument comme vous," Caylus wrote to the archaeologist Paolo Maria Paciaudi, in 1765, "sur l'excès de l'encre et du foin de Piranesi, mais que voulez-vous? C'est sa manière . . ." (*Correspondance,* 1877, vol. 2, p. 95). Caylus could admire only the early works. But by then Pierre Patte was selling copies of Piranesi's etchings in Paris. Piranesi's reputation remained strong and his works continued to sell. The feud with the French was soon forgotten. Just before he died, in 1778, he produced the boldest, most somber of his works, a sheaf of etchings of the temples at Paestum, the title in French, *Différentes vues de quelques restes de trois grands édifices qui subsistent encore dans le milieu de l'ancienne ville de Pesto.* The solemn magic of these plates, more than anything else, perhaps, was to reveal to architects the solid splendor of Greek antiquity.

There were other propagandists, however, the greatest of them Johann Joachim Winckelmann (1717–1768), with whom we still associate the ideal of the "noble simplicity and quiet grandeur" of Greek art. Like Caylus, Winckelmann never visited the temples of Greece itself, though he was invited on three occasions to do so. He preferred that Greece remain a remote landscape. He wanted an ideal image, not reality. When he wrote his first invocation to Greek art, the *Gedanken über die Nachahmung der griechischen Werke in der Malerei und Bildhauerkunst,* in Dresden, in 1755, he had not even traveled to Rome. For his ideas on Greek art he relied on the writings of Pliny the Elder and Pausanias. He visualized Greek art

*83. Jean-François de Neufforge, designed for a paneled interior, section, 1757*

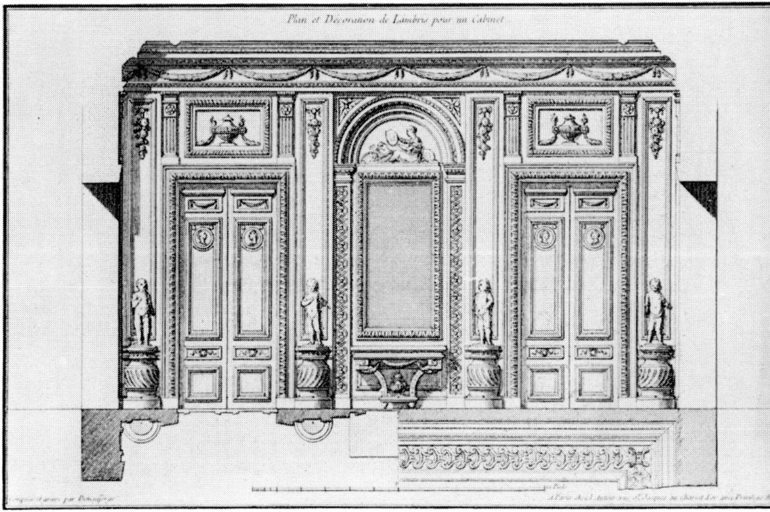


*84. Jean-Laurent Legeay, design for a circular temple, 1765*

*85. Jean-François de Neufforge, church with a Corinthian portico, elevation, 1757*

entirely in terms of that of Raphael—in particular, the *Sistine Madonna,* with which he was familiar in Dresden. Raphael's smooth and rounded forms established Winckelmann's ideal. This was sapless and colorless. "Color," Winckelmann wrote in the second chapter of his *Geschichte der Kunst,* "should have but little share in our consideration of beauty, because the essence of beauty consists not in color but shape, and on this point enlightened minds will at once agree." Elsewhere he wrote that great art should have no flavor, but should be like pure water.

Plan et Elevation de l'ordonnance d'un Portail d'Eglise composé d'un grand ordre Corinthien contenant trois
sortes d'entrecolonnements, la hauteur de la Colonne à 20 modules et l'entablement 4 modules 12 parties
3.

Winckelmann's interest, as one might expect, was focused on sculpture, on the *Apollo Belvedere* and on the *Laocoön.* He did not know the works of Phidias, never saw a statue dating from before the fifth century B.C., and never really experienced the noble simplicity of the Greek art that he extolled. His concern for architecture was strictly limited. He described the temples of Agrigento, but summarily, in 1759, in *Amerkungen über die Baukunst der alten Tempel zu Girgenti in Sizilien,* relying on the observations of the Scottish architect Robert Mylne (1734–1811), and, for the rest, limiting himself to general remarks on the subject of Greek and Roman architecture. He lauded rather the works of Michelangelo, as represented at St. Peter's. None of his writings was illustrated in a way calculated to stir architects. His direct influence on architecture may thus be dismissed. Yet he did prompt a reassessment of Greek art among connoisseurs that was to affect architecture. For however shaky his premises, however personal his interpretations, his accounts of the stylistic evolution of Greek and Roman art, couched in elevated and rapturous language, riveted the attention of his contemporaries (and even his successors, as late as the end of the nineteenth century, when Walter Pater was still quoting him with the highest admiration). There can be no denying the dramatic impact of Winckelmann's writings, in particular the *Geschichte der Kunst des Altertums,* of 1764, the first systematic account of the evolving forms of antique art. He was the most important propagator of the Greek myth in the late eighteenth century. His books were translated into French almost immediately on publication, though they were less quick to appear in English. The Swiss painter Henry Fuseli translated some of Winckelmann's earlier works in the late 1760s but the *History of Ancient Art Among the Greeks* did not appear until 1849, and then in America.

Winckelmann's life, one may note, also had its dramatic side, not uninteresting to his contemporaries. Son of a Prussian cobbler, he rose rapidly from schoolmaster, to reader, to librarian; then, like Jean-Jacques Rousseau, he turned to Catholicism to further his career. In 1755, at the age of thirty-eight, he moved to Rome to become librarian to Cardinal Archinto. Archinto died, and three years later Winckelmann graduated to the library of Cardinal Albani, where he may have advised Anton Raphael Mengs on the famous ceiling fresco *Parnassus,* of 1760, and the architect Carlo Marchionni on the three *tempietti greci* just being completed outside the cardinal's villa.

*86. Plate from Giambattista Piranesi's* Prima parte di architetture e prospettive, *1743, showing the vestibule of a temple*

*87. Plate from Giambattista Piranesi's* Diverse maniere d'adornare i camini, *1769, design for a fireplace*

In 1763 Winckelmann moved to the Vatican itself, where he became Keeper of Antiquities. He was an active and influential propagandist, regarded as a man of the highest sensibility, but on occasion his perception failed him. His friend Mengs, whom he had even known in Dresden, painted a fresco of Jupiter and Ganymede in the antique style in imitation of one from Herculaneum. Winckelmann acclaimed it as an antique original. He liked the cupbearer. "Jove's paramour," he wrote to his friend Friedrich Reinbolt von Berg, "is certainly one of the most extraordinarily beautiful figures that has come down to us from antiquity, and I could not hope to find anything to compare with his face, it breathes so great a voluptuousness that his whole soul seems to be drawn into this kiss." Goethe, too, liked this Ganymede.

There were shadows in Winckelmann's life. In 1768 he was brutally murdered by a hustler in Trieste. Such scandalous incidents served, however, to attract more than usual attention not only to the man, but also to his work and all that he upheld. The French were particularly intrigued, but they were not to be spurred to the extent of initiating a Greek Revival.

England made the most determined effort to apply the new archaeological information to the creation of a new architecture directly inspired by the antique. English architects were less troubled by theory and ideas than their French counterparts and their powers of invention were further stimulated by the growth of the Picturesque tradition.

The new wave of enthusiasm for the antique, which enables us to see the middle of the eighteenth century as a turning point in British architecture, had been anticipated by Lord Burlington (Richard Boyle; 1694–1753) and his neo-Palladian circle. Thus, although England could scarcely parallel the long French tradition of theorists proposing a new rational architecture shorn of Baroque trimmings, many of the forms that were to be characteristic of neoclassical architecture had already been exploited by the Burlingtonians—in particular, the sequences of domed and apsed spaces derived from the Roman Baths. Lord Burlington was determined to purify British architecture of Baroque extravagance by recapturing that classical harmony which, he believed, had been codified and enshrined in the architecture and theory of Palladio. This obsession with the antique, if only at second hand through the eyes and researches of Palladio, made England unique in Europe at the beginning of the eighteenth century and helps explain why English architecture was out of step with, and, in some ways, stylistically in advance of, that of the rest of Europe.

One of the most influential products of Burlington's ruthless and doctrinaire classicism was the Assembly Rooms at York, which he designed in 1730. In his search to discover how the ancients would have designed a festival hall he was directed, probably by Giacomo Leoni (1686–1746), to Palladio's reconstructions of a hall in the "manner of the Egyptians," based on a description in Vitruvius, and of the courtyard of a Greek house.

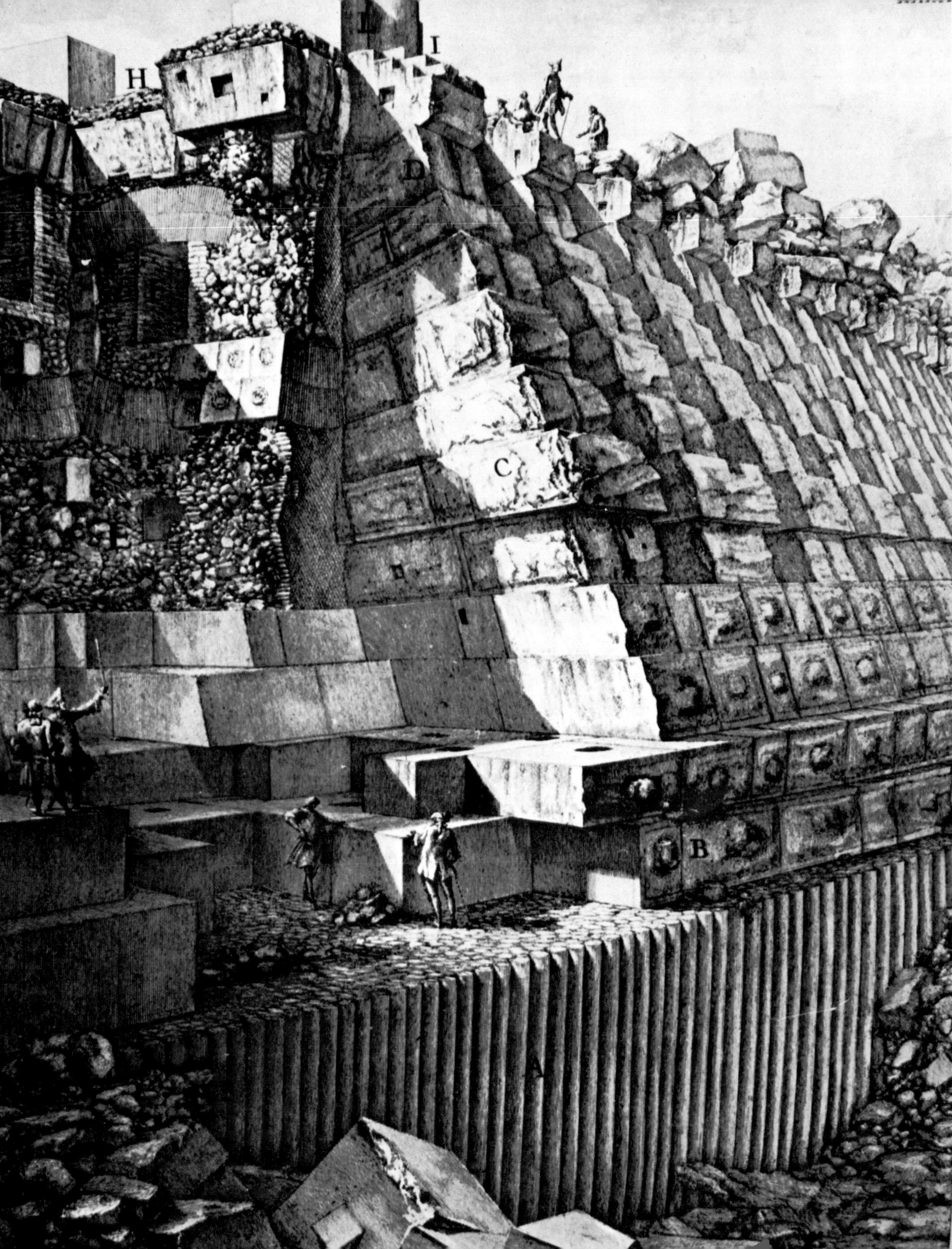
H
I
D
C
B

88. *Plate from Giambattista Piranesi's* Antichità romane, *1756 onward showing the foundations of the Theater of Marcellus*

89. *Plate from Giambattista Piranesi's* Prima parte di architetture e prospettive, *1742*

90. *Plate from Giambattista Piranesi's* Antichità romane, *1756, showing visitors in the Tomb of Arruntius*

Leoni himself had published a similar design in his *Designs for Buildings both Publick and Private,* which appeared in 1726–29. However, the credit for realizing the idea for the first time in an actual building must go to Burlington, since not even Palladio had been able to carry his scheme into execution. Similarly, at Holkham Hall, William Kent and Lord Burlington were able to realize a plan type invented though never fully executed by Palladio. Burlington's chill hall at York, with its insistent freestanding columns carrying an unbroken horizontal entablature, set a precedent that was to be followed throughout the eighteenth century and later, from Mereworth church, Kent (1744–46; anonymous), via Adam's hall at Kedleston, Derbyshire (1760–70), to Leo von Klenze's throne room at the Munich Residenz (1832).

In the same year as his York design, 1730, Burlington printed for private circulation an edition of Palladio's original drawings for the restoration of the Roman Baths that Burlington had bought from the Bishop of Verona. Entitled *Fabbriche antiche disegnate da Andrea Palladio Vicentino,* this important contribution to archaeology gave Burlington the inspiration for the round and apsidal rooms that flank the great colonnaded hall at York and also for the remarkable entrance facade (now destroyed) with its curved portico containing windows similar to those of the Baths of Diocletian.

Burlington was an important forerunner of the architect as archaeologist, as exemplified during the next hundred years in England by Stuart and Revett, Adam, William Wilkins, C. R. Cockerell, and Henry W. Inwood. Another architect who had been interested in Palladio's reconstruction of Vitruvius' Egyptian Hall was Inigo Jones's pupil John Webb (1611–1672). We should not forget that the seventeenth century in England had enjoyed its own Palladian Revival. In the 1630s Jones added a colossal Corinthian portico to Old St. Paul's cathedral on a scale that still impressed Cockerell two centuries later, and about 1655 Webb provided The Vyne, Hampshire, with a giant Corinthian portico probably inspired by Palladio's chapel at the Villa Barbaro, Maser. Webb's was the first portico ever to adorn an English country house and is thus the father of the countless examples erected in Europe and North America during the following century.

Burlington was a learned and influential architect but he lacked flare and panache as a designer. Those qualities were possessed in abundance by his intimate friend and follower, William Kent. Burlington and Kent's collaboration on the design of Holkham Hall, Norfolk, for Lord Leicester, produced one of the most spectacular interiors of eighteenth-century Europe: the entrance hall of about 1734. To the basic theme of Palladio's Vitruvian Hall, as revived at York, has been added a great apse partly inspired by Palladio's reconstruction of the antique basilica and partly by his own Venetian churches. The rich frieze, the coffered cove, and the details of the eighteen fluted Ionic columns from the Temple of Fortuna Virilis in Rome are based on plates in that popular work of archaeology Desgodets's *Édifices antiques de Rome* (1682). The light coloring of the Derbyshire

*91. Plate from Giambattista Piranesi's* Différentes vues de quelques restes... de l'ancienne ville de Pesto, *1778, showing the Temple of Neptune*

alabaster and the prominent Greek-key and Vitruvian-scroll friezes also help to create a thoroughly classical effect in a room whose disposition obviously has a certain Baroque or threatrical drama.

Of the many sides to Kent's genius that cannot be fully explored here, one of the most significant is his interest in the Etruscan or Pompeian type of interior decoration that had been revived by Raphael and Giovanni da Udine in Renaissance Rome and that was to be given prominent emphasis in a number of celebrated interiors by Robert Adam. Kent painted ceilings in this festive classical taste in the Audience and Council chambers at Kensington Palace, London (1724), and in the parlor at Rousham, Oxfordshire (1738–40). The Rousham ceiling, framed within a striking Greek-key border, is especially noteworthy since it contains two Romantic landscape paintings by Kent, which also point the way to future developments in painting.

From Kent's revolutionary interiors of the 1720s and 1730s it is but a step to what is sometimes regarded as the first neoclassical interior in England, James Stuart's Painted Room at Spencer House, London (1759), and to Clérisseau's celebrated room in the Hôtel Grimod de la Reynière, Paris (1774 or 1775). To mention the name of James Stuart is to recall the Society of Dilettanti. Founded in 1733-34, this remarkable institution may justly be regarded as the fountainhead of English neoclassical architecture. A group of about forty rich young noblemen and gentlemen, mostly in their late twenties and in the process of making their *grands tours,* got together to form a club to promote what they called "Greek taste and Roman spirit." Their aim was to institutionalize, as it were, the interest in the antique expressed more indirectly by Burlington and his circle, and for the next century successive members of the society, by acting as patrons of designers and architects and by financing archaeologists and scholars, were able to exercise great influence over the development of taste. In some ways the most characteristic members were the architects Stuart and Revett in the mid-eighteenth century, and Wilkins and Cockerell in the early nineteenth, for all four combined the roles of archaeologist and architect. But the patrons, following in the footsteps of Lord Burlington, were almost as important: such men as Sir George Beaumont, elected in 1784, and Thomas Hope, elected in 1800. Though the Society of Dilettanti was aristocratic in impetus, its membership reflected both the social mobility of England and the strength of the Whig oligarchy. Nothing like it could have existed in any other European country.

James Stuart (1713-1788) was born into humble circumstances. He first found employment with Louis Goupy, a fan painter who had accompanied Lord Burlington on an Italian tour. Goupy's fans were decorated with views of classical buildings. Stuart set out for Rome in 1742; there, he acquired a reputation as a connoisseur of pictures and probably acted as *cicerone* to Englishmen on the *grand tour.* In 1748 he accompanied Gavin Hamilton, Matthew Brettingham, and his future partner, Nicholas Revett, on an

*92. Plate from Giambattista Piranesi's* Parere su l'architettura, *1765*

*V. Robert Adam, Kedelston Hall, Derbyshire, the Marble Hall, 1760–70*

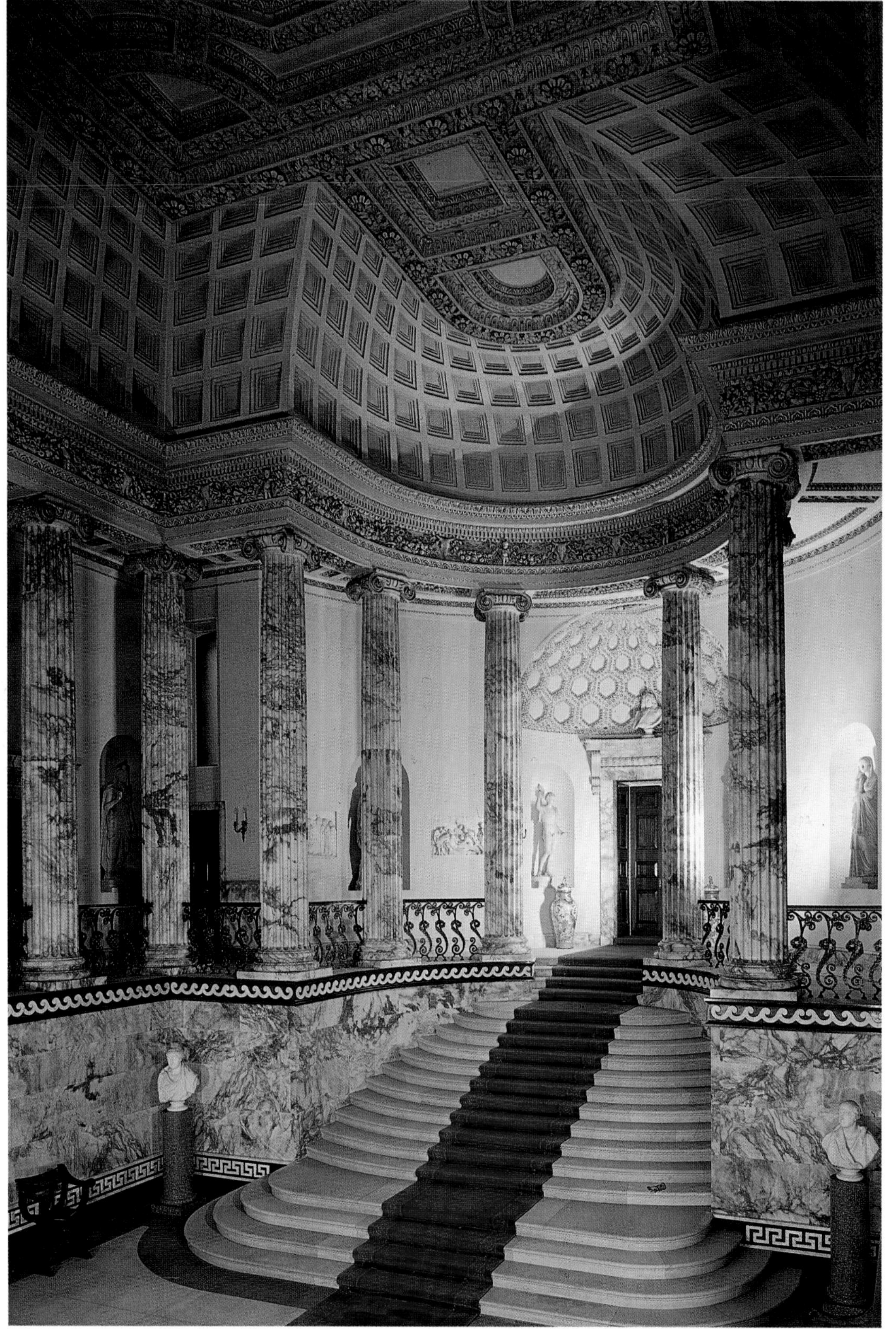

*VI. William Kent, Holkham Hall, Norfolk, hall, c. 1734*

93. *James Stuart, Spencer House, London, Painted Room, 1759*

expedition to Naples, during which the plan to visit Athens was first discussed. Revett (1720-1804), the son of a Suffolk squire, was very different in background from Stuart. In 1742 he traveled to Rome to study painting with Cavaliere Benefiale. The friendship of these four widely different men—Hamilton, Brettingham, Stuart, and Revett—led to their decision to measure the buildings of Athens, and they were encouraged by such English dilettanti in Rome as Lord Malton, Lord Charlemont, James Dawkins, and Robert Wood. Money was raised to finance the expedition, though in the end Brettingham and Hamilton were unable to take part. In 1748 Stuart and Revett issued their "Proposals for Publishing an Accurate Description of the Antiquities of Athens." Their aim was to parallel the way in which "Rome, who borrowed her Arts, and frequently her Artificers, from Greece, has by means of Serlio, Palladio, Santo Bartoli, and other ingenious men, preserved the memory of the most excellent sculptures and Magnificent Edifices which once adorned her." They also pointed out that "A work so much wanted will meet with the approbation of all those Gentlemen who are lovers of Antiquity, or have a taste for what is Excellent in these Arts, as we are assured that those Artists who aim at perfection must be infinitely more pleased and better instructed the nearer they can draw their Examples from the Fountain-head."

This clear statement of a neoclassical aesthetic in 1748 emphasizes the close connection between the study of archaeology and the practice of architecture. Stuart and Revett left Rome for Greece in 1750. They spent some time on the way in Venice, where the British Resident, Sir James Gray, procured their election to the Society of Dilettanti. They arrived in Athens in March 1751 and returned to England four years later to prepare their drawings for publication. Naturally, those members of the Society of Dilettanti who had helped finance the expedition were impatient for the results. In Germany Winckelmann himself shared their impatience as we know from the preface to his *Anmerkungen über die Baukunst der Alten* (1762), written in 1760, two years before Stuart and Revett's first volume was published.

Between 1748 and 1762 Stuart and Revett changed their ideas as to the contents of the first volume, so that it eventually contained not the major buildings of the Acropolis but the smaller, later, and minor buildings in the city of Athens. These, they modestly hoped, might furnish hints concerning "the different Grecian modes of decorating buildings." Indeed, the buildings they chose to illustrate, such as the Choragic Monument of Lysicrates, the Tower of the Winds, and the Gateway to the Agora, were Hellenistic, note Greek, and lent themselves particularly to a process of transformation into garden ornaments for English parks. This is an early instance of the way in which, in England, the tradition of the Picturesque tended to dissolve any expression of pure neoclassicism. Stuart himself had contributed to this process even before the first volume of his *Antiquities of Athens* appeared in 1762, so that the first Greek Revival building in Europe is, characteristically, a garden ornament in an English landscaped park. This is the temple at Hagley Park, Worcestershire, designed by Stuart for Lord Lyttelton in 1758. Built of red sandstone originally covered with stucco, it is not an exact copy of any Greek building but, being Doric hexastyle with a column at each side of the cella entrance, it was perhaps inspired by the Theseum in Athens. In October 1758 Lord Lyttelton wrote to Mrs. Elizabeth Montagu: "Stuart is going to embellish one of my little hills with a true Attic building, a Portico of six pillars, which will make a fine effect to my new house, and command a most beautiful view of the country." Thus, the Greek Revival was conceived from the start as part of the Picturesque impact of contrived landscape scenery.

Six years after Hagley, Stuart began to develop in a quite extraordinary way this theme of reducing Greek architecture to garden ornaments. From 1764 on, at Shugborough, in Staffordshire, for another Whig landowner, Thomas Anson (a founder-member of the Society of Dilettanti), Stuart dropped a succession of Picturesque buildings based on the minor

94. *Lord Burlington, Assembly Rooms, York, plan, 1730*

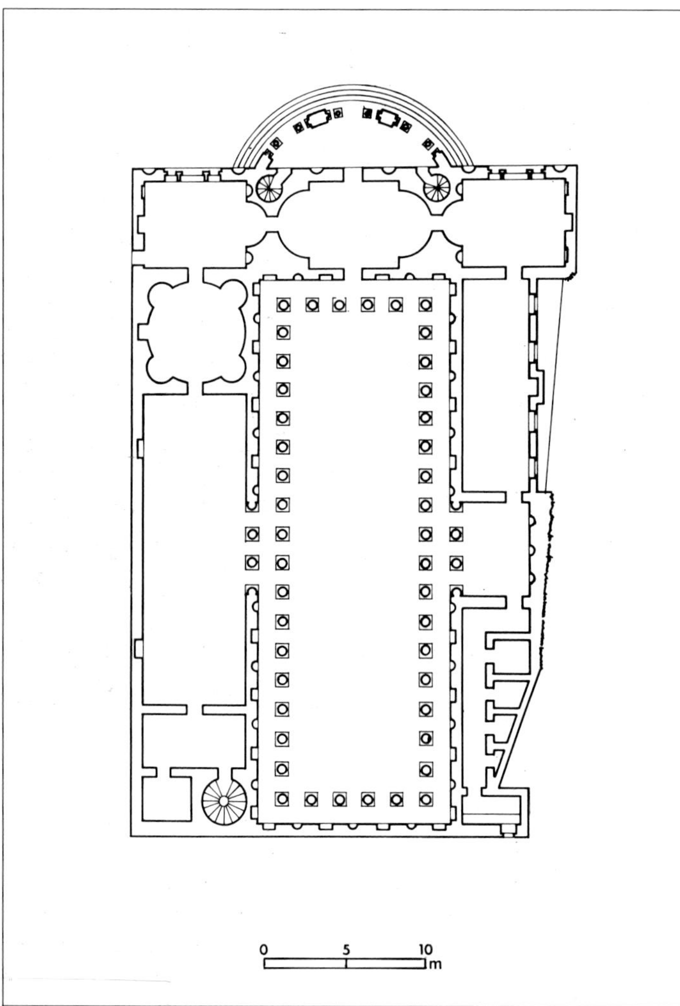


architecture of Athens into a park that had long been adorned with garden ornaments and ruins of different shapes and sizes, including Chinese.

In some ways Stuart was more successful at adapting his archaeological knowledge to modern design in furniture and interior decoration than to architecture. Soon after his return to England from Greece he was invited to design interiors for two Whig landowners who were to subscribe to the first volume of *Antiquities of Athens.* Stuart's tripod stands of about 1757 for Lord Scarsdale at Kedleston, Derbyshire, and a related pair of candelabra for Lord Spencer at Spencer House, London, of 1759–60, are based upon the tripod at the top of the Choragic Monument of Lysicrates, but develop it in a novel, beautiful, and functional way. Stuart's interiors for Kedleston were not executed, but his Painted Room of 1759 at Spencer House survives as the first "Etruscan" Revival room in Europe. It was conceived as a unity with its furniture, which included a set of four fantastic sofas and six armchairs with side pieces made up of gilt griffins. These derive from antique Roman marble seat furniture Stuart may have seen in the Vatican or in other Italian collections. Their flashy drama anticipates Regency and Empire style furniture and is astonishing for 1760.

Stuart's only remaining work of real consequence was his rebuilding and redecoration, after a fire, of Christopher Wren's chapel at the Royal Hospital, Greenwich. This was carried out with the assistance of Stuart's very talented Clerk of the Works, William Newton, between 1779 and 1788. Reflecting the impact of the mature Adam style, it is dominated by a rich but filigreed ornament, the details of which are Greek in origin though the overall impression is certainly not. The most imaginative feature of the chapel is the pulpit, obviously inspired by Stuart's favorite building, the Choragic Monument of Lysicrates.

It will have become clear that Stuart's career was marked by a certain failure of nerve and that he never created the new architecture for which his contemporaries were waiting. His procrastination delayed until 1789 the publication of the important second volume of the *Antiquities of Athens,* which illustrated the Parthenon. Nicholas Revett had in fact resigned his interest in the joint publishing venture even before the publication of the first volume. As a gentleman of leisure he certainly maintained his interest in Greek architecture and archaeology, and in 1764 was chosen by the Society of Dilettanti to go on an expedition to the coast of Asia Minor with Richard Chandler and William Pars. This resulted in his editorship of the *Antiquities of Ionia,* which appeared in two volumes in 1769 and 1797. The buildings depicted were of equal interest to those in the first volume of the *Antiquities of Athens*—in particular, the splendid Temple of Apollo at Didyma, near Miletus—but, rather unaccountably, they did not influence contemporary architecture as they could and perhaps ought to have done. One reason why they did not was that Revett himself used them in only one of his own buildings. His name can be connected with the design of only three important buildings, and in two of these he used the order based

*95. Lord Burlington, Assembly Rooms, York, interior, 1730*

on the Temple of Apollo at Delos, which he had illustrated in the first volume of the *Antiquities of Athens.* Revett adapted this late fourth-century Delian Doric style at Standlynch (now Trafalgar) House, Wiltshire (c. 1766), for his friend Henry Dawkins, and at the church at Ayot St. Lawrence, Hertfordshire (1778). At Standlynch the composition of the Doric portico is still basically Baroque and at Ayot St. Lawrence the whole composition, with a central pavilion linked to side wings by colonnades, is of Palladian origin. Evidently Revett could not think in a really Greek way, though at West Wycombe Park, Buckinghamshire, in 1770, he provided for Sir Francis Dashwood, a founder-member of the Society of Dilettanti, an undeniably impressive western portico, based on the Temple of Dionysus at Teos, of the second century B.C., which he had included the year before in the *Antiquities of Ionia.*

Other important archaeological publications that influenced taste were Robert Wood's *Ruins of Palmyra* and *Ruins of Balbec.* Thus, a late-Palladian building such as Henry Flitcroft's west front of Woburn Abbey, Bedfordshire (1757–61), incorporates in the State Bedroom a version of the ceiling of the vestibule at the south end of the cella of the Temple of the Sun at Palmyra of the early first century A.D., as illustrated in Wood's book. It is interesting to compare Flitcroft's straightforward imitation of antiquity with Adam's more fanciful adaptation in the drawing room at Osterly Park, begun in the 1760s and completed in 1773. The ceiling of Adam's Great Drawing Room at Syon House of the 1760s is an imaginative mingling of Wood's illustrations with Raphael's and Giovanni da Udine's decorations in the vaulting of the loggia of Villa Madama, Rome.

The engravings for Wood's *Ruins of Palmyra* were prepared in London in 1751 by Giovanni Battista Borra, a Piedmontese architect, after drawings he had made at Palmyra. From 1752 to 1755 he incorporated Palmyrene themes in the ceiling of his State Bedchamber at Stowe House, Buckinghamshire. In 1775 the painter-architect Vincenzo Valdrè (c. 1742–1814), of Faenza, created the magnificent oval saloon at Stowe, flanked by sixteen, freestanding columns supporting a full Doric entablature and a crowded frieze depicting a Roman triumphal procession. This hermetic, monumental interior, windowless, domed, top-lit, leads into a richly Pompeian music room of 1777, also by Valdrè. In the drawing room the Greek Corinthian order was adapted by Valdrè from that of the Choragic Monument of Lysicrates as illustrated in Stuart and Revett; the Bacchic frieze in the south portico was also taken from Stuart and Revett.

A decade after the Pompeian music room at Stowe another Italian-born architect working in England produced a room of greater archaeological accuracy. This was the Pompeian Gallery at Packington Hall, Warwickshire, designed for Lord Aylesford by the eccentric Joseph Bonomi (1739–1808). Bonomi, a Roman, was a pupil of Clérisseau who had been engaged in 1765 by Robert Adam as tutor, guide, and companion. In 1767 Bonomi came to England to work for Adam and married the niece of Angelica Kauffmann, one of Adam's decorative painters. On the collapse of the Adam brothers' Adelphi speculation (a development of terraced houses on the Thames), Bonomi left their office, possibly in 1774, for that of Thomas Leverton (1743–1824). The project for decorating the Long Gallery at Packington, initiated in 1782, seems to have been Bonomi's first independent commission. Lord Aylesford was a remarkable figure, a gifted painter, an architect manqué, a traveler and connoisseur, a friend of the Picturesque theorist Sir Uvedale Price and of the collector Sir George Beaumont. He was the dream patron for any neoclassical architect. The Pompeian Gallery that Bonomi created for him at Packington was the work of one English and three Italian craftsmen: Benedetto Pastorini, a painter and engraver who had been employed by Robert and James Adam to make the plates for their *Works in Architecture;* Domenico Bartoli, a scagliola manufacturer; Joseph Rose, Jr., Adam's plasterworker; Giovanni Borgnis, a fresco painter; and, perhaps most important, John Francis Rigaud, a painter from Turin who came to England by way of Paris in 1771. The lower part of the walls up to the shelf of the chimneypiece was of scagliola, imitating panels of porphyry surrounded by borders of Siena marble: This arrangement corresponds with

*96. William Kent, Holkham Hall, Norfolk, hall, c. 1734*

what had been discovered at Pompeii. The strong black and terra-cotta coloring recalls the Greek vases that Lord Aylesford enthusiastically collected, although the real source for the decoration was neither Greek nor Pompeian but Roman. It was taken from the plates either in Ludovico Mirri's and Giuseppe Carletti's *Antiche camere delle terme di Tito e loro pitture* (1776) or in Vincenzo Brenna's, Ludovico Mirri's, and Franiszek Smuglewicz's *Vestigia delle terme di Tito* (c. 1780), which were both later used by Nicolas Ponce in his *Description des bains de Titus; ou, collection des peintures trouvées dans les ruines des thermes de cet empereur* (1786). As interesting as the bold archaeological decoration of the gallery is the design of a set of eight Greek Revival chairs that still adorn it. Bonomi based the klismos form of these—a type subsequently popularized by Thomas Hope—not on Roman furniture but on the chairs depicted in Greek vase paintings.

After his tour de force in the gallery Bonomi turned his attention to the design of a new church in the park at Packington. The plans were prepared in 1788 with the active assistance of Lord Aylesford, and the foundation stone was laid in April 1789. This grim, gaunt building is Revolutionary in the manner of Ledoux's *barrières,* which Bonomi presumably knew. Its interior is no less remarkable for its confident use of the still-revolutionary Greek Doric order. It seems to be based on the Temple of Neptune at Paestum, which had been illustrated in T. Major's *The Ruins of Paestum* (1768), though without the entasis so prominent at Packington. Lord Aylesford's etchings of Greek ruins can be seen in the fourth volume of Henry Swinburne's *Travels in the Two Sicilies* (1783), and it may be that the addition of entasis is due to him rather than to Bonomi. The Doric groin-vaulted interior seems to have influenced several interiors by Sir John Soane and James Wyatt in the 1790s: Soane's Tyringham Hall, Buckinghamshire; Bentley Priory, Middlesex; an unexecuted House of Lords project; and Wyatt's remarkable chapel at Dodington Park, Gloucestershire, designed some time between 1798 and 1805.

The stark and deliberately unprecedented air of the exterior of the Packington church is also echoed in the Berlin Mint (1798–1800; demolished 1886), by Heinrich Gentz (1766–1811). Gentz was a pioneer in the introduction of the Greek Doric style to Germany. He visited Paestum and Sicily, and also traveled in England, Holland, and France. He was a friend of the artist Asmus Jakob Carstens and the publisher Wilhelm Tischbein and he married the sister of Friedrich Gilly (1772–1800), the most original architect of late eighteenth-century Germany. Although so many German architects looked to the Paris of Ledoux for inspiration at this time, it was English neoclassical architecture, with its archaeological interest in the revival of the Greek Doric, that was closest in spirit to German architecture at the end of the century. Indeed, it was in Germany—not in England, and least of all in France—that the first building based on the Athenian Propylaea was erected. This was the Brandenburg Gate (1789–91) by Carl Gotthard Langhans (1732–1808), the gateway not only to Berlin

*97. Joseph Bonomi, Packington Hall, Warwickshire, Pompeian Gallery, c. 1786*

98. *Robert Adam, Kedleston Hall, Derbyshire, hall, 1760–70*

*99. Joseph Bonomi, church in the park at Packington, Warwickshire, 1789*

*100. Joseph Bonomi, church in the park at Packington, Warwickshire, interior, 1789*

*101. James Wyatt, chapel at Dodington Park, Gloucestershire, interior, c. 1805*

but also, in a sense, to German neoclassicism itself. It was probably inspired by Le Roy's striking reconstruction of the Athenian Propylaea published in his *Ruines des plus beaux monuments de la Grèce.* Langhans had visited Italy in 1768–69, and Holland, France, and England in 1775. He became director of the Royal Office of Public Buildings in Berlin in 1788, and his striking Greek Revival gateway has always impressed visitors to that city. In December 1794, for example the influential connoisseur, patron, and designer Thomas Hope was so much affected by the gateway when he saw it that ten years later, when he came to write a pamphlet on the style he believed ought to be adopted at Downing College, Cambridge, he recommended it as a model for the entrance to the college. And sure enough, Hope's protégé, the dutiful William Wilkins, provided designs in 1806 for a more than usually extensive porter's lodge à la Propylaea. Whereas Wilkins's Greek Doric style was accurate and based on firsthand study of the originals in Greece—his *Antiquities of Magna Graecia* was published at Cambridge in 1807—Langhans had merely employed a sort of stripped Roman Doric style. His overattenuated columns have bases, unlike the Greek Doric order, and are unequally spaced in the side pavilions; also, there are demi-metopes at the ends of the frieze, whereas the Greeks ended their friezes firmly with a triglyph.

The examples of Langhans and Wilkins were followed by the architect Thomas Harrison (1744–1829) in his gateway at Chester Castle (1810–22), the design of which he had been cogitating since the 1780s. The theme was brought to a triumphant and imaginative conclusion by Leo von Klenze (1784–1864) in his Propylaeon, of 1846–60, on the west side of the Königsplatz in Munich. The project was first proposed in 1817, and Klenze's early sketches followed the Athenian prototype more closely than his final scheme with its powerful pylons.

Greek Doric was employed with varying degrees of accuracy by Benjamin Latrobe, James Wyatt, and Joseph Gandy. Shortly before embarking on his successful career in North America in 1796, Latrobe designed Hammerwood Lodge, Sussex, with Paestum-style Doric capitals. In the 1790s Wyatt transformed an unremarkable house, Stoke Poges Park, Buckinghamshire, into a neoclassical fantasy by surrounding it with stocky Greek Doric colonnades; similar stylistically was Storrs Hall, Westmorland, of 1808, by the eccentric Joseph Gandy, who later turned a temple inside out for the design of Doric House, Sion Hill, Bath (c. 1810). One of the noblest of all antique-inspired English houses is Belsay Hall, Northumberland. An austere product of the collaboration between 1806 and 1817 of three men—its owner Sir Charles Monck, the connoisseur Sir William Gell, and the architect John Dobson—Belsay Hall is the quintessence of what everyone in Europe had learned to feel about Greek art since Winckelmann first praised its noble simplicity and calm grandeur. The striking Villa Giulia at Palermo, Sicily (1789–92), by the French architect Léon Defourny (1754–1818), is close in form to Belsay, but Dobson's building has a quality

*102. William Wilkins, project for the entrance to Downing College, Cambridge, 1806*

*103. Thomas Harrison, Chester Castle, gateway, 1810–22*

and an air of absolute authority that made it unique in Europe for its time. Karl Friedrich Schinkel gave his buildings the same stamp of conviction, as can be seen in his first important commission, the Royal Guard House in Unter den Linden, Berlin (1816). Two years later came an even greater masterpiece in the center of Berlin, the State Theater, of which Schinkel wrote: "I tried to emulate Greek forms and methods of construction insofar as this is possible in such a complex work." Apart from the Greek Ionic portico, the most memorable feature of the building is the frequent use of a kind of functionalist pilaster strip. For these Schinkel cited a Greek source, the Choragic Monument of Thrasyllus (illustrated in the second volume of Stuart's and Revett's *Antiquities of Athens,* 1789, and since destroyed), and also argued that, when used in windows, these pilasters admitted the maximum amount of light. Schinkel's theater was imitated by Sir Charles Barry in his Royal Institution, Manchester, now the City Art Gallery (1823–35).

C. R. Cockerell is in some ways the most characteristic of archaeologist-architects. His staggeringly successful seven-year tour of Greece, Turkey, and Italy resulted in the discovery of the pediment sculpture at Aegina, the Bassae frieze, and the use of entasis at the Parthenon. His early buildings show the difficulty he experienced in trying to incorporate this new knowledge of what Greek architecture was like into the classical tradition as practiced then in England. His staircase hall, of 1823, at Oakly Park, Shropshire, includes casts of the Bassae frieze with a version of the unique Ionic order from Bassae and details taken from the capitals of the Tower of the Winds in Athens. (However, Cockerell increasingly relied on Italian Renaissance and Mannerist sources to enliven his classical vocabulary, and will thus be considered later in the book).

Two buildings of the greatest archaeological interest are Wilkins's Grange Park, Hampshire (1809), and, exactly contemporary with Oakly Park, St. Pancras church, London (1819–22), by William Inwood (c. 1771–1843) and his son Henry William (1794–1843). Henry Inwood had traveled to Greece to study Athenian architecture in 1819 and had formed a small collection of Greek antiquities which was later given to the British Museum. In 1827 he published *The Erechtheion at Athens, Fragments of Athenian, Architecture and a Few Remains in Attica, Megara and Epirus.* Meanwhile, at immense expense, he and his father produced their own version of the Erechtheum—St. Pancras church, which, with its astonishing caryatid-flanked porches, has never failed to surprise generations of visitors.

Equally surprising is Wilkins's Grange Park, the grandest temple-like house in Europe. Its vast portico, alas only of brick and plaster, was based on the Theseum in Athens, and the monumental piers on the sides of the building are developed from those on the Choragic Monument of Thrasyllus. The effect was rather like a stage set, although beneath the Athenian drama Wilkins left the original seventeenth-century red-brick house more or less intact. Blending into its beautiful Hampshire landscape,

*104. Leo von Klenze, Propylaeon, Munich, 1846–60*

*105. Sir Charles Monck, Sir William Gell, and John Dobson, Belsay Hall, Northumberland, detail of the exterior, 1806–17*

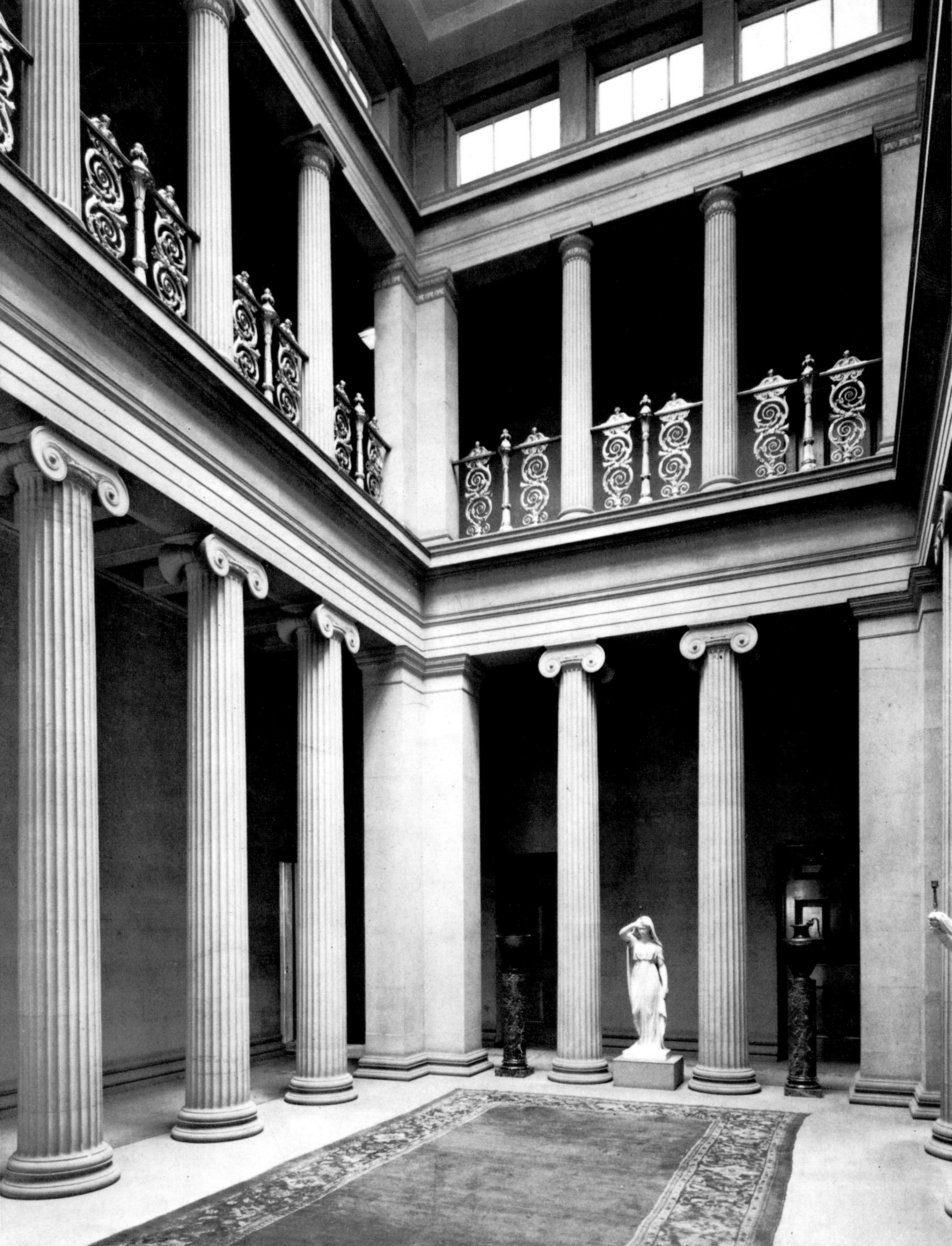

*106. Sir Charles Monck, Sir William Gell, and John Dobson, Belsay Hall, Northumberland, interior, 1806–17*

*VII. James Stuart, Spencer House, London, Painted Room, 1758*

*VIII. Leo von Klenze, Walhalla, near Regensburg, 1830–42*

*107. Friedrich Gilly, project for a monument to Frederick the Great, gateway, 1797*

*108. Thomas Hamilton, Royal High School, Edinburgh, 1825–29*

richly wooded and watered, Grange Park epitomizes the archaeological and the Picturesque side of English neoclassicism. It is thus a fulfillment of what Stuart initiated at Hagley Park fifty years earlier with his little Greek garden temple described by Lord Lyttelton as "a true Attic building . . . which will . . . command a most beautiful view of the country." That image of a Greek temple set in a high place remained powerfully in men's minds from the mid-eighteenth to the early nineteenth century. Nowhere was it more powerful than in Germany. Friedrich Gilly's entry of 1797 in the first of the many competitions for a monument to Frederick the Great in Berlin, though it departed from the terms of the competition, inspired a whole generation of architects with its solemn Doric temple set in a sacred precinct. The passionate desire to erect an adequate monument to Frederick's glory was linked to the process of establishing German national unity and self-identity, so that, in a sense, the real monument to Frederick was the foundation of the German Empire in 1871.

The competition for the monument to Frederick the Great did not, in fact, result in the erection of any single building. Curiously, something of the mood of Gilly's influential design can perhaps best be sensed in Scotland and in the north of England. In Edinburgh, for example, there are the Royal High School (1825–29) by Thomas Hamilton (1784–1858), the Royal Scottish Academy (1822–35) by W. H. Playfair (1789–1857), and Cockerell's and Playfair's uncompleted National Monument, or Walhalla, of 1821. The grim but dramatic Penshaw Monument in County Durham, modeled on the Parthenon (as was the Scottish National Monument), was erected in 1830 from designs by Benjamin Green (died 1858). As a bizarre but undoubtedly impressive footnote we should add that hybrid combination of Parthenon and Pantheon situated high up in the mountains above the village of Possagno, the Tempio del Canova (1819–33), designed by Antonio Canova (1757–1822) himself, possibly with help from Giannantonio Selva. The Walhalla near Regensburg in Bavaria (1830–42) is surely the culmination of the Picturesque vision of setting a temple on high and endowing it with that ennobling power with which Winckelmann had credited Greek art. But before examining this masterpiece by Leo von Klenze, we will turn again to France, since the design of the Walhalla was influenced by a new wave of archaeological discovery and debate, largely about polychromy, that was emanating from Paris.

During the early years of the nineteenth century a doctrinaire classicism was fostered in France, in particular by Antoine-Chrysostome Quatremère de Quincy (1755–1849), an unsuccessful sculptor who became *Secrétaire Perpétuel de l'Académie des Beaux-Arts* in 1816, a position he was to retain for twenty-three years, to be succeeded by a classicist of almost equally limited outlook, Désirée-Raoul Rochette (1790–1854).

Quatremère de Quincy upheld Winckelmann's ideals, though he was prepared to adapt them at times to accommodate new discoveries as they occurred. When he traveled to London in 1816 to see the Elgin Marbles,

*109. Karl Friedrich Schinkel, Royal Guard House, Berlin, 1806–18*

*110. Karl Friedrich Schinkel, State Theater, Berlin, 1818–21*

*111. Charles Robert Cockerell, Oakly Park, Shropshire, staicase, 1823*

which he viewed with C. R. Cockerell, he was greatly moved, and thereafter altered his canons somewhat. But such small flexibility in his outlook was to destroy almost the image of classical rectitude for which he labored throughout his life. Already in 1815 he had produced a major study, *Le Jupiter Olympien; ou, l'art de la sculpture antique,* in which he had indicated that the great cult statues of the Greeks might not be of pure white marble, but might incorporate gold and ivory, lapis lazuli and semiprecious stones. He scarcely intended to evoke a colorful image of antiquity, but was following, rather, the scholarly lead of such men as Edward Dodwell—who had noticed traces of color on Greek fragments in Sicily in the early years of the century—and, more important, of that great French scholar and enthusiast of the Doric, Léon Dufourny—architect of the marvelously robust early essay in the Greek Revival, the Villa Giulia, in the Orto Botanico, Palermo. Dufourny had reported his findings directly to Quatremère de Quincy, whose rash interpretation of this discovery was to be taken up many years later by Jacques-Ignace Hittorff, who, as we have already seen would attempt to revise totally the accepted image of antique architecture, to present it in the most vivid array of colors, as a basis for a livelier and more colorful contemporary style. This was the last occasion on which archaeological study was to make a fresh and vital impact on current design.

In Rome, in 1823, Hittorff encountered Thomas Leverton Donaldson (1795–1885), later to become president of the Royal Institute of British Architects, who had just written a brief essay on the discoveries of a group of young English scholars and architects—William Kinnaird, Joseph Woods, C. R. Cockerell, and Charles Barry—who had noticed traces of color on Greek buildings. Hittorff was hoping to make an archaeological discovery on his own account, and when he heard that William Harris and Samuel Angell had made similar observations in Sicily, he dashed there at once, overtaking Leo von Klenze, who was on the same trail. At Selinunte and at Agrigento Hittorff put eighteen excavators to work. He found what he wanted there and wrote at once to the editors of learned journals to stake his claim. When Hittorff returned to France, in 1824, he started a campaign to publicize his notions of a colorful image of antiquity. He believed that Greek temples had been covered completely with yellow paint, the sculpture and moldings heightened with lively patterns of bright blue, green, red, and gold paint. His short manifesto *De l'architecture polychrome chez les grecs; ou, restitution complète du temple d'Empédocle dans l'Acropolis d'Empédocle* was printed both in Italy and in France in 1830, starting an active and most acrimonious debate. Rochette defended the orthodox position; Antoine-Jean Letronne, professor of classical archaeology at the Collège de France, argued on Hittorff's behalf. Soon the debate became widespread. In 1834 Gottfried Semper voiced his theory that vapory red, rather than yellow, had served as the base color, and Franz Kugler produced his less fanciful reconstructions in the following year. In England a select committee was set up in 1837 to inspect the Elgin Marbles for traces of color, and Donaldson, Francis

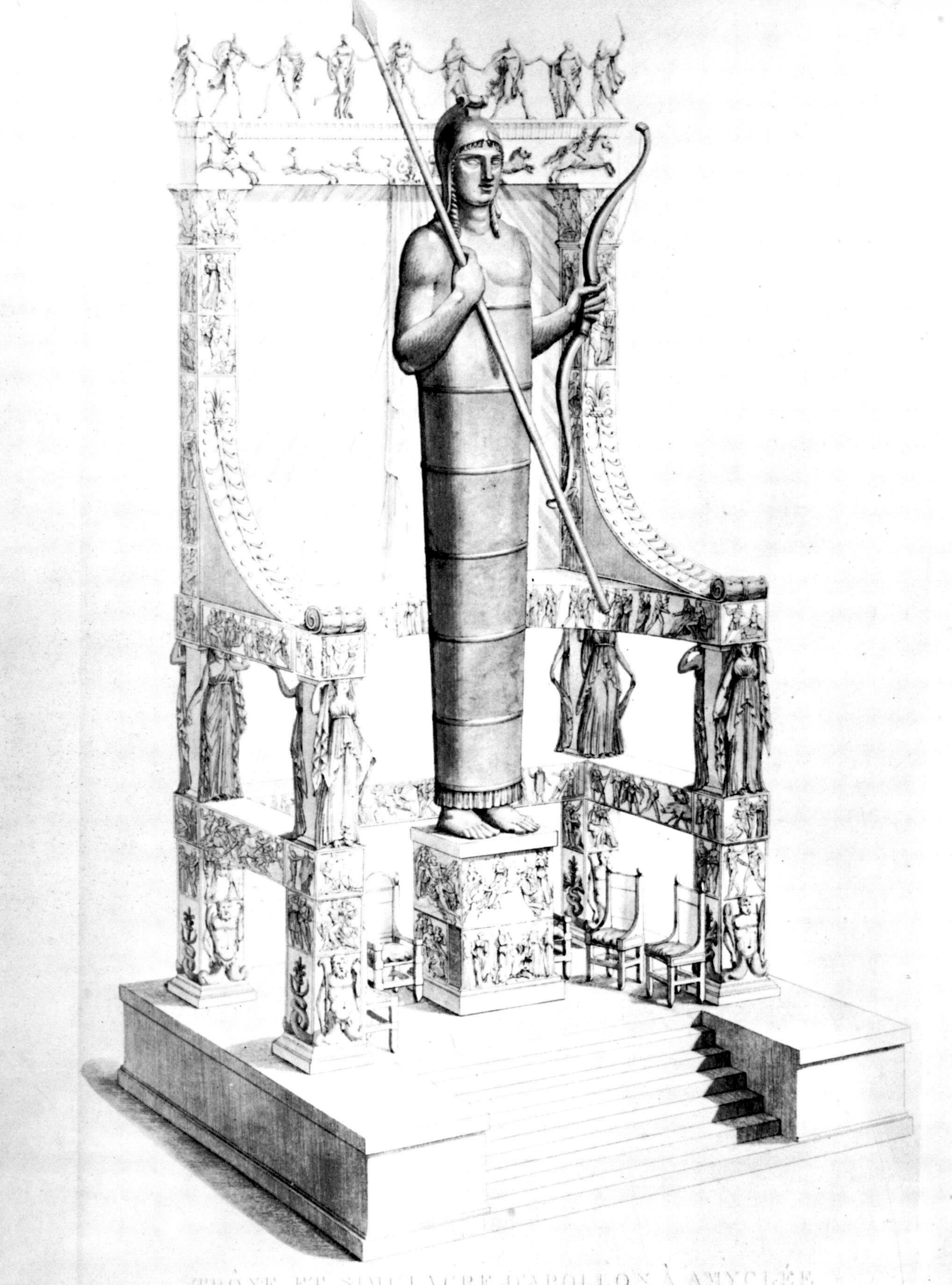

TRÔNE ET SIMULACRE D'APOLLON À AMYCLÉE

*112. Antoine-Chrysostome Quatremère de Quincy, reconstruction in gold, ivory, and lapis lazuli of the throne of Apollo, from his* Le Jupiter Olympien, *1815*

Cranmer Penrose, and Cockerell were to continue afterward to take a very active interest in the subject, though it was not until 1854 that Owen Jones and Sir Matthew Digby Wyatt erected the highly colored Greek court at the Crystal Palace at Sydenham. The influence of their ideas was enormous, especially in the field of decorative design. In France Hittorff, too, had attempted to infuse his ideas into contemporary design: His colorful portico for the Cirque Nationale, set up on the Champs-Élysées, Paris, in 1840, was one such experiment. Later, in 1852, he was to build another at the Cirque d'Hiver; it still stands in the Boulevard des Filles-du-Calvaire, though its present appearance is now toned down. His most important demonstration of architectural coloring, however, was the church of St.-Vincent-de-Paul, Place Lafayette, Paris, which was begun in 1824, though Hittorff took over only in 1830. Sixteen years later he began to cover the external portico wall with brightly colored enamel plaques depicting scenes from the Bible, but they were soon removed at the request of the clergy, who were incensed by the color and by the nudity of Adam and Eve.

The internal decorative scheme—a variant of that of the Norman cathedral in Monreale, Sicily—was also not begun until the 1840s. Something of Hittorff's intentions, though in muted form, was realized in the house built in 1858 by the architect A. A. Jal for the artist Pierre-Jules Jollivet at 11 Cité Malesherbes. But though Hittorff's own attempts to give expression to his ideas were of no great consequence, and though his final summation of his theories, the *Restitution du temple d'Empédocle à Selinonte; ou, l'architecture polychrome chez les grecs,* was probably not much read when it finally came out, between 1846 and 1851, there can be no doubt that he vitally influenced a whole range of architects, as disparate as Henri Labrouste and Charles Garnier, and showed them that a reassessment of antiquity was possible and most desirable. Hittorff was an indifferent archaeologist and an awkward, lackluster designer, but, almost unaided, he broke the spell of the doctrinaire classicists in France and prepared the way for the exuberance of the architecture of the Second Empire.

Leo von Klenze, Hittorff's rival in Sicily, was also influenced by the debate about polychromy, as is clear from the rich use of color, particularly colored marbles, in his Walhalla near Regensburg, and from its elaborate openwork roof, which resembles that of Hittorff's St.-Vincent-de-Paul. In 1833 Klenze designed the temple in the English Garden in Munich, which was described at the time as the "first example of lithochromy in the present day." The notion of the Walhalla was initially suggested to Crown Prince Ludwig of Bavaria by the defeat of Napoleon at Leipzig in 1813. The competition was announced in 1814 and its terms demanded Greek forms because, it was argued, the Parthenon had been closely linked to the Greek victory over the Persians from which Greek unity derived. In 1815 the architect Haller von Hallerstein (1774–1817) submitted a project from Athens, where he was visiting Greek sites in the company of C. R. Cockerell. In 1829 the competition was reframed and Klenze's plan for a monumental temple on

*113. A. A. Jal, Jollivet House, 11 Cité Malesherbes, Paris, 1858. Majolica decoration*

114. *Leo von Klenze, Walhalla, near Regensburg, 1830–42*

an enormous substructure was chosen. What exactly is the Walhalla? In Norse mythology it is the place in which the souls of slain heroes feast, having been brought there by the Valkyrie. For Ludwig it was also to be "to excellent Germans a monument, hence a Walhalla," and he emphasized that one was intended to be more German on leaving it than upon entering. It was a pantheon of political and intellectual portrait busts of, for example, Leibnitz, Schiller, Gluck, Mozart, Mengs, Thomas à Kempis, and Blücher. The Valkyrie also appear inside, but in the form of Greek caryatids wearing Nordic bearskins! Outside, one sculptured tympanum shows the defeat of Napoleon at Leipzig, the other the defeat in A.D. 9 of Augustus's legions by the united tribes of central and north-western Germany, who thereby saved the country from Roman domination.

Faced with a building, so classical yet so Romantic, so archaeological yet so much a part of nineteenth-century Germany, we are reminded forcibly of the paradox that neoclassicism can justly be regarded as one aspect of the Romantic movement. That point is neatly underlined by the fact that the painter J. M. A. Turner chose as the subject of and entitled one of his most remarkable paintings *The Opening of the Walhalla* (1842).

115. *Joseph Mallod William Turner,* The Opening of the Walhalla, *detail, 1842. London, Tate Gallery*

116. *Leo von Klenze, Walhalla, near Regensburg, 1830–42*

*117. Giovanni Niccolò Servandoni, design for the west front of St.-Sulpice, Paris, with the addition of a third order, c. 1752*

FRANCE: *From Gabriel to Ledoux*

The ideas that were to condition the changes in the form of architecture in late eighteenth-century France were generated early, by Perrault, Frémin, Cordemoy, and others; by 1753 these had been encapsulated and expressed with the utmost lucidity in the Abbé Laugier's *Essai sur l'architecture.* But the vital visual inspiration that was to make precise and alive the new style emerged but fitfully. L.-J. Le Lorrain's three designs for the Festa della Chinea of 1745, 1746, and 1747—borrowing motifs from Perrault's Louvre facade and also from Piranesi's *Prima parte*—provided the key for much that was to follow. Many formal devices and details can be traced to Le Lorrain's designs, but for a new boldness of massing, sudden changes of scale, contrasts of richness and stark wall surfaces, architects were to be indebted directly to Piranesi. His vision was to dominate architecture. The ruins of Rome, or rather an interpretation of them, were the mainspring of the new style.

Fittingly, the first architect who was to capture something of the new spirit, Giovanni Niccolò Servandoni (1695–1766), was trained in Rome by Piranesi's own forerunner G. P. Panini, and also by the Florentine architect Giuseppe Ignazio Rossi; he began his career as a stage designer, and he traveled in this capacity throughout Europe to Lisbon and London, Brussels, Stuttgart, and Vienna. Far too little is known of his designs, but he appears to have made his debut in France (whence came his father, coachman from Lyons) in 1726, with lavish sets for *Pyramus and Thisbe.* By 1732 he had won a competition for the west front of the church of St.-Sulpice in Paris. His design was not advanced—indeed, it had less to recommend it in the way of geometrical clarity than one drawn up six years earlier by Gilles-Marie Oppenordt—and was evidently derived from the west front of St. Paul's in London. But as work went slowly ahead the detail was modified and changed. In 1742 Servandoni engraved a variant that showed the entablature above the first order extending unbroken across the facade; by 1752 the entablature at the second level had also become an unbroken line across the facade. At this stage a third order was erected between the towers and a square planned in front of the church. Only the robust house that Servandoni designed and built for himself on the square from 1752 to 1757, on the corner of the Rue des Canettes, Paris, survives. The third order was taken down after Servandoni's death in 1766 and a giant pediment put in its place; this was struck by lightning in 1770 and replaced in turn by the simple balustrade that stands today—a reversion to the initial project by Oppenordt.

The north tower was then finished off by Jean-François-Thérèse Chalgrin, a pupil of Servandoni. "Plein des beautés de l'antique," Blondel wrote of Servandoni in his *Cours d'architecture,* "il a su soutenir le style grec dans toutes ses productions, tandis que Paris, de son temps, n'enfantoit guère que des chimères" (vol. 3, p. 351). No exaggeration surely was intended, for when it was finished in 1777 the west front of St.-Sulpice seemed to contemporaries to have the firmness of geometry, the regularity, and the columnar rhythms of a Greek temple. Certainly it was one of the starkest and most startling buildings in Paris. But its design had been evolved over a long period and by many architects, Chalgrin no less than Servandoni.

The chief architects of the years of transition were Pierre Contant d'Ivry and J.-G. Soufflot, whose designs for churches—especially Soufflot's Ste.-Geneviève—first suggested the form that the new architecture might take. But Contant d'Ivry did not visit Rome, and Soufflot was first there in the 1730s, before that interlude of enterprise and interaction between the French *pensionnaires* and the Italian painters of views, the *vedutisti.* In consequence, Soufflot's vision was to include little of novelty. The two architects took over an established tradition: Contant d'Ivry one that was French, Soufflot a late Renaissance formula. Neither was in any case greatly interested in novel formal devices. The spur to their architecture was structural finesse. The focus of interest in Contant d'Ivry's churches—at Condé-sur-l'Escaut, Arras, and, even more, the Abbaye Royale de Penthémont (106 Rue de Grenelle, Paris), of 1747 to 1756, and his unfinished project for the Madeleine, designed in 1761—is the refinement of construction. He experimented continually to reduce the mass of his structures and to make more daring his vaulting techniques.

Soufflot's concern for the way in which a building was made and how it might operate efficiently was evident from the start in the theater he began in 1754 in Lyons, in which the shape of the auditorium was conditioned by the sight lines and acoustics already tested in the theaters of Italy—though he went further than the Italians in introducing heating systems, tanks of water for fire fighting, and new lighting devices. His facades were creditable but dull. And at Ste.-Geneviève itself, as we have seen, though he was greatly concerned with the formal geometry, building the whole up from a regular grid, and slowly developing the design of the dome so that it became more and more pure in form, it was the manipulations of structure that drew forth his best energies and his delight—and led also, it was said, to his death (from worry). Considering that he presented himself as a reformer of architecture, and operated with the fullest support of the Marquis de Marigny, how disappointing is his output—in particular, those buildings in which structural experiment could play but a small part: the sacristy of Notre-Dame, of 1756; the École de Droit, facing Ste.-Geneviève, of 1771–83; and the buildings for Marigny himself, which included a house in the Faubourg du Roule, of 1769, notable for its Palladian window, and the orangery and nymphaeum at the Château de Ménars. Soufflot relied too readily on what he had learned in Italy.

The first architect to provide a model for a new and reformed classical style and to infuse into it the well-considered grace and decorum of the French tradition, which—despite the rococo irruption—had continued strong from the reign of Louis XIV onward, was Ange-Jacques Gabriel (1698–1782). He did not go to Italy, but trained with his father, *Premier*

*118. Giovanni Niccolò Servandoni, design for the west front of St.-Sulpice, Paris, 1732*

*119. Giovanni Niccolò Servandoni, St.-Sulpice, Paris, west front, 1732–77*

*120. Pierre Contant d'Ivry, Abbaye Royale de Penthémont, Paris, interior of the dome and vaults, 1747–56*

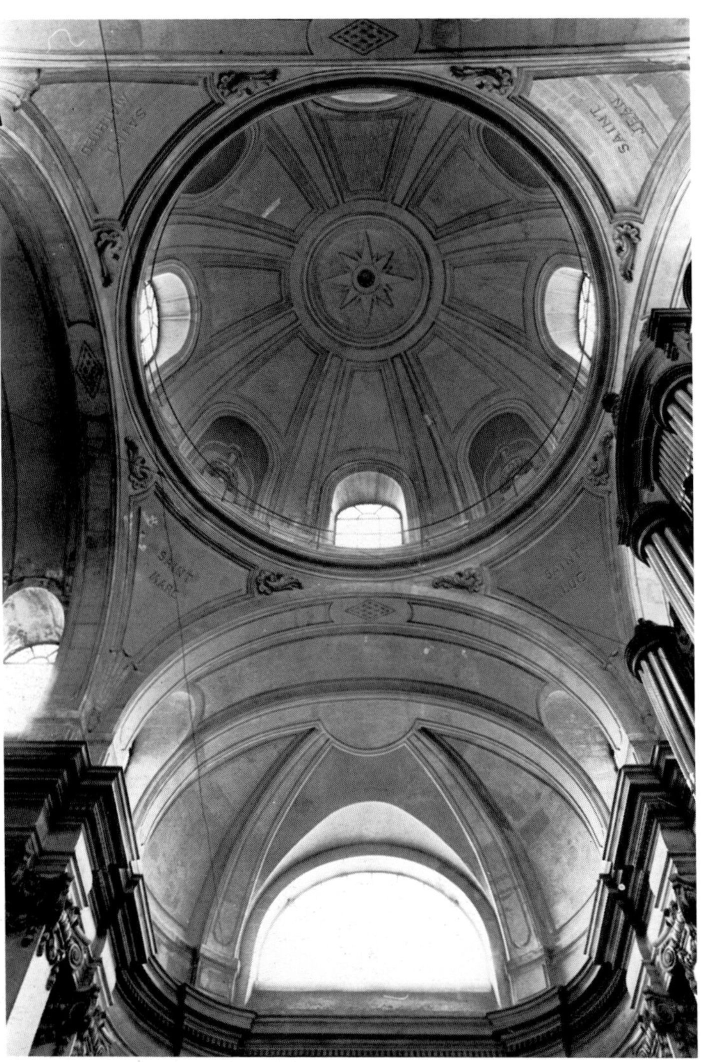

*Architecte du Roi,* and succeeded to that title (as well as to *Directeur de l'Académie d'Architecture)* with the fullest confidence in his ability, in 1742; he retained the title until he retired, in 1774. He worked only at the king's command: Far too much of his time and energy was to be taken up with complex and futile schemes of alteration and extension to the royal palaces at Versailles, Fontainebleau, Compiègne, and Choisy. His *grands projets* no less than his *petits appartements*—and certainly the splendid and now beautifully restored theater that he built at Versailles for the dauphin's wedding in May 1770—are all deserving of study, and no doubt served to influence the course of architecture, but it was rather the succession of small and comparatively simple buildings that he erected for the court in the 1750s that was to indicate to his contemporaries how architecture might be reformed—Mme. de Pompadour's Pavillon Français (1749–50) at the Petit Trianon, Versailles, and her Ermitage (1749) at Fontainebleau, and the hunting lodges of Le Butard (1750), St.-Hubert (1755-57), Les Fausses-Reposes (1756; virtually unrecorded), and La Muette (1764), in the forests around Versailles. They were all neat and restrained in treatment. The culmination of his career was the Petit Trianon itself, promised to Mme. de Pompadour in 1761, begun in 1762, but not taken up in earnest until 1764, one year after the Seven Years' War, and the year of her death. The interiors, with paneling by Honoré Guibert, were not completed until 1769. This is a perfect example of the most refined taste of the period, the forerunner of the architecture of Boullée, Ledoux, and others. All admired Gabriel's work, but it was in Paris that its impact was to be most forcibly felt, once again on the initiative of Mme. de Pompadour. Even before her brother became *Directeur Général des Bâtiments,* in 1751, Gabriel had been called upon to design the imposing École Militaire, begun that year, greatly revised in 1765, and continued by a succession of architects until 1788.

In 1748 architects had been asked to submit proposals for a towplanning venture to frame a commemorative statue of the king. About one hundred fifty projects were sent in for sites all over Paris. But the king, alarmed at the cost of acquiring the sites proposed, ceded a large area of ground at the end of the Tuileries gardens and ordered another competition in 1753. Only nineteen architects submitted on this occasion. Gabriel's design was finally chosen in 1755 and work was begun —and continued until 1775—to provide Paris with the noblest and also the most unusual square in Europe, the Place Louis XV (today the Place de la Concorde). The rectangular space was defined by ditches and balustrades, with small pavilions, topped with statues, to mark the cutoff corners. The whole was dominated by two majestic colonnaded buildings, fittingly commemorating Perrault's example at the Louvre. "On aurait beaucoup mieux fait," Laugier carped in his *Observations,* of 1765, "de retrancher l'énorme soubassement de ces deux façades, d'établir la péristile au rez-de-chaussée sur un perron, élevé de plusieurs marches, et de lui donner toute la hauteur du bâtiment" (p. 35). But Ledoux, less intractable, wrote in his *L'architecture,* "Voyez les colonnes

*121. Pierre Contant d'Ivry, Palais-Royal, Paris, grand staircase, 1756–70*

*122. Pierre Contant d'Ivry, St.-Vaast, Arras, interior, designed 1754*

*123. Pierre Contant d'Ivry, the Madeleine, Paris, plan, 1761*

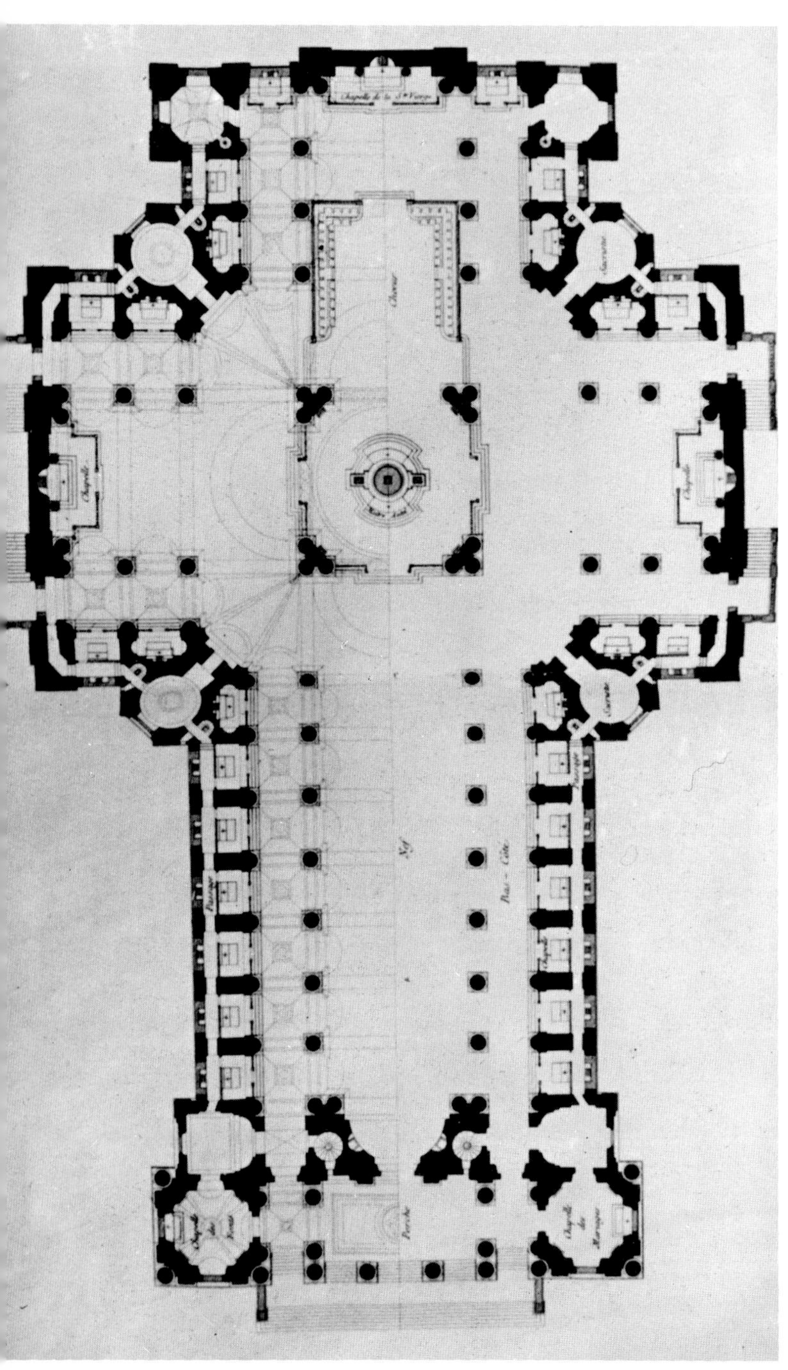

de la place Louis XV . . . on les aperçoit du quai du nord, à plus de trois cent toises; elles sont si bien conçues qu'elles s'effacent aux yeux, pour laisser à la pensée sublime idéal qui tient du prodige. C'est là, c'est dans ce fastueux édifice que brille le sentiment inépuisable de l'architecture française" (vol. 1, 1804, p. 108). One cannot be altogether sure that no sarcasm was intended here, for, like Laugier, Ledoux ridiculed the fussines of the detail. Yet Gabriel's influence on later generations of architects was enormous. He was the exact counterpart of Jacques-François Blondel, a man of moderation and common sense in all things, wanting restraint and no great novelty, balance without violent movement or contrast. Together they provided a sound basis for the future.

With the signing of the Treaty of Paris in 1763 and the ending of the Seven Years' War, building activity began once again in Paris on an unprecedented scale. Whole new quarters sprang up within a few years on the site of the northern ramparts, where the new boulevards were laid out. Farther to the north toward Montmartre, to the west bordering the Champs-Élysées, and in scattered pockets to the south, a succession of small and elegant villas was built in imitation of Italian casinas, Vitruvius's *aedes pseudourbanae.* These marked the beginnings of a suburban development and were termed *folies,* not to account for any whimsicality—though many were bizarre enough—but because they were intended as retreats, hidden by foliage and trees. A new generation of architects emerged, then, to take control and impose their ideas, a generation inspired by Blondel, Gabriel, and Soufflot, but aiming at something different, something more severely classical, more starkly monumental and large in scale.

"La plupart de nos élèves s'y trompent-ils tous les jours," Blondel wrote in the fourth volume of his *Cours d'architecture,* in 1773, "il leur parât plus aisé d'arriver aux compositions gigantesques, qu'aux proportions de la belle architecture" (p. lxx). Yet he was able to appreciate the largeness of scale and the simple geometry of the circular Halle aux Blés that Nicolas Le Camus de Mézières was to build right in the heart of the Marais, on the site of the old Hôtel de Soissons, between 1763 and 1767. This was not, strictly, a classically inspired work though contemporaries did liken it to an antique amphitheater and Laugier himself was moved to write, in 1765, even before its completion, that it was likely to become the finest building in Paris. When, in 1782 and 1783, Jacques-Guillaume Legrand (1743–1808) and Jacques Molinos (1743–1831) covered the circular central court with a giant dome, thirty-nine meters (one hundred twenty-nine feet) in diameter, of a light timber construction—similar to that proposed by Philibert de l'Orme for a nun's dormitory at Montmartre—the building appeared the most complete expression in France of the current liking for bold geometrical form. It was referred to as an equivalent of the Panthéon, which it almost equaled in size, and was to be inordinately admired by architects of the new generation.

The architects with whom we will deal first, Peyre, de Wailly, and

*124. Pierre Contant d'Ivry, the Madeleine, Paris, interior, begun 1764*

*125. Jacques-Germain Soufflot, design for the Hôtel de Marigny, Faubourg du Roule, Paris, 1769*

*126. Jacques-Germain Soufflot, nymphaeum for the Marquis de Marigny, Château de Ménars (Loire), 1764*

127. Ange-Jacques Gabriel, Pavillon Français, garden of the Petit Trianon, Versailles, 1749–50

128. Ange-Jacques Gabriel, Le Butard, a hunting lodge near Marly, 1750

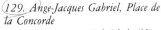

129. Ange-Jacques Gabriel, Place de la Concorde

130. Ange-Jacques Gabriel, building on the north side of the Place de la Concorde, Paris, 1758–75

Moreau-Desproux, had all been to Rome, though only two had won the Grand Prix. The most advanced was Marie-Joseph Peyre (1730–1785), an innovator of great power. His influence flashed suddenly into the international sphere with the publication, in 1765, of his *Oeuvres d'architecture,* dedicated to the Marquis de Marigny, and was instantly absorbed and lasted longer than that of most of his contemporaries. He was a pupil of Blondel, Denis Jossenay, and Louis-Adam Loriot. In 1571 he won the Grand Prix with a design for a public fountain, a grand affair with projecting side pavilions made up of Doric columns *in antis* supporting unadorned entablatures and pediments. The skyline is enlivened with statues and a dome, topped with a feature that looks something like an antique sarcophagus. But it is in no sense a design in the antique spirit; it is very characteristically a product of Blondel's school. In the spring of 1753 Peyre reached Rome, where he was to find at least one fellow pupil, William Chambers, and was to be joined within eighteen months by two more, Charles de Wailly (1730–1798) and Pierre-Louis Moreau-Desproux. Together with them Peyre was to explore the monuments of the city and measure the thermae, the circuses, and, in particular, Hadrian's Villa.

He soon put these studies to use. Not long after his arrival in Rome he entered and won a competition at the Accademia di San Luca for a cathedral and two related palaces, one for an archbishop and the other for the canons. His designs show that, though he had studied carefully both Michelangelo's and Bernini's work at St. Peter's, he was also incorporating aspects of antique architecture into his work. From this period dates his extraordinary fondness for freestanding columns. His cathedral, a Greek cross surmounted by a great dome with four subsidiary cupolas, is set in a circular colonnade circumscribed by a circular space and an even larger colonnade, copied directly from Bernini. The two palaces, square buildings planned around open courtyards, are set laterally on either side of the circle thus formed. The scheme is vast. But it is no less vast, though perhaps less advanced, than that for an academic center he prepared a few years later, in 1756. The main building this time is square in plan, though diminished in area by the inclusion of two grand semicircular courts. It is far more overtly antique in conception in that it contains a variety of rooms and halls of different geometrical shapes, all toplit, cleverly counterpointing one another and derived for the most part from Hadrian's Villa, but also no doubt from Piranesi's own variations on this theme. The main building, topped by a colonnaded drum, is again encompassed by columns, and is placed in a square court delimited by a range of buildings screened by more freestanding columns. This court is flanked by a "cirque . . . pour les révolutions militaires" and a naumachia, modeled, naturally, on Roman circuses, but terminating in hemicycles of serried columns.

The giant formality of these designs—though not at all unusual within the context of the competitions of the Accademia di San Luca—profoundly affected the future of architecture when they were published, together with

*131. Ange-Jacques Gabriel, Place Louis XV (now Place de la Concorde), Paris, designed 1753, executed 1755–75. Engraving by G. L. Le Rouge*

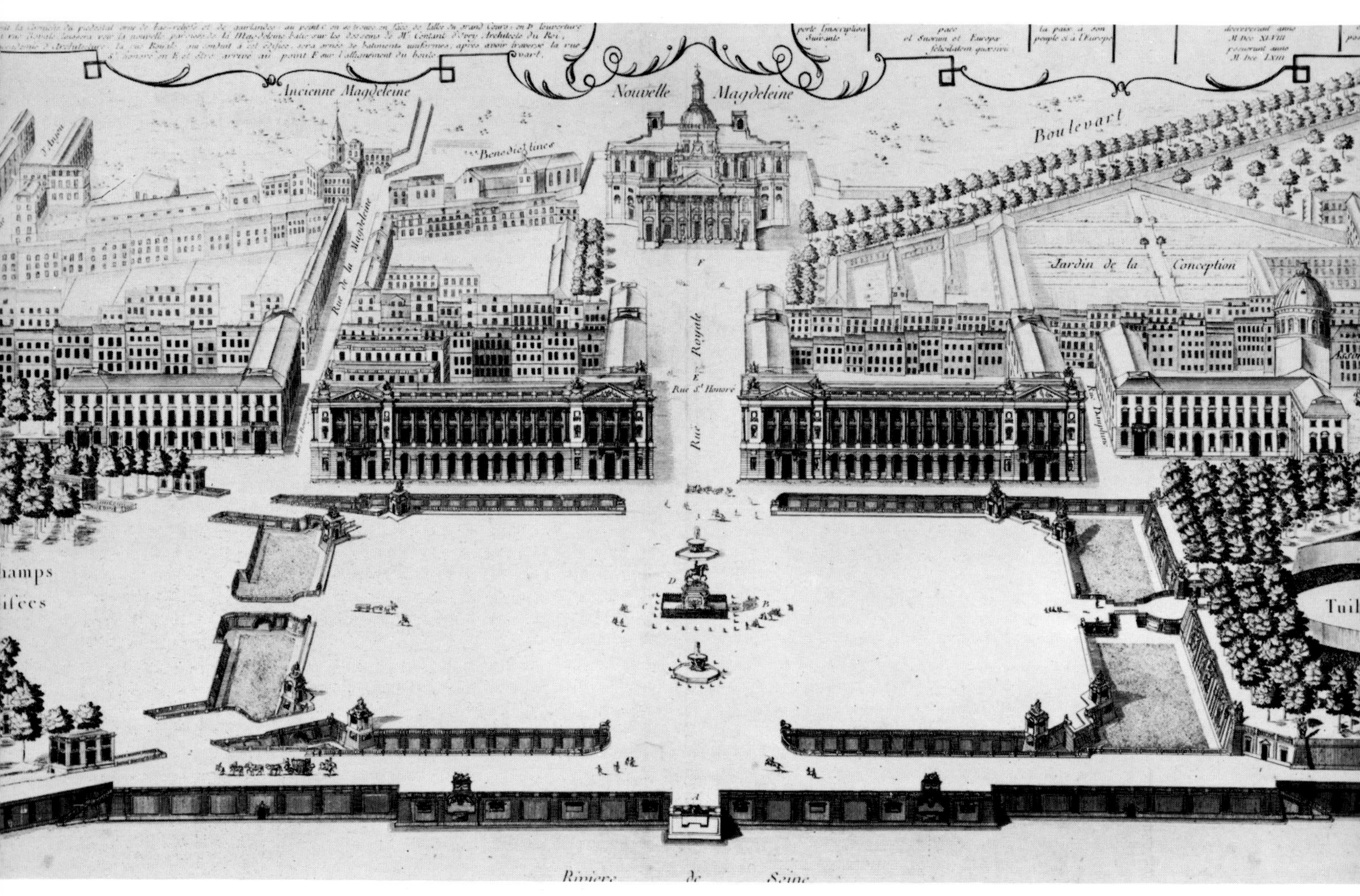

132-134. Ange-Jacques Gabriel, Petit Trianon, Versailles, garden facade, courtyard facade, entry staircase, 1763, 1764–68

a similar though slightly more commonplace project for a sovereign's palace, in the *Oeuvres d'architecture,* in 1765. They had no doubt exercised their potent influence on a number of architects even before their publication. Certainly their sheer magnificence of scale finds its parallel in the drawings of the Grand Prix winners of the early 1760s. And Peyre's insistence on the use of columns, so that all architecture appears as a sequence of columnar episodes (calling to mind Frézier's horrified comment on Cordemoy, "Il nevoulait partout que des colonnes, isolées et dégagées"; *Mémoires de Trévoux,* 1704, p. 161), can be traced in the works of such architects as Jacques Gondoin and Robert Adam long before it served to transform the late eighteenth-century architecture of France and England. Peyre's strong liking for toplighting was also to be echoed in the undertakings of Gondoin, Adam, and George Dance, the younger, before the end of the 1760s. Peyre wrote several articles at this time for the *Mercure de France* (reprinted in the second edition of his *Oeuvres d'architecture,* in 1795), one of which dealt with the planning arrangements of the ancient Romans, upholding for imitation their single-story buildings, with service areas below, made up of rooms of different shapes and sizes packed together and lit from above. "Les romaines," he wrote, "étaint si persuadés de l'effet et de la beauté des grandes pièces éclairées par les voûtes, que, non seulement ils les pratiquaient dans les palais de leurs empereurs et dans les monuments publics, mais aussi dans les maisons des particuliers, et on y voyat toujours quelques salles principales dans ce genre" (p. 11).

In only a handful of buildings in Paris, however, all of a fanciful kind, were the vastness of scale, the complexity of planning, and the experimental lighting effects to be realized. The most ambitious was the Colisée, built between 1769 and 1771 to the designs of Louis-Denis Le Camus, at the top end of the Champs-Élysées. This pleasure dome soon deteriorated and was demolished within fifteen years, though its spectacular effects were recorded in sketches by Gabriel de Saint-Aubin. In 1770 Victor Louis proposed a similar, if less elaborate, layout for a vauxhall in the Bois de Boulogne, which was never built, although a related enterprise, the Cirque Royal, designed by Nicolas Lenoir le Romain or Jacques Cellerier (1742–1814), was opened on the boulevards in 1775. Between 1774 and 1785 Henri Piètre (c. 1725–after 1785), a pupil of Jean-Silvain Cartaud, together with A.-T. Brongniart, completed a smaller, though private and permanent and thus more remarkable, pavilion for the Duc d'Orléans in the Rue de Provence, adjoining the house that Brongniart had built for the duke's morganatic wife, Mme. de Montesson. The Pavillon d'Orléans, an altogether charming work, was closest in appearance to Peyre's ideal, especially as illustrated—no doubt inaccurately—by J.K. Krafft and P.-N. Ransonnette in the *Plans, coupes, élévations des plus belles maisons et des hôtels construits à Paris et dans les environs,* in 1802.

Although Peyre had returned to Paris from Rome in 1756, it was not until 1762 that he was called upon to build his first—but very remarkable—

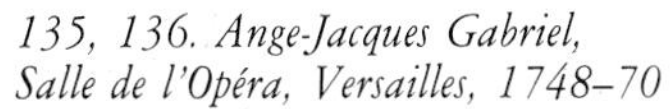

*135, 136. Ange-Jacques Gabriel, Salle de l'Opéra, Versailles, 1748–70*

work, a *folie,* the Hôtel Leprêtre de Neubourg, at Clos Payen, south of Paris. This was built in the same year in which Gabriel produced the revised design for the equally remarkable but more elegant and less reserved Petit Trianon, and four years after Stuart's Doric temple at Hagley Park in Worcestershire was completed. Unlike Stuart, however, Peyre was not concerned with imitating antique architecture, but, following Palladio, he wished to distill its effects and infuse them into his work. The Hôtel Leprêtre de Neubourg is, in essence, neoclassical. It is, perhaps, the first strictly neoclassical building in France (though in appearance it is not at all unlike William Kent's Wakefield Lodge, at Potterspury in Northamptonshire, built about 1745 or soon after). Like many of Jules Hardouin Mansart's houses, it rests on a stylobate and consists broadly of two pedimented blocks joined by a rectangular mass to which a portico of six Doric columns, carrying a horizontal entablature, is appended. Leading up to the portico is a divided flight of stairs. The composition is compact, with unadorned wall surfaces—apart from a few niches—and well-spaced door and window openings, without surrounds; despite all its symmetry, there is a true neoclassical reluctance to emphasize the center. The principal entrance itself is placed not on the main axis of the house but at the side, and the planning reflects this fondness for underemphasis. The stair is enclosed and played down, as Peyre had noted was usually the case in antique architecture. The entrance and stair hall, decorated with columns, lead to the dining room, which opens in turn on to the salon and then to the principal bedchambers and dressing rooms. There are no passages. Gone is the marvelous complexity and refinement of arrangement that Blondel had lauded as the great French contribution to architecture. Here is a baldly empirical arrangement, almost antique in character, suggesting that Peyre's innovations were applicable on even the smallest of domestic scales.

*137, 138. Nicolas Le Camus de Mézières, Halle aux Blés, Paris, exterior and interior, 1763–67. Drawings by Maréchal*

Peyre's next design was less severe. In April 1763 he drew up the plans of a house for the Prince de Condé, intended for a site opposite the Palais du Luxembourg, delimited today by the Rue de Condé, the Rue Monsieur-le-Prince, and the Rue de Vaugirard. The exaggerated aspect of his Roman projects is at once apparent in the perspective sketch (illustrated in the *Oeuvres d'architecture*), though the plan has none of that novelty. It is, indeed, not unlike that for an ideal château that Blondel drew for his pupils, though the central feature of Peyre's design—a low-domed rotunda containing a freestanding circle of columns behind which four symmetrical flights of stairs rise, preceded by a flat-topped portico—is an updated and purified version of the Panthéon. The most striking feature, however, is a columnar screen, with a triumphal arch enclosing the entrance court. This theme can be traced back to Cordemoy, and to Delamair'sa Hôtel de Soubise of the same period, and it was to be illustrated with flourishes by both Blondel and Neufforge in the 1750s. It was taken up in 1764 by Gabriel for the château at Compiègne, and a few years later suitably flattened, by Gondoin at the École de Chirurgie, Paris. The most direct transcription from Peyre, however, was the derivative masterpiece of Nicolas-Marie Potain's son-in-law, Pierre Rousseau (1751–1810), the Hôtel de Salm (now the Palais de la Légion d'Honneur), at 64 Rue de Lille, Paris, built between 1782 and 1785. In England, Robert Adam introduced the idea for the Admiralty Screen at Whitehall in 1759, soon after his return from Italy, but missed the point in placing a blank screen-wall immediately behind the colonnade.

From the first, Peyre was conscious of himself as an innovator. His purpose, he declared in the *Oeuvres d'architecture,* was to show how the works of the ancient Romans might be imitated to counteract the established French tradition, yet after the publication of his book he did very little work of importance. He became *Contrôleur* at Choisy. In 1767 he was admitted to the Académie, and throughout the rest of his life he submitted a number of schemes for reconstructions and new buildings (at least two of his houses in Paris survive today: the Hôtel de Nivernais, 10 Rue de Tournon, and the adjoining 11 Rue Garancière). But his only significant work was the Théâtre-Français (later Théâtre de l'Odéon, new Théâtre de France), designed in collaboration with his friend Charles de Wailly.

A pupil of Legeay and Blondel, de Wailly won the Grand Prix in 1752 with a design for a facade for a vast palace with a concave central feature screened with giant Corinthian columns, the whole preceded by a triumphal arch and a much lower curved colonnaded screen adapted from Bernini's at St. Peter's. Clearly, Peyre was to be indebted to this design for his *grands projets.* De Wailly generously offered to share his prize with his friend Pierre-Louis Moreau-Desproux, who, for three successive years, had come was a man of no great talent: He built, as we have seen the Hôtel de Chavannes (1756–58), the Théâtre de l'Opéra at the Palais-Royal (1763–70), and the Pavillon Carré de Beaudouin, on the heights of Ménilmontant (1770). All these works are of interest, and show promise, but all are

*139. Marie-Joseph Peyre, competition project for a cathedral submitted to the Accademia di San Luca, Rome, 1753*

*140. Marie-Joseph Peyre, project for an academy, designed at Rome in 1756*

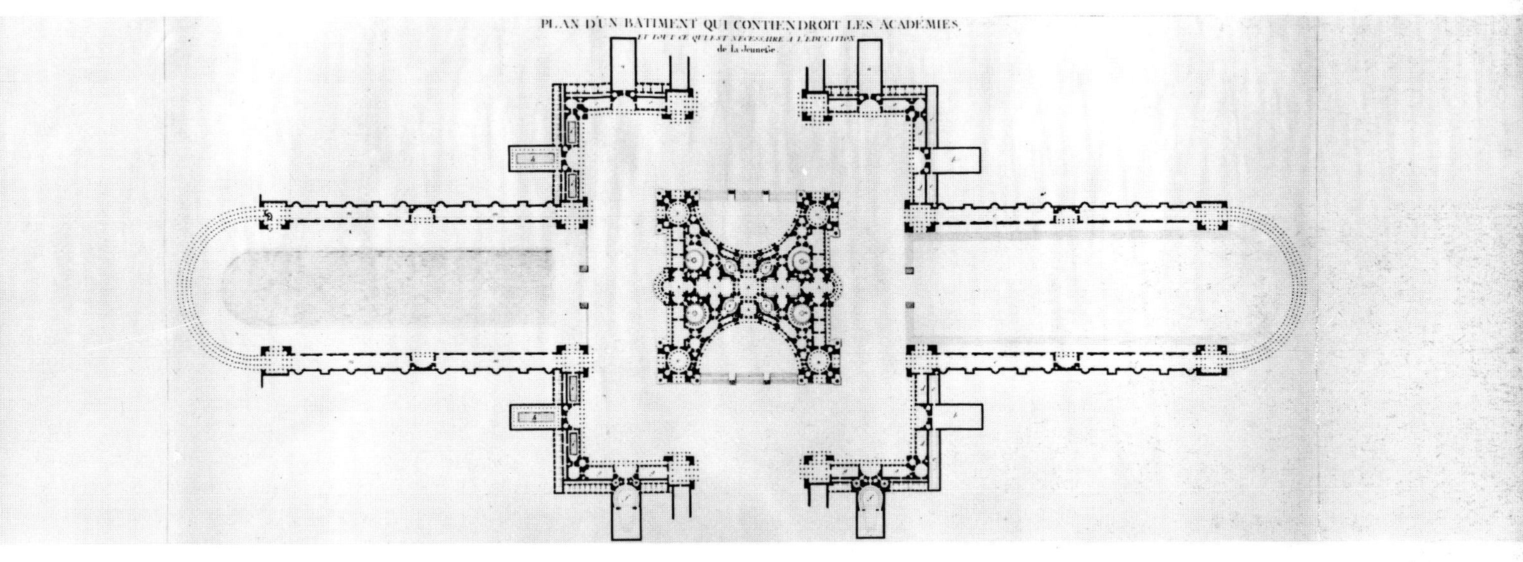


unsatisfactory in that they lack tension of design. Moreau-Desproux was sustained by the family post he inherited in 1763, the *Maître des Bâtiments de la Ville de Paris.* He was the last to hold that title. De Wailly, however, was a challenging man. On his return from Rome he opened an *atelier* where he taught a number of architects—among them the Russians Vasili Ivanovich Bazhenov (1737–1799), Ivan Yegorovich Starov (1743–1808), and Fiodor Ivanovich Volkhov (1755–1803). In 1767 de Wailly became *Contrôleur* at Versailles under Gabriel, and in the same year he was literally forced into the *première classe* of the Académie Royale de Peinture et de Sculpture by Marigny, who greatly admired his work. Four years later he was elected to the Académie Royale de Peinture et de Sculpture, the only architect to achieve this distinction apart from that maverick recorder of ruins Clérisseau. Charles-Louis Clérisseau (1722–1820) was the painter of the Ruin Room at S. Trinità dei Monti, in Rome, that was so admired by Piranesi, designer of the early arabesque decorations for Grimod de la Renière's salon in the Rue Boissy-d'Anglas (1774/75), and architect of the Palais du Gouverneur (now the Palais de Justice), in Metz (built between 1776 and 1789). De Wailly's activity was almost as diverse but his development was less consistent. Indeed, his ouput is baffling. In Rome, for instance, he made drawings of the ceiling of Il Gesù and of Bernini's *Throne of Saint Peter* with an obvious interest in the richness of form and the atmospheric qualities of lighting. Many of his interiors, such as the *salone* of the Palazzo Spinola in Genoa (1772–73), the Chapelle de la Vierge in St.-Sulpice (1777–78), and even the rooms of the old Hôtel d'Argenson (redecorated in 1784), are overabundant and exuberant in a Baroque sort of way. For the Marquis d'Argenson's country house, Les Ormes, he designed an elaborate stair in about 1771 (with which Sir William Chambers was in some way involved), derived from that by G. B. Piacentini, built in 1695 into the Palazzo dei Ranuzzi (now di Giustizia) in Bologna, where de Wailly had been made a member of the Academy in 1755. For the Marquis de Marigny, at the Château de Ménars, he designed a garden pavilion in 1768 or 1769, with partially fluted Doric columns like those of the Temple of Apollo at Delos, the only direct imitation of the Greek Doric in France, and for the crypt of St.-Leu-St.-Gilles, in Paris (1773–80), he used columns derived from the temples at Paestum, but with a square base and reeding rather than concave fluting—Gothic in effect rather than classical. In his whole manner of composing buildings there is this same discordance of vision: Some are made up of small, contrasting elements of divergent shapes and scale; others consist of large, simplified geometrical masses. Yet his major works, if not always as hard and stark as those of his contemporaries, are undeniably neoclassical.

The first and boldest of de Wailly's country houses, Montmusard, on the outskirts of Dijon, was designed in 1764 for Olivier Fyot de la Marche, first president of the Parlement of Burgundy. The plan was marked by a complex yet wonderfully lucid geometry and was consciously antique in spirit; it was to be the first secular building in eighteenth-century France to be dedicated as a temple, a temple to the muses. This was clearly expressed in its arrangement. Only a fragment was built, but de Wailly's original plan survives, as does a painting by Panini's pupil Jean-Baptiste Lallemand (1716–1803), to convey the architect's intention. The plan is rectangular, almost square, with just the suggestion in the articulation of four corner pavilions. On the garden side a domed circular salon projects to form a semicircle; at the entrance front an open colonnaded temple is formed, cutting into the mass of the building. The detailed planning was more intricate than usual. The facades, though, were treated as single story, with an attic above and a balustrade over, the whole unified by an overall pattern of rustication. There were no moldings around the window and door openings. Had it been completed in this form, the house would have been the most daring yet noble in France. But money ran out in 1772, long before the building was finished. In the following year de Wailly exhibited a design at the Salon for an even grander variant on the theme for Catherine the Great, dedicated this time to Minerva. Much later, in 1812, J. K. Krafft was to publish an altogether different design for the Château de Montmusard, consisting of a cylinder linked to two cubic blocks. The *raison d'être* of this arrangement was the domed open circular *salon d'été* at first-floor level, surrounded by two rows of columns with the staircase rising between them. This, no doubt, was derived from Peyre's stair hall for the Hôtel de Condé, though it may be distantly linked also to Balthasar Neumann's oval stair at the Episcopal Palace at Bruchsal, in Baden-Württembert, built in 1731. Such central focus on the stair hall is unusual in France. In England experiments with a circular domed and colonnaded stair hall began with a design of 1759 for York House, Pall Mall, by Sir William Chambers; he, as we have seen, seems to have collaborated in 1774 with de Wailly on the latter's more complex variation at the Château d'Ormes. The most notable of these stair halls, however, was that designed in 1770 by James Paine for Wardour Castle, in Wiltshire.

The five town houses that de Wailly planned for the Rue de la Pépinière, Paris (only two were built—the sculptor Augustin Pajou's in 1776, and his own, in 1778—and a third was begun in 1779), consist of an array of simple blocks, some of them surmounted by small pediments, others by rounded gables; they were evidently intended to form a unified architectural panorama of lively interest. The handling of the forms is wonderfully resourceful, if we are to judge by the illustrations in Krafft's and Ransonnette's *Plans . . . des plus belles maisons . . . à Paris.* Another circular colonnaded stair hall is introduced to give a central focus. But the constant setbacks in the composition, made up of small and varied elements, would have weakened the total effect.

In 1767 de Wailly was called upon with Peyre to design his greatest work, the Théâtre-Français (later Théâtre de l'Odéon, today Théâtre de France), on the site of the Hôtel de Condé. In the following years he traveled to England, Germany, and twice to Italy in order to study theaters. The history of the building is complex, with many changes of site and client and much rivalry involving a takeover at one stage by Moreau Desproux, who had not only benefited from de Wailly's friendship, as a student, but was by then the brother-in-law of Peyre. But the building that was started in May 1779 on the foundations set down by Moreau-Desproux (to be completed in 1782) was in most respects similar to his and de Wailly's joint project approved in 1770. The circular auditorium is contained entirely within a rectangular block, rusticated all over, with arcades on the ground floor along the sides and the rear, rectangular windows on the second floor, and circular openings in the attic story. The whole is surmounted by a high pyramid roof. In front of the building is a Doric portico with a horizontal entablature, at one time intended to carry two reclining figures and a lyre, a symbolic dedication to Apollo. Later, in 1786, when the theater was to be converted into an opera house, de Wailly prepared a design in which two lodges and, further back, a pavilion with a Venetian window, niches, and sculptural decorations were to be set above the portico, providing a trinity of features in a different key from the rest. But the building that was erected, sober and severe in form, was made only marginally more severe when, after a fire in 1799, it was rebuilt by Chalgrin.

The bare account offered of the careers of Peyre and de Wailly gives some indication of the dramatic changes that took place in domestic architecture after 1763: changes in massing and the treatment of wall surfaces; changes in planning, from reliance on the simple *enfilade* to a complexity of

*141, 142. Marie-Joseph Peyre, project for the main building of an academy, designed at Rome in 1756*

interlocking rooms of different shapes and sizes; and changes also of detail. In the whole range of building types there were similar significant developments. More public buildings were erected than ever before. Theaters, which multiplied throughout France in this period, provide a particularly fruitful field for study. The practical demands of acoustics, sight lines, lighting, fire precaution, and construction resulted in notable departures from the norm. A progression—indeed, a progress—may be traced, starting with the new theater at Metz, or, more properly, with Soufflot's theater in Lyons begun in 1754, and including no less than twenty in Paris, dominated by Peyre's and de Wailly's designs for the Théâtre-Français. The building of theaters extended also to the provincial centers: to Amiens, where Jean Rousseau built a theater in 1778; to Besançon, where Ledoux was active from 1775 to 1784; and especially to Bordeaux, where the most magnificent theater in all of France, a great rectangular block preceded by a portico of twelve giant Corinthian columns, was erected between 1773 and 1780. This, containing a stair hall that is one of the splendors of eighteenth-century architecture, is still virtually intact. The designer was Louis-Nicolas-Victoire Louis (1731–c. 1807), a pupil of L.-A. Loriot, who called himself Victor Louis after he won the equivalent of the Grand Prix in 1755 and went to Rome for three years. Upon his return to France he established an extremely fashionable practice, first under the protection of Mme. Geoffrin, as architect to the king of Poland, then as designer of a majestic temporary ballroom for the Spanish ambassador's reception in honor of the dauphin's marriage in 1770 (Chalgrin set up an equally noble ballroom for the Austrian ambassador). But Louis made a name and a living for himself chiefly in Bordeaux, where he built a number of *hôtels* in the new quarters adjoining his theater—the Hôtels Saige (1774–80), Fontfrède (1774–76), Legrix, de la Molère, de Rolly, and de Nairac (begun 1775). He was also responsible for several country houses, such as the Château de Virasel, near Marmande. The most ambitious by far was the Château de Bouilh, at St.-André-de-Cubzac, for the Marquis de la Tour du Pin, begun in 1786 but realized only in part. Even the unfinished fragment reveals it as one of the grandest country houses of the century. Louis's project of 1785 for the Place Louis XVI, on the site of the Château Trompette (now the Place des Quinconces), Bordeaux was of an equivalent heightened scale: a hemicycle of linked houses, 400 meters (1, 320 feet) in diameter, was to open on to and extend along the Garonne River, but they were never begun. In 1772, while still busy in Bordeaux, he planned

*143. Louis-Denis Le Camus, Colisée, Champs-Élysées, Paris, plan, 1769–71*

*144. Gabriel de Saint-Aubin,* La Fête du Colisée. *London, Wallace Collection*

*145. Henry Piètre with Alexandre-Théodore Brongniart, or, more likely, Brongniart alone, Pavillon d'Orléans, Paris, elevation and plan, 1774*

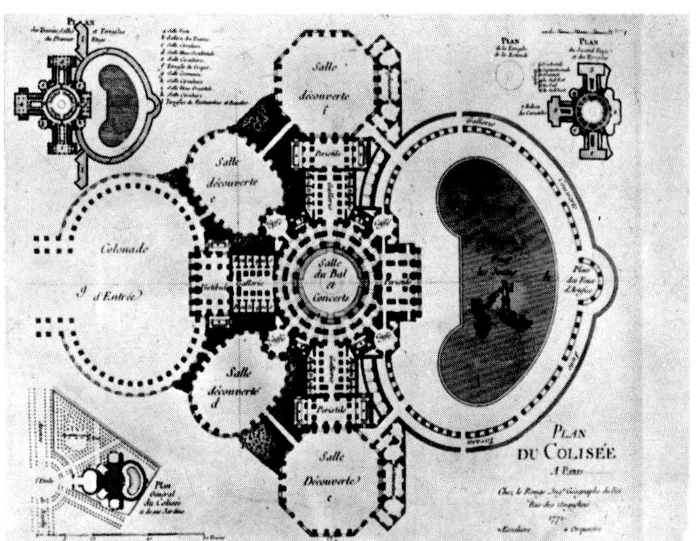

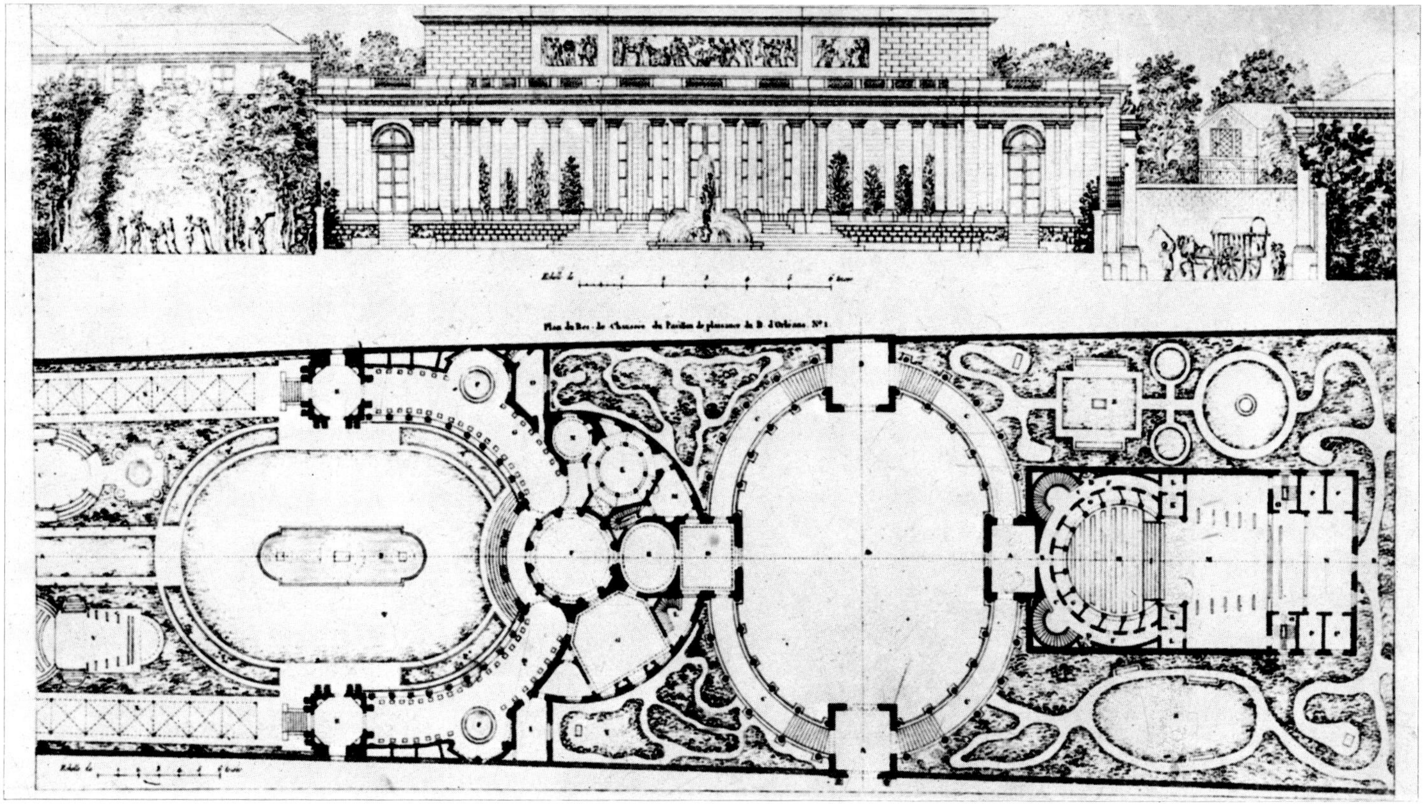

the Hôtel de l'Intendance (now the Préfecture) in Besançon, to be carried out faithfully during the next four years by a pupil of Blondel, Nicolas Nicole (1702–1784). Later, Louis was to return to Paris, upon which he conferred his expansive vision in 1781 in the form of the Galeries du Palais-Royal and a related theater, rebuilt by Julien Guadet in 1902, after a fire. The theater was notable for its cast-iron trusses and reinforcements, all lovingly phototraphed by Guadet's son Paul in their ruined state.

One of Louis's earliest works, the Chapelle des Âmes du Purgatoire in the church of Ste.-Marguerite-de-Charonne, Paris, designed in 1763, was no less distinctive a contribution to the evolution of church design than his theaters. The chapel—seemingly flanked by rows of Ionic columns supporting a horizontal entablature, without a projecting cornice, designed in imitation of a frieze from a sarcophagus, and carrying a coffered barrel vault—was, in fact, a *trompe l'oeil* painting by Paolo Antonio Brunetti, who, together with his father, Gaetano, and Charles-Joseph Natoire, had painted the scene of ruins on the walls of the chapel in Boffrand's Enfants-Trouvés (1746–51). It was a startling novelty, hailed by the Abbé Laugier in his *Observations* as "un des plus beaux dessins d'architecture que nous ayons à Paris" (p. 115). The revolution in church design that Louis thus acknowledged, proclaimed first by the Perraults with their project for Ste.-Geneviève and later by Cordemoy and Laugier, and culminating at just this time *en grand* with Soufflot's Ste.-Geneviève and Contant d'Ivry's Madeleine, was given convincing form a year or two later in the designs of three basilican churches: St.-Philippe-du-Roule, in Paris; St.-Symphorien, at Versailles; and St.-Louis, at St.-Germain-en-Laye. These, one should note, were preceded by St.-Vincent-des-Augustins, in Lyons—built in 1759 by Léonard Roux (1725–c. 1794), an associate of Soufflot—which was finished only in 1789 and was thus not to achieve the fame or the influence of the Parisian exemplars of the genre.

The most famous of these, of course, is St.-Philippe-du-Roule, the work of another pupil of Loriot and also of Boullée, Jean-François-Thérèse Chalgrin (1739–1811).

He won the Grand Prix at the age of nineteen, and traveled to Rome the following year. From Rome, he corresponded with Soufflot. On his return to France he became *Inspecteur des Travaux de la Ville de Paris,* under Moreau-Desproux, and in this capacity supervised the building of the Hôtel de Saint-Florentin, just off the Place Louis XV, according to the designs of Gabriel. Chalgrin himself designed the gateway and entrance door. He was commissioned in 1764 by the Comte de Saint-Florentin, as *Ministre de la Maison du Roi,* to design a new church. But the site was not acquired until May 1767, the plans approved by the Académie only in August 1768, and work finally begun in 1772, to be completed in 1784. The arrogant novelty of the design—with its freestanding Ionic columns ranged down the nave and continuing around the curve of the apse, a coffered barrel vault above, and a squat Tuscan portico outside—was thus not to be appreciated until

*146. Marie-Joseph Peyre, Hôtel Leprête de Neubourg, Clos Payen, near Paris, 1762. Engraving by Durand*

*147. William Kent, Wakefield Lodge, Northamptonshire, c. 1746.*

very late in the century. Today the church has lost the coherency and the feeling for classical unity so evident in old engravings, for it has twice been altered, once in 1846 by Étienne-Hippolyte Gode—who introduced windows into the vaults and built the Chapelle de la Vierge at the east end, opening up a vista through the screen of the apse—and in 1853 by Victor Baltard, who added the Chapelle des Catéchismes. Some of the initial quality was captured, however, by Chalgrin's pupil Jean-Baptiste Kléber (1753–1800), the future general, who copied the arrangement in 1774 for the Capuchin chapel at Strasbourg. Indeed, Kléber's version was even closer to Chalgrin's original intentions, for he retained the vault of stone complete with its flying buttresses that was omitted at St.-Philippe-du-Roule when a timber and plaster vault was built instead for economy.

Long before Chalgrin's church was complete, a similar basilica, designed in 1764 with partially fluted Doric columns supporting a horizontal entablature and surmounted by a coffered barrel vault (broken to accommodate windows), and preceded by a portico with freestanding Tuscan columns, was erected at Versailles. This was the church of St.-Symphorien de Montreuil, consecrated in 1770. The architect was Louis-François Trouard (1729–1794), once again a pupil of Loriot, who won the Grand Prix in 1753, arrived in Rome in the autumn of 1754, and spent three years there before returning to work at Versailles, where he was responsible for the barracks of the Gardes-françaises and other large and unremarkable buildings. He became architect at Orléans cathedral and at the Économats Royaux (an administration that spent the income from vacant bishoprics and estates confiscated from Protestants). In this capacity he was to design both St.-Symphorien and the Chapelle des Catéchismes at the east end of St.-Louis, in Versailles, in 1764–70. This chapel, divided with screens of columns, appears to have been derived directly from a plate in Piranesi's *Prima parte.* Another Italian-inspired church once attributed to Trouard but now more convincingly shown to be the work of Étienne-François Legrand—Trouard's successor at both the Économats Royaux and Orléans cathedral—is St.-Louis, in Port Marly (Yvelines), dating from 1778, the year in which Nicholas Revett built a comparable church at Ayot St. Lawrence, in England.

Legrand's successor at Orléans, in turn, was Trouard's pupil Pierre-Adrien Pâris (1747–1819). Pâris did not win the Grand Prix, but nonetheless traveled to Rome in 1770–71, in the company of Trouard's son; he returned to France in 1774 and four years later joined the Menus-Plaisirs, the administration responsible for royal fêtes, festivities, and spectacles, and to serve the world of fashion as well with designs for neat, precise, and altogether charming town and country houses. Pâris's chief claim to distinction, though, derives from his larger works—a vast Italianate palace at Porrentruy, for the Prince Bishop of Basel, begun in 1776 but never completed; the town hall at Neuchâtel, erected between 1784 and 1790 by the local builder Raimond; and the hospital at Bourg-en-Bresse. When he died in 1819 he left to his native Besançon an unrivaled collection of drawings by such artists as François Boucher, Jean-Honoré Fragonard, and Hubert Robert, together with an even more extensive array of his own drawings done on his early visit to Italy. He made other drawings during later visits to Rome in 1783, and with his students, after 1806, when he became director of the Académie de France à Rome. These illustrate all the buildings he studied, whether antique, Renaissance, or later, and include not only Palladio's works and those of Giulio Romano and the Sangallos but also Pirro Ligorio's buildings and other oddities such as the Collegio Elvetico, in Milan (so admired by Gondoin), and the Certosa, at Ema (which would prove so exciting to Le Corbusier). All Pâris's original designs are still in Besançon, demonstrations of the exotic range of his sources, and, as such, urgently requiring investigation.

The third of the basilican churches being considered here, St.-Louis, in St.-Germain-en-Laye, was, like St.-Symphorien, also designed in 1764, though work was not begun for two years; it was interrupted and resumed only in 1787, just before the Revolution, and was finally built in 1823–24 by Alexandre-Jacques Malpièce and A.-J. Moutier. The original architect was Nicolas-Marie Potain (1713–1796), a man of Soufflot's generation, who had won the Grand Prix in 1738 and had remained in Rome until 1744, where, like Soufflot, he measured St. Peter's, and then traveled through Italy studying theaters. The result, in 1763, was an unusual project for a theater on a corner site. The auditorium, with its axes on the diagonals, was

*148. Marie-Joseph Peyre, Hôtel de Condé, Paris, 1763*

*149. Pierre Rousseau, Hôtel de Salm (now Palais de la Légion d'Honneur), Paris, entry colonnade, 1782–85*

*150. Pierre Rousseau, Hôtel de Salm (now Palais de la Légion d'Honneur), Paris, facade on the Quai Anatole France, 1782–85*

*151. Charles de Wailly, Grand Prix design for a palace, 1752*

*152. Charles-Louis Clérisseau, design for the Ruin Room in the monastery of S. Trinità dei Monti, Rome, c. 1765*

*153. Charles-Louis Clérisseau, decorative panels for the salon of the Hôtel Grimod de la Reynière, Paris, 1774 or 1775. London, Victoria and Alberto Museum*

elliptical in plan, with receding tiers or seats. The wide proscenium opening, divided up by columns, was to be recalled by Peyre and de Wailly. The elevations, however, are less striking: Two prostyle porticos of Ionic columns with balustrades above give the building an air of boldness, but the pattern of window openings and the decoration betray a fondness rather for Gabriel's brand of classicism. Potain was to work as Gabriel's assistant on the Place Louis XV from 1754 to 1770. His work was, not altogether surprisingly, much admired by Marigny. When, therefore, in 1762, Soufflot's fullest energies were required in Paris on Ste.-Geneviève, Marigny decided on Potain to replace him as architect of the new cathedral in Rennes. Soufflot's appointment dates from 1754; Potain's designs for the cathedral, based on those of Soufflot, were submitted to the Académie on July 26, 1762. They were revised the following year, and approved by the king on May 9, 1764. The surviving plan shows freestanding columns along the nave, on the foundations of a destroyed Gothic church. The nature of the vaulting is not indicated. Construction was started in 1786, to be stopped by the Revolution. Although the cathedral as it stands today was built between 1811 and 1844, it is tempting to think that this exemplary basilica, with its Ionic columns alongside the nave and continuing around the apse, its horizontal entablatures, and its coffered barrel vault, reflects Potain's early designs and thus, indirectly, Soufflot's first project (1754). Certainly this plan would have provided a prototype for all three basilicas designed about 1764, and would in some measure account for their simultaneous conception.

A number of churches of this type were to be built in the years that followed. One of the least visited, but the most elegant, is St.-Symphorien, at Gy, by the engineer Henri Frignet and the local architect Charles Colombot, constructed between 1769 and 1785 for the Bishop of Besançon. By the early nineteenth century the pattern was ubiquitous, accepted as as

*154. Charles-Louis Clérisseau, design for the wall of the salon of the Hôtel Grimod de la Reynière, Paris, 1774 or 1775*

*155, 156. Charles-Louis Clérisseau, Palais de Justice, Metz, facade and courtyard, 1776–89*

*157. Charles de Wailly, Chapelle de la Vierge, St.-Sulpice, Paris, 1777–78*

*158. Charles de Wailly, pulpit, St.-Sulpice, Paris, 1789*

*159. Charles de Wailly, crypt, St.-Leu-St.-Gilles, Paris, 1773–80*

*160. Charles de Wailly, Château de Montmusard, Dijon, elevation and ground-floor plan as illustrated by J. K. Krafft, 1812*

*161. Charles de Wailly, Château de Montmusard (now part of the École St.-Dominique), Dijon, 1764–72*

*162. Detail of a painting of c. 1770 by Jean-Baptiste Lallemand, showing the Château de Montmusard as Charles de Wailly designed it in 1764. Dijon, Musée des Beaux-Arts*

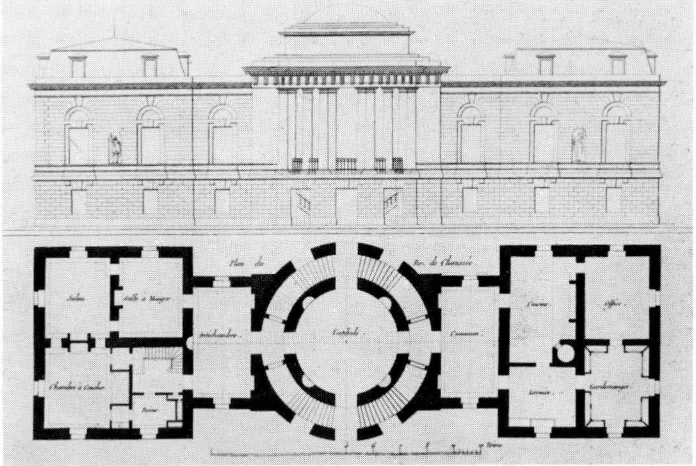

*163. Charles de Wailly, the architect's house in the Rue de la Pépinière, Paris, section, 1778*

*164. Charles de Wailly, houses in the Rue de la Pépinière, Paris, elevation and plan*

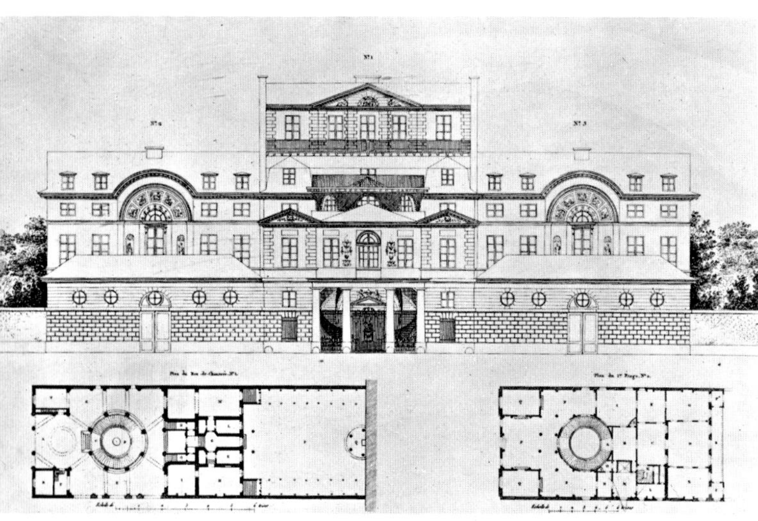

trite and well-tried formula; no one then cared about, or was aware of, the play of Gothic that had been so important an aspect of the eighteenth-century experiment.

Peyre, de Wailly, Louis, and Chalgrin have been presented as the first true representatives of the revised classical style of late eighteenth-century France, but no less important are Boullée, Jacques-Denis Antoine, Ledoux, Gondoin, Brongniart, and Bélanger—not one of whom was to win the Grand Prix, though Gondoin did travel to Italy. They made their debuts in the 1760s. Not all, though, were innovators. The youngest members of the group, Alexandre-Théodore Brongniart (1739–1813) and François-Joseph Bélanger (1744-1818), were indeed fashionable exponents rather than precursors of the new style. Heirs to Gabriel, excellent planners, and designers of taste, they managed to capture much of the elegance and grace of his best mid-century work and to infuse it into their new, more sober—if sometimes even grander—Parisian manner.

Brongniart, a pupil of Blondel and Boullée, began his career in 1765, when he built the theater at Caen, a building of little enough merit, which shows a liking for the works of Soufflot and, naturally, Blondel. The numerous houses that he built in Paris in the years following, however, reflect the influence of de Wailly and the smooth and flattening tastes of advanced classicism. All his *hôtels* are restrained in outline and pure in form, beautifully planned, with most of the rooms rectangular or square but a few of a circular or other geometrical shape to provide a degree of variety. The facades of the houses are, almost invariably, composed with regular roundheaded openings on the ground floor and rectangular bas-relief panels or windows above, each unit separated by giant pilasters. The roof line is always horizontal. Later he was to forego the pilasters, retaining only the most restrained and even rustication. His first mature work, the Hôtel de Montesson, of 1770 to 1771, in the Chaussée-d'Antin, thus has affinities with the late buildings of Gabriel, though it is understandably more reserved and crisply geometrical. This has now been demolished, along with his most ambitious work, the Hôtel de Sainte-Foix, of 1775, on the Rue Basse-du-Rempart, but many of his later *hôtels* survive, if only in part, and may easily be visited—the Hôtel de Monaco (now the Polish Embassy), of 1775–77, at 57 Rue St.-Dominique, and a nearby group: the Hôtel de Mlle. de Bourbon-Condé, of 1780–81, at 12 Rue Monsieur (now minus Clodion's relief panels); the Hôtel de Montesquiou, of the following year, at 20 Rue Monsieur; his own house, of the same date, at 49 Boulevard des Invalides; the Hôtel Chamblin, of about 1789, at 3-5 Rue Masseran; and the Hôtel Masserano, dating from 1787, at 11 Rue Masseran.

Before the Revolution Brongniart built only two important buildings outside the domestic range: the church of St.-Germain-l'Auxerrois, at Romainville, Paris, of 1785–87, recalling St.-Philippe-du-Roule in its internal arrangement but with far sturdier Doric columns in the nave, and the Couvent des Capucins de la Chaussée-d'Antin (now the Lycée Condorcet

*165, 166. Marie-Joseph Peyre and Charles de Wailly, Théâtre-Français (later Théâtre de l'Odéon, now Théâtre de France), Paris, section and view of the foyer and staircase showing the design of 1770*

*167. Marie-Joseph Peyre and Charles de Wailly, Théâtre-Français, Paris, 1779-82. Rebuilt after a fire in 1799. The house on the left, for the sculptor Augustin Pajou, was begun in 1776*

INTÉRIEUR DE LA NOUVELLE SALLE DE COMEDIE FRANÇAISE DE L'ANCIEN PROJET.

*168. Jacques-Germain Soufflot, Grand Théâtre, Lyons, plan, 1753*

*169. Jean Rousseau, theater, Amiens, facade, 1778*

*170. Victor Louis, Grand Théâtre, Bordeaux, cross section, 1773–80*

*171. Victor Louis, Grand Théâtre, Bordeaux, view of the auditorium*

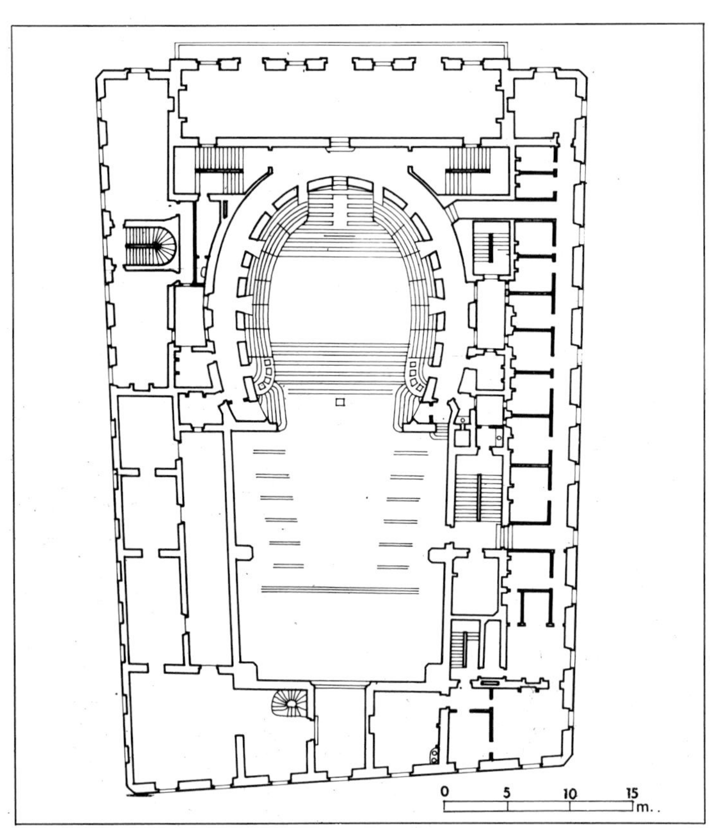

172. Victor Louis, Grand Théâtre, Bordeaux, perspective view

173. Victor Louis, Grand Théâtre, Bordeaux, longitudinal section

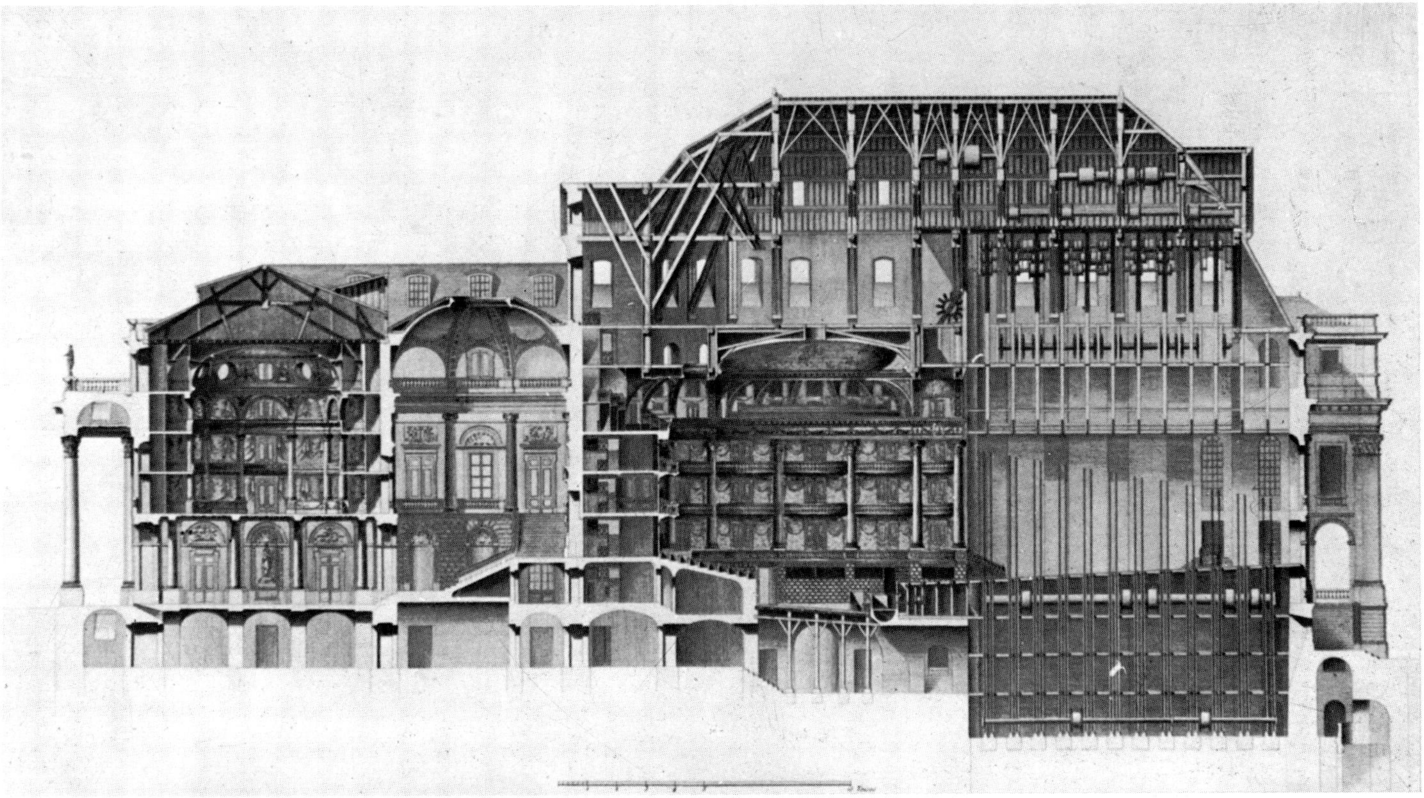

*174. Victor Louis, Grand Théâtre, Bordeaux, exterior, 1773-80*

*175. Victor Louis, Grand Théâtre, Bordeaux, staircase, 1773–80*

*176. Victor Louis, project for the Château de Bouilh, St.-André-de-Cubzac, begun 1786*

*177. Victor Louis, project for the Place Louis XVI, on the site of the Château Trompette (now Place des Quinconces), Bordeaux, 1785*

*178. Victor Louis, Hôtel de l'Intendance (now Préfecture), Besançon, built between 1772 and 1776 by Nicolas Nicole*

*179. Victor Louis, Galeries du Palais-Royal, Paris, 1781*

*IX. Ange-Jacques Gabriel, Salle de l'Opéra, Versailles, 1748–70*

and the church of St.-Louis d'Antin), of 1780–83, where he showed for the first time an original temper of mind. In the courtyard he introduced columns of the Paestum type, but with smaller capitals and without fluting. The main facade is also more robust and geometrical. Two pedimented pavilions linked by a lower mass, each with its own doorway, are otherwise sparsely punctuated with no more than empty niches and two elongated bas-relief panels. The whole, however, is inclined to be precise rather than powerful.

His great post-Revolutionary work, the Bourse, designed in 1807 when he was sixty-eight, was likewise not the creation of a man fitted for design in the grand manner. Yet it seemed to contemporaries to embody many of their ideals, and even Perrault's and Cordemoy's theories find their fullest expression there. Giant Corinthian columns supporting a simple entablature and cornice surround the solid rectangle of a structure pierced by regularly spaced, arched rectangular openings. Even before it was transformed into a Greek cross in 1903, the building did not convey an impression of either magnitude or magnificence. It lacked the weight needed for success.

Bélanger, taught by Le Roy and Contant d'Ivry, began his career in 1767, when, at the age of twenty-three, he was appointed *Dessinateur aux Menus-Plaisirs.* The previous year he had perhaps traveled to England, recording some of his impressions in a notebook that is today in the library of the old École des Beaux-Arts. He was certainly in England in 1778, when he prepared a design—he was one of a succession of such designers, from Robert Adam in 1773 to Robert Smirke in 1819—for Lord Shelburne's gallery in Lansdowne House, off Berkeley Square. But, for the rest, his activity and work were to be concentrated in Versailles and Paris; through the Menus he came into contact with the Comte d'Artois, whose architect he became, and also with the great singer Sophie Arnould, whose lover and architect he became. During the next twenty years he designed almost exclusively for her distinguished group of admirers, thus earning the title "faiseur à la mode." But he was an architect of the highest competence and finesse. He established himself early, in 1769, with the Pavillon Lauraguais in the garden of the Hôtel de Brancas, in the Rue Taitbout—a dazzling temporary confection in which he was assisted by Clérisseau—but his most spectacular feat was the Pavillon de Bagatelle, designed, erected, and furnished between September 21 and November 26, 1777, the result of a wager between the Comte d'Artois and Marie Antoinette. The famous *jardin anglais* there was laid out from 1778 onward, with the advice of the Scotsman Thomas Blaikie, who had been employed first by the Comte de Lauraguais in Normandy. But Bélanger was soon to prove adept at this genre, too, notably at the Folie Saint-James in nearby Neuilly-sur-Seine (also begun with the help of Blaikie in 1778), and later, starting in 1784, on the grandest of scales, on the estate of the court banker Jean-Joseph de Laborde at Méréville, near Étampes. Here he would be succeeded by Hubert Robert, who was to claim the garden as his own.

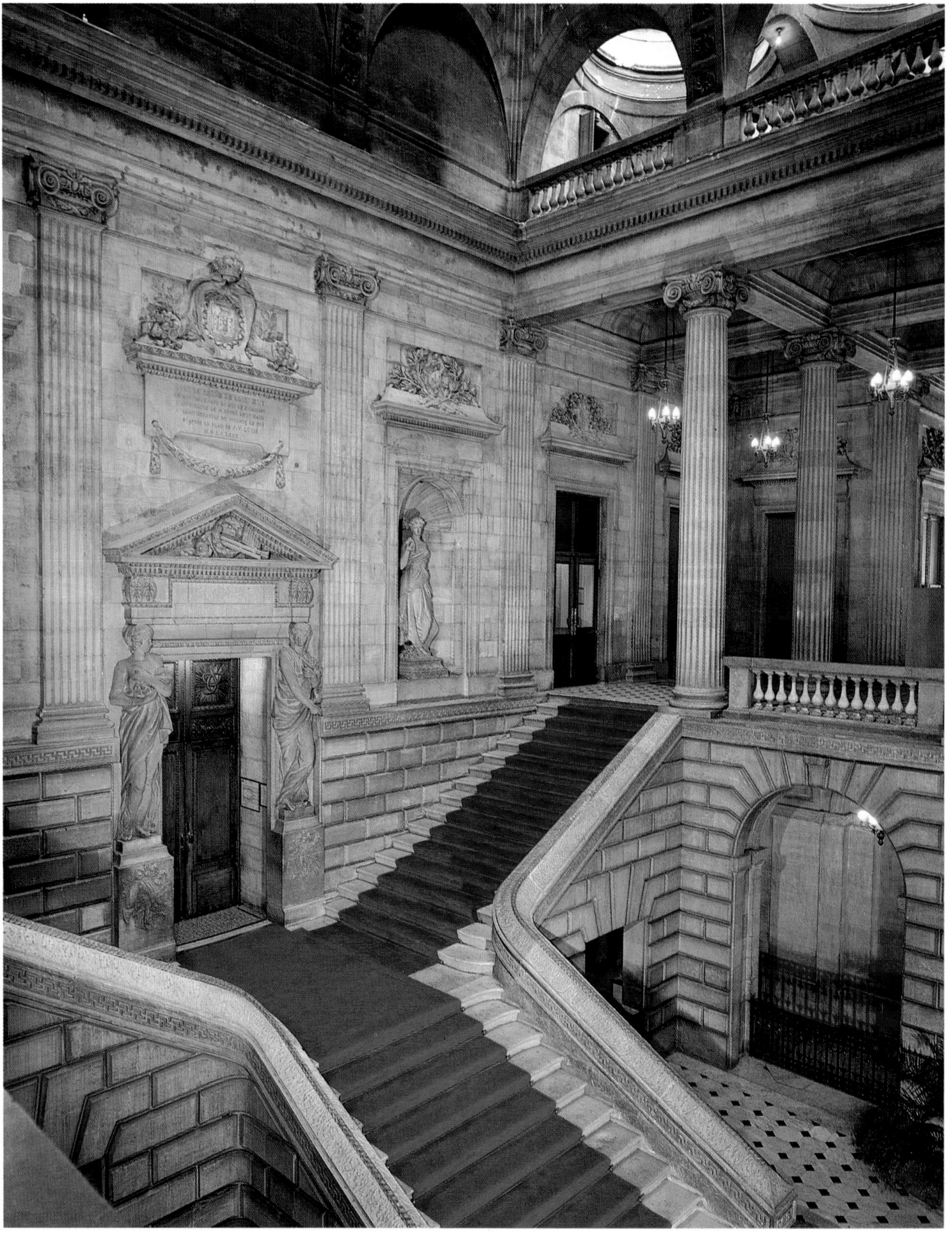

*X. Victor Louis, Grand Théâtre, Bordeaux, staircase, 1773–80*

*180. Victor Louis, Chapelle des Âmes du Purgatoire. Ste.-Marguerite-de-Charonne, Paris, 1763–65 (painted by Paolo Antonio Brunetti)*

*181. Jean-François-Thérèse Chalgrin, St.-Philippe-du-Roule, Paris, interior, approved 1768, built 1772–84. Engraving by J.-N.-L. Durand*

*182. Jean-François-Thérèse Chalgrin, St.-Philippe-du-Roule, Paris, approved 1768, built 1772–84*

*183. Louis-François Trouard, Ste.-Symphorien de Montreuil, Versailles, east facade, 1764–70*

*184. Louis-François Trouard, St.-Symphorien de Montreuil, Versailles, west facade, 1764–70*

*185. Louis-François Trouard, St.-Symphorien de Montreuil, Versailles, interior, 1764–70*

Boullée, Ledoux, and Gondoin were not all as adept and as busy but they were innovators of influence and power. All three were pupils of Blondel, though Boullée intended a career as a painter and studied first with Jean-Baptiste Pierre and later with the architects Pierre-Étienne Lebon and Jean-Laurent Legeay; Ledoux worked also for Louis-François Trouard. Not one of them won the Grand Prix; Gondoin, however, the son of a skillful gardener at Choisy, was sent to Rome in 1761 at the instigation of the king, and during his stay of two years he became—and remained—a close friend of Piranesi. Rome, in the imaginations of Boullée and Ledoux, remained the pretentious place of Piranesi's assembled engravings, although the exaggerated fantasies for which they are held today in such uncritical esteem were not done, as one might expect, in their young and student days when Piranesi's influence was at its highest, but in the years that immediately preceded the Revolution and, in particular, in the idle years that followed. Their early works were, in comparison, almost restrained.

Étienne-Louis Boullée, by far the oldest member of the group, built little of importance. He made his reputation and demonstrated his ability as a teacher. At the early age of nineteen, it seems, he began to teach at the École des Ponts et Chaussées. Later he opened an *atelier* of his own from which emerged such distinguished architects as Brongniart, Chalgrin, J.-N.-L. Durand, N.-C. Girardin, Jacques-Pierre de Gisors, Antoine-François Peyre, Pâris, and Jean-Thomas Thibault. Though he taught for over fifty years, Boullée was not merely a pedagogue. His career began in 1752, when, together with his master, J.-B. Pierre, and the sculptor Étienne-Maurice Falconet, he began work on a dramatic *trompe l'oeil* decoration, greatly admired by Soufflot, in the Chapelle du Calvaire at St.-Roch, in Paris. But the works that first served to establish his reputation were the redecoration of the Hôtel de Tourolle (some of his *boiserie* survives) and a design for the entrance to the Hôpital de Charité, in the Rue Jacob, both dating from 1762. Thereafter, in quick succession, came eight *hôtels* in Paris—the Hôtel Alexandre (1763–66), the two Hôtels de Monville (1764), the Hôtel de Pernon (1768–71), the Hôtel de Thun (1769–71), the redecoration of the Hôtel d'Évreux (1774–78), the Hôtel de Brunoy (1775–79), and a speculative venture in the Rue Royale (1777–78). He worked on four houses near Paris: the financier Nicolas Beaujon's house at Issy-les-Moulineaux (1760–73), the Château de Perreux (begun 1761), the Château de Chaville (1764–66), and an extension to the Château de Chauvry (1783). Of these, only the first, the Hôtel Alexandre, at 16 Rue de la Ville-l'Évêque, survives, but drawings for the larger Hôtel de Brunoy enable us to imagine their effect. The planning is straightforward, consisting largely of rectangular rooms in *enfilade.* The compositions are of unusual rectangularity and compactness, the masses, packed tightly against each other, related by continuous cornices and stringcourses. The facades of the *corps de logis* (main building) are articulated, as a rule, with giant Ionic pilasters, each bay thus formed being punctuated with a rectangular or round-headed doorway and

*186. Jean-Baptiste Kléber, design for the Chapelle des Capucins, Strasbourg, 1774*

*187. Louis-François Trouard, Chapelle des Catéchismes, St.-Louis, Versailles, 1764–70*

*188. Plate from Giambattista Piranesi's* Prima parte di architetture e prospettive*, 1743, showing a Doric atrium*

*189. Étienne-François Legrand, St.-Louis, Port Marly, west facade, 1778*

*190, 191. Pierre-Adrien Pâris, design for a palace for the Prince Bishop of Basel, Porrentruy, details of exterior and plan of the ground floor*

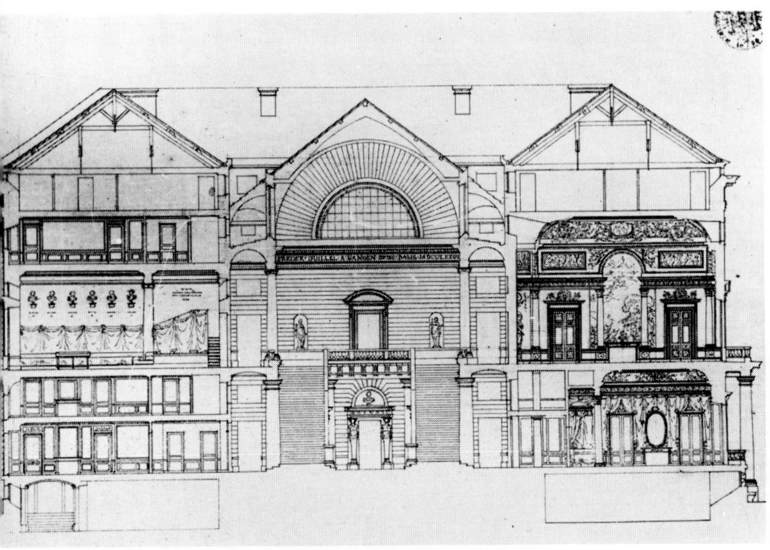

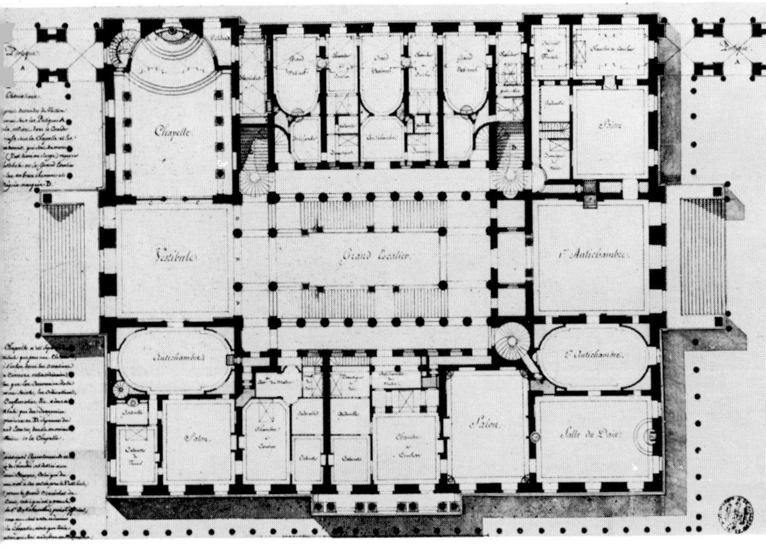

a bas-relief panel above. The result is a closely woven surface pattern, the grid of pilasters overlying the stringcourses and moldings—a theme to be taken up soon enough by Brongniart. The entrance fronts of the Hôtel Alexandre and the Château de Chaville offer a variation in the format of a portico with freestanding columns *in antis,* flanked by rectangular openings, each with a wreathed oval medallion above. But the effect is not much different. Only on the garden front of the Château de Chaville is something novel attempted, an overall pattern of rustication punctured by rectangular openings. The handling of the detail is not at all unlike that of de Wailly's exactly contemporary Château de Montmusard.

During the first phase of his career Boullée was also responsible for a series of projects for the Hôtel des Monnaies, starting in 1755 and continuing until 1767, when the commission was awarded to Jacques-Denis Antoine (1733–1801). Antoine, the son of a joiner who had gained his knowledge of architecture from a building contractor, was to take up Boullée's proposals with considerable success, to produce that noble structure, more than three hundred meters (almost one thousand feet) long, on the Quai de Conti, its regular pattern of close-set openings broken only by a slightly advancing central pavilion, with a giant Ionic order on an arcuated and rusticated ground floor, and, above, a heavy cornice with a high attic and statues in front. The effect, however, is one of monotony rather than monumentality. As Le Camus de Mézières was to remark, the architecture was too well-ordered to face the sunless north; it lacked movement. The only entirely satisfactory feature was the triple-arched vaulted entry, with coupled columns, and the great stair hall, which led from the entry to an equally magnificent salon above. In 1764 Boullée prepared a scheme for the conversion of Giovanni Giardini's Palais-Bourbon into an establishment for the Prince de Condé, a design that M.-J. Peyre, who also submitted a plan, was to describe to his nephew as "une machine immense," though today it does not seem particularly shocking but rather a suitably enlarged version of his early domestic projects. In 1775 Boullée became *Intendant des Bâtiments* to the Comte d'Artois, for whom he designed a sumptuous suite in the Enclos du Temple, including a room in the Turkish style. Two years later he resigned this position, but in 1780 he prepared drawings for the Comte d'Artois for a palace on the site of the Pépinières du Roule. This was an immense affair, whose giant formality and colonnaded vistas presaged the phantasmagoria to come. Yet it was the Hôtel de Brunoy rather that marked the change both in his approach and in his activity. Though his earlier works are clear and consistent in design, they are lacking in the vigor of this composition, where a raised central feature, screened by a portico of six Ionic columns, is integrated with perfect fluency and restraint with a lower arcaded range, and is topped with a curious stepped roof terminating in a statue of the goddess Flora, recalling Pliny's description of the Mausoleum at Halicarnassus. This was Boullée's self-conscious archaeological twist. The house was, of course, known as the Temple de

*192-194. Pierre-Adrien Pâris, design for a palace for the Prince Bishop of Basel, Porrentruy, elevations, and section of a garden terrace, 1776. Besançon, Bibliothèque de la Ville*

*195, 196. Pierre-Adrien Pâris, Hôtel de Ville, Neuchâtel, 1784–90*

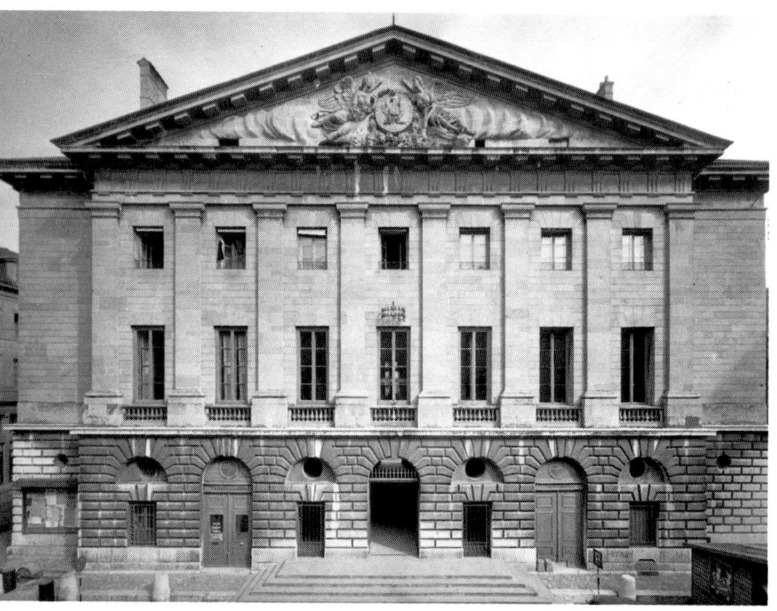

Flore. Thereafter Boullée designed in a new key, overblown and arrogant. He decided, it seems, to become a genius, or, at very least, to resume his early interest in painting. He virtually forsook domestic work. In October 1778 he became *Contrôleur des Bâtiments à l'Hôtel Royal des Invalides;* two years later he was appointed to a similar post at the École Militaire. He thus embarked on an official career in architecture, the aim of most members of the profession. Unaccountably, however, he resigned both positions in 1782. He continued with other minor official commissions, but he was more intent to indulge his fantasies. Unfortunately, as we shall see, they were of the histrionic kind. They were to ensure that his influence was enormous—in particular, in post-Revolutionary France. Almost all architects of the period derived something of their style from his sophisticated and superbly rendered designs. No one, however, endowed his work with Boullée's spectacular spirit as successfully as Ledoux.

Yet the early buildings of Claude-Nicolas Ledoux (1736–1806) are not unconventional. A pupil of Blondel and an assistant to Trouard, he competed unsuccessfully for the Grand Prix and, like Boullée, he did not travel to Rome. In 1762, at the age of twenty-six, he started his career with the design of the *boiserie* for a military café, the Café Godeau, once in the Rue St.-Honoré (now in the Museé Carnavalet), made up of panels supporting trophies divided by wreathed clusters of spears topped with plumed helmets. The design and execution, though of a seventeenth-century kind, are exceptionally bold. For the next four years, however, Ledoux was to be active in the provinces, in Champagne, Franche-Comte, and Burgundy, working for the Service des Eaux et Forêts, building and supervising the execution of bridges, fountains, schools, and five small churches, none of particular distinction. By 1766 he was able to return to Paris to rebuild the Hôtel de Bouligneux, at 28 Rue Michel-le-Comte, for the Comte d'Hallwyl, a building of note—in particular, for the cononnades that flank the walls of the garden, and, in *trompe l'oeil* perspective, terminate the garden on the wall of a property beyond, thus imitating Jacques Rousseau's seventeenth-century perspective on the wall of the Hôtel de Dangeau—but one that, on the strength of engravings in the second, greatly enlarged edition of *L'architecture considérée sous le rapport de l'art, des moeurs et de la législation* (published only in 1847, as *L'architecture de Claude-Nicolas Ledoux*), has generally been thought to have been more advanced than it was. The heavy unbroken cornice shown in his engraving of the street facade gives an unusual coherence and tension to the architecture and reinforces the importance of the recessed central portion. But on the building as it stands today the cornice is more conventionally designed to follow the outline of the plan, which has two end pavilions with a setback in the center. The effect is altogether unlike Ledoux's Hôtel d'Uzès, based once again on an existing structure and designed a few months later in competition with two other architects, Pierre-Noël Rousset and Mathurin Cherpitel, and similarly lacking in vigor. The building is composed of rectangular masses, but

*197. Nicolas-Marie Potain, St.-Louis, St.-Germain-en-Laye, interior, designed 1764. Drawing by P. A. Demachy*

*198. Henri Frignet and Charles Colombot, St.-Symphorien, Gy, interior, 1769–85*

*199, 200. Alexandre-Théodore Brongniart, Hôtel de Sainte-Foix, Paris, elevation and ground-floor plan, 1775*

*201. Alexandre-Théodore Brongniart, Hôtel de Mlle. de Bourbon-Condé, Paris, garden facade, 1780–81*

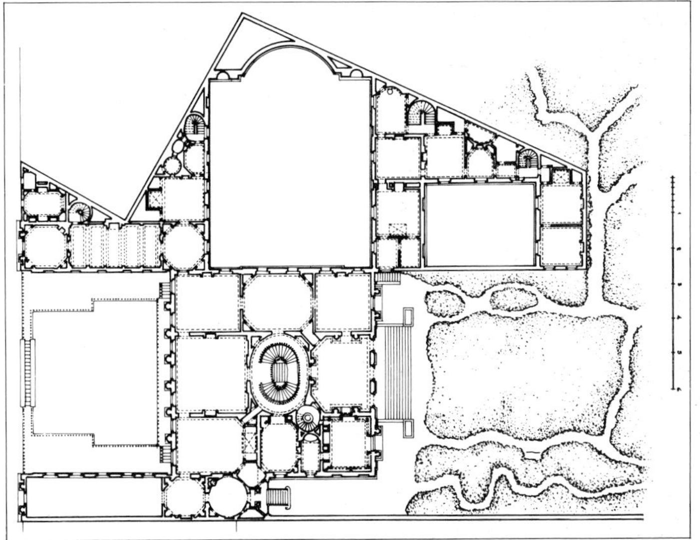

202. *François-Joseph Bélanger, design for the bedroom of the Comte d'Artois, Pavillon de Bagatelle, Paris, 1777*

203. *François-Joseph Bélanger, Pavillon de Bagatelle, Bois de Boulogne, Paris, 1777*

dramatic tension is lost with the use of close-set openings—some rectangular, some roundheaded, all in the same run—and an uneasy pattern of overall rustication. The forecourt, however, with its portico of four giant Corinthian columns supporting a far-projecting cornice and heavy balustrade, illustrates forcibly the boldness inherent in his powers of composition. These were more successfully displayed in the interior paneling, carved in 1769 by Jean-Baptiste Boistou and Joseph Métivier, some of which is now also in the Musée Carnavalet. Ledoux's first country house, the Château de Bénouville (Calvados), also a remodeling—begun in 1770 and completed in 1777—is once again similar in treatment. It consists of a number of rectangular elements broadly composed to create a horizontal mass. The whole is pierced with very narrowly proportioned windows and is screened in part by a portico of giant Ionic columns. His engraved design of the building, not published until 1804, is, as before, bolder in conception than the executed work. There is no doubt that Ledoux updated his designs for publication. The great stone stair hall within, however, even as it stands, compares favorably with Antoine's contemporary stair at the Hôtel des Monnaies.

Ledoux's maturity begins with his next group of Parisian *hôtels,* starting in 1770 with the Hôtel de Montmorency, entered, exceptionally, on a corner (Boulevard de Montmorency and Rue de la Chaussée-d'Antin). The building is a cubic mass reinforced with a screen of Ionic columns on each of the two street facades, which suggests an unusual derivation from Potain's theater project of 1763, though it relates rather to the equal claims to the Montmorency lineage of the prince and princess, whose independent suites of rooms are thus expressed on the facades. The interior contains a succession of spaces, circular, oval, and some less straightforwardly geometrical, all brilliantly planned around a diagonal. Ledoux surpassed this tour de force in the same year with a pavilion nearby for the dancer Marie Madeleine Guimard. Here he scored a triumph. The open, semidomed apse of the porch, screened by four Ionic columns carrying an entablature, and, above, a statue of Terpsichore, provides an altogether successful and ingenious focus for the design. The conception was inspired, no doubt, by the measured studies of Roman Baths carried out by Peyre and de Wailly, but the parallel between the Temple of Venus at Stowe—dated as early as 1732 and usually ascribed to William Kent—and Robert Adam's similar themes in the interiors of Syon House, Kenwood, and Newby is suggested irresistibly, the more so as Ledoux is known to have traveled to England, where he is said to have designed a house for Lord Clive. The attracting feature was used a year later, but in a slightly different form, for the pavilion Ledoux designed at Louveciennes for Mme. du Barry. The exedra of the entrance porch is screened as before by four Ionic columns, but the semidome rises up instead behind the entablature and balustrade of the facade. The planning here, though exemplary, is also less adventurous than in the Guimard pavilion.

*XI. Victor Louis, Galeries du Palais-Royal, Paris, 1781*

*XII. Claude-Nicolas Ledoux,*
boiserie *for the Café Godeau, 1762.*
*Paris, Musée Carnavalet*

*204. François-Joseph Bélanger, project for the gallery of Lord Shelburne in Landsdowne House, London, longitudinal section, 1778*

*205. François-Joseph Bélanger, Pavillon Lauranguais, in the garden of the Hôtel de Brancas (Hôtel de Lassay), Rue Taitbout, Paris, facade elevation, 1769*

*206. J. Métivier, Hôtel Gouthière, Paris, entrance on the courtyard, 1780*

*207. François-Joseph Bélanger and Thomas Blaikie, plan of the* jardin anglais, *Parc de Bagatelle, Paris, 1778–80. Engraving by Le Rouge*

*208. François-Joseph Bélanger, Folie Saint-James, Neuilly-sur-Seine, 1778–84*

*209, 210. Étienne-Louis Boullée, Hôtel Alexandre, Paris, elevation and ground-floor plan 1763–66*

*211. Étienne-Louis Boullée, Hôtel Alexandre, Paris, 1763–66*

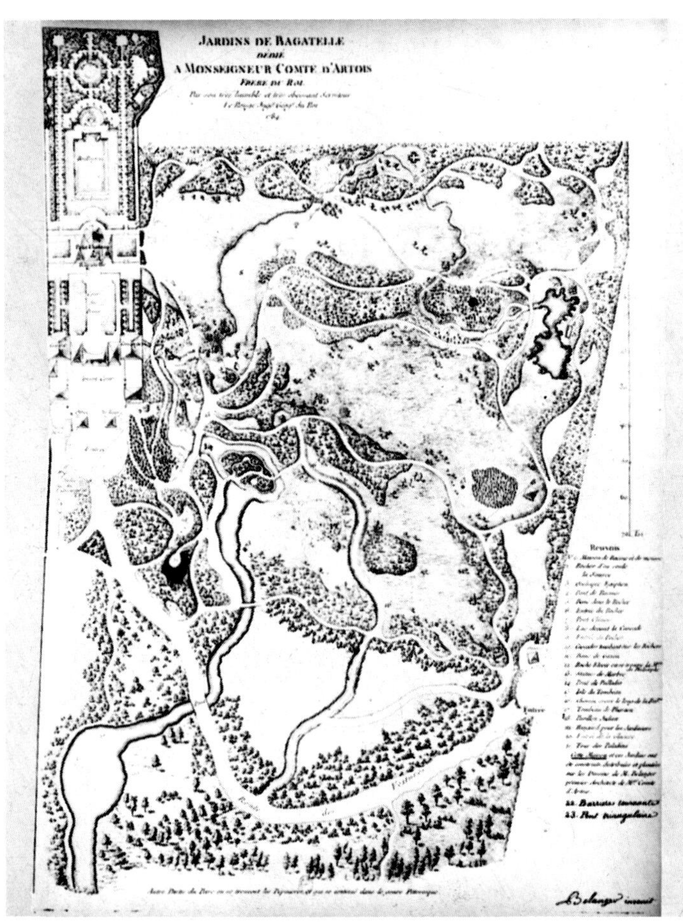

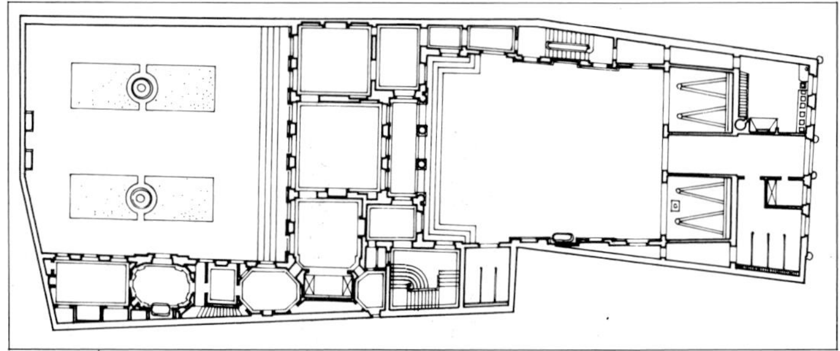

From this period dates a whole succession of small and costly *hôtels,* wonderfully resourcefully planned and with much variation in design, often of a Palladian sort, beginning with the Hôtel Tabary, in the Faubourg Poissonnière, in 1771—which may be compared with Soufflot's slightly earlier handling of the same themes for Marigny's house in the Faubourg du Roule—and culminating in the magnificent and altogether overindulgent Hôtel de Thélusson in the Rue de Provence, dating from 1778 to 1783. This was approached through a triumphal arch, designed as if half-buried, as in Piranesi's Roman views.

All Ledoux's great works date from his middle years. In 1771 he was appointed *Inspecteur des Salines de la Franche-Comté,* as adjunct to Perronet, and within three years had designed and started to build his famous project for the Salines d'Arc-et-Senans; both the remaining heavily rusticated buildings of the saltworks, completed in 1779, and the outlandish unexecuted designs that he was to evolve later show him to have been at once an admirer of the reserved and dignified architecture of Louis XV's reign and an unbridled experimentalist with a pronounced liking for a conglomeration of heavy simplified masses and unadorned wall surfaces. This aspect of his character was to find its fullest expression in the *barrières,* or tollhouses, for Paris, built between 1785 and 1789, which seem at first sight supremely monumental in the traditional French manner, though on inspection reveal that the characteristic forms and measures of classical architecture have been interpreted with a waywardness and a willful wrong-headedness peculiar to Ledoux. They are the most powerful architectural works of the century. The promise of Piranesi finds its fulfillment here. However, when Ledoux attempted something of the sort on a larger scale the result was less immediately successful. At Aix-en-Provence he began a Palais de Justice and related prison in 1786. Work progressed slowly, and was stopped altogether in 1790; the structure was replaced in the nineteenth century by M.-R. Penchaud's Maison d'Arrêt. But Ledoux's engraved drawings show one of the buildings, the prison, as a solid simplified mass that is deliberately top-heavy. The roofs of the four corner pavilions dominate the whole, and all the richness and incident in the architecture, the curious squat porticos apart, are concentrated at the eaves. Nothing quite like it was to be built in eighteenth-century France. Yet many of the remarkable and altogether surprising projects that Ledoux prepared from 1786 onward (in particular, in the idle years that followed his fourteen-month stay in the prison of La Force, beginning in December 1793, when he was suspected of undermining the Revolution), and that he published, in part, together with his equally idiosyncratic theories, in 1804, in *L'architecture,* all exemplify his notion of architectural beauty as something large in scale, simple and lumpish, enclosed and amplified by a clear-cut, if broken, outline. It was an ideal that many of his contemporaries shared and one that they derived, most probably, from Boullée; though more strictly classical in spirit, Ledoux tended to prefer continuous masses and

*212, 213. Étienne-Louis Boullée, Hôtel de Brunoy, Paris, plan and elevation of the garden facade, 1775–79*

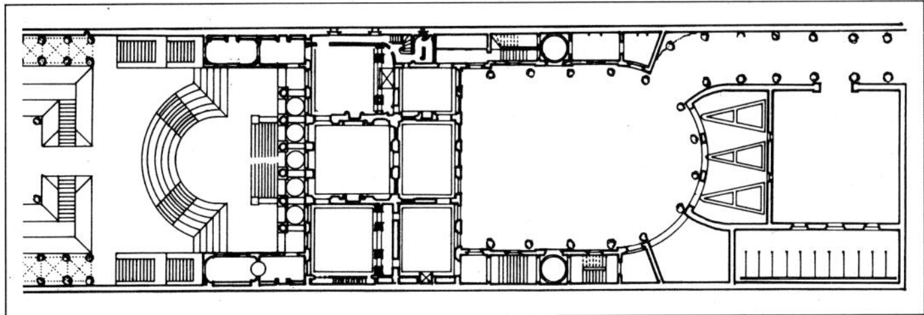

*214. Jacques-Denis Antoine, Hôtel des Monnaies, Paris, principal facade, begun 1767*

215. *Jacques-Denis Antoine, Hôtel des Monnais, Paris, salon, begun 1767*

216, 217 *Claude-Nicolas Ledoux,* boiserie *for the Café Godeau, 1762. Paris, Musée Carnavalet*

unbroken outlines. Ledoux may thus have been the forerunner of much of the turgidity of nineteenth-century architecture.

Neigher Boullée nor Ledoux, however, would have come to his early understanding of continuity and the unbroken line without Gondoin. Jacques Gondoin (1737–1818) was nine years younger than Boullée, one year younger than Ledoux, and he made his architectural debut about five years after the latter, yet he appears to have remained throughout his life a strict and consistent classicist. Indeed, he is remembered for one building and hardly any other, the École de Chirurgie in the Rue de l'École de Médecine in Paris, which might be said to epitomize the classical movement of the late eighteenth century: "Un seul mot doit faire l'éloge de ce monument," that upholder of classical orthodoxy, Quatremère de Quincy, was to write in the early nineteenth century. "Il est le monument classique du dixhuitième siècle" ("Notice sur . . . M. Gondoin," 1821, in *Recueil de notices historiques . . . ,* Paris, 1834, p. 201).

Commissioned, designed, and begun in 1769, three years after Gondoin had returned from Italy—via Holland and England—the École de Chirurgie was finished by 1775. The problem of planning a surgical college in 1769 called for no great ingenuity, and the detailed arrangements are of little interest. But the semicircular lecture hall, with its rising tiers of seats, its blank curved wall, and its coffered half-dome and demi-oculus, was a creation of genius and not surprisingly was reflected in all the assembly halls of the Consulate and Empire periods—the Chambre des Députés, built between 1795 and 1797 by J.-P. de Gisors and Étienne-Chérubin Leconte; the Salle du Sénat at the Palais du Luxembourg, designed in 1804 by Chalgrin; and the Salle du Tribunat, installed a few years later by C.-E. de Beaumont in the Palais-Royal. Yet it was rather Gondoin's conception of a facade composed of a triumphal arch embedded in a continuous screen of Ionic columns, some engaged, some freestanding, and at the far end a giant Corinthian portico—in short, the dramatic interpenetration of continuous columnar screens—that makes the École de Chirurgie so remarkable and so stunning a work. The notion had been a part of French architectural thought from Perrault onward, and had recently been reinforced by Peyre, yet the liberating stimulus came from Italy, from the arrangement of the Temple of Isis at Pompeii—the École de Chirurgie was conceived as a Temple of Aesculapius—and, more surprisingly, from the first court of the Collegio Elvetico in Milan, begun in 1608 by Fabio Mangone. There, freestanding columns are used with even greater uniformity and obsession, while the continuous, unbroken line of the cornice and the columns running the entire length of the facade, which seemed so rude a departure from the French tradition of composed elements, also came from Italian sources—perhaps from the Raphaelesque Palazzo Vidoni-Caffarelli, in Rome, begun in 1515 but greatly extended in the mid-eighteenth century, when it was engraved by Piranesi for his *Varie vedute di Roma.* But to Gondoin's contemporaries the design of the École, with its related yet contrasting

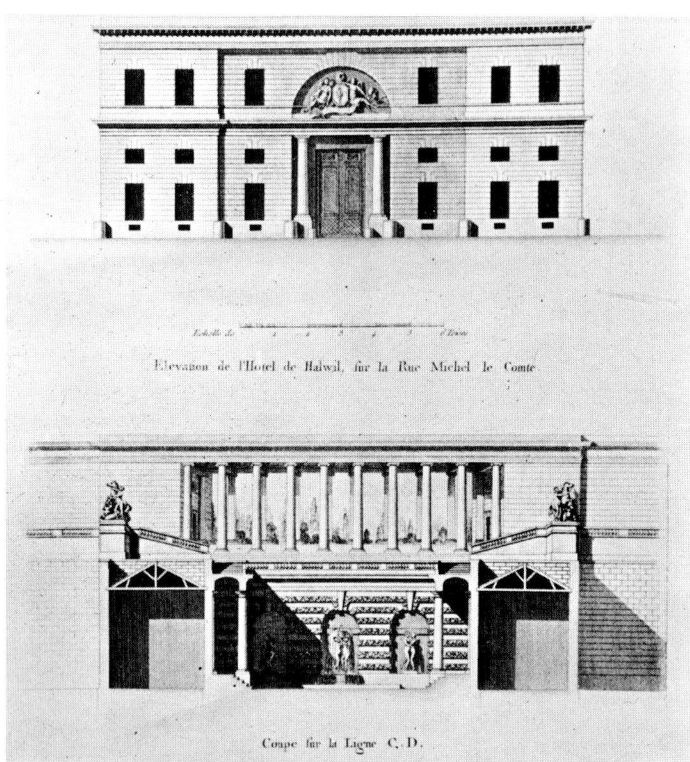

*218. Claude-Nicolas Ledoux, Hôtel d'Hallwyl, Paris, elevations of the street and garden facades, 1766–67*

*219. Claude-Nicolas Ledoux, Hôtel d'Hallwyl, Paris, 1766–67*

*220. Claude-Nicolas Ledoux, Hôtel d'Uzès, Paris,* cour d'honneur, *1767-68*

*221. Claude-Nicolas Ledoux,* boiserie *for the Hôtel d'Uzès, Paris, 1769 (panels carved by J. B. Boistou and J. Metvier, 1769). Paris, Musée Carnavalet*

square and fountain in front, was a revelation and altogether original. Many attacked it. Blondel reluctantly recognized its peculiar antique power and Peyre defended it with vigor. J.-G. Legrand wrote of it in C.P. Landon's Annales du musée in 1803: "Tout le système de la vieille architecture française fut renversé par cet exemple inattendu, et les partisans de la routine furent stupéfaits de voir une façade sans avant-corps au milieu, sans arrière-corps, et dont la corniche suivant d'un bout à l'autre sans ressaut ni profil, contre l'usage reçu en France, et dont les Contant, les Gabriel, les Soufflot, venaient de donner de si récens et si dispendieux exemples dans l'École Militaire, dans la Madeleine, et dans la nouvelle Sainte-Geneviève. Cependant l'opinion publique se prononça en faveur du nouveau système, la critique se tut, et l'École de Chirurgie fut proclamée par tous les gens de goût, le chef-d'oeuvre de notre architecture moderne" (vol. 5, p. 127).

The success of this work won many commissions for Gondoin. In 1769 he became *Dessinateur du Mobilier de la Couronne* and started at once to design furniture for Marie Antoinette; he is said to have built a number of town and country houses, though only minor works such as the Hôtel Saint-Léonard, at 12 Rue Victor Hugo, Falaise (Calvados), and the Hôtel de Ville in the same town can yet be attributed to him. He also began a house for himself on the banks of the Seine, near Melun, in the late 1780s, and building continued in the years that followed the Revolution. He became wealthy. When, in 1775, he traveled to Italy for the second time, he sought to buy Hadrian's Villa at Tivoli. This proved impossible, as too many disputatious individual landowners were involved. He was thus forced to content himself with making measured drawings of the villa, which he gave to his friend Piranesi, who had been excavating there for several years with Gavin Hamilton and Clérisseau. Gondoin's drawings presumably served as the basis for the great site plan issued after Piranesi's death in 1781.

The classical movement of the eighteenth century was, as Quatremère de Quincy insisted, "une communauté d'instruction et de connaissance, une certaine égalité du goût et du savoir . . . entre toutes les contrées de l'Europe" (L. Hautecoeur, *Rome et la renaissance de l'antiquité à la fin du XVIIIe siècle,* 1912, p. 224).

ENGLAND: *From Chambers to Wyatt*

The architects at whom we shall be looking in this section—principally Sir William Chambers, Robert Adam, James Wyatt, and Henry Holland—are more famous and were more prolific than those who figured in the earlier chapter on the influence of the antique. It is not that Chambers, Adam, Holland, and Wyatt were not interested in the antique—far from it—but they did not allow either archaeology or theory to interfere with their large and successful practices: They were ambitious, fashionable, popular, and stylistically omnivorous. Again we should begin by appreciating the pioneering achievements of the architects in the Palladias tradition, in particular of two second-generation Palladian architects, Sir Robert Taylor

*222. Claude-Nicolas Ledoux, Hôtel d'Uzès, Paris, garden facade, 1767–68*

*223. Claude-Nicolas Ledoux, room in the Hôtel d'Uzès, Paris, 1767–68. Paris, Musée Carnevalet*

224. *Claude-Nicolas Ledoux, Château de Bénouville (Calvados), facade, 1770–77*

225. *Claude-Nicolas Ledoux, Château de Bénouville, grand staircase, 1770–77*

226. *Claude-Niocolas Ledoux, Hôtel Guimard, Paris, principal facade, designed 1770, built 1773–76*

227. *Claude-Nicolas Ledoux, Hôtel Guimard, Paris, plan, 1770*

228. *Claude-Nicolas Ledoux, Pavillon de Mme. du Barry, Louveciennes, 1770 onward*

229. *Claude-Nicolas Ledoux, Pavillon de Mme. du Barry, Louveciennes, plan*

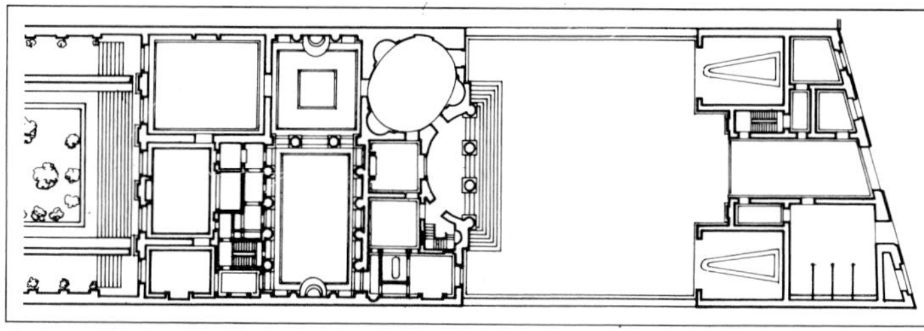

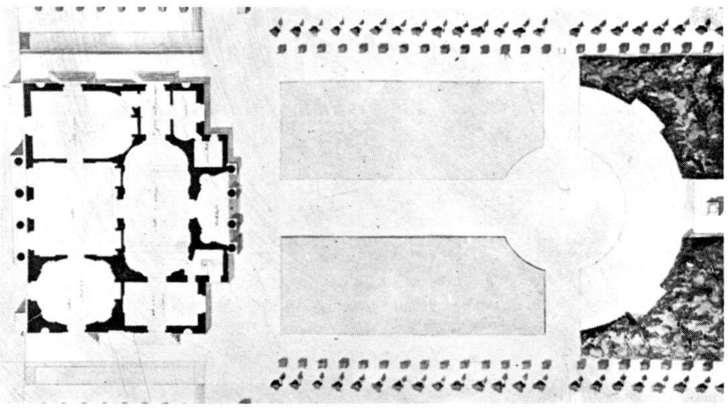

230. *Claude-Nicolas Ledoux, Hôtel Tabary, Paris, elevation, 1771*

231. *Claude-Nicolas Ledoux, Hôtel de Thélusson, Paris, plan 1778–83*

232. *Claude-Nicolas Ledoux, Hôtel de Thélusson, Paris, facade and main entrance in form of a triumphal arch, 1778–83*

(1714–1788) and James Paine (1717–1789). Adhering basically to the Palladian canon, Paine created such powerful buildings as Stockeld Park, Yorkshire (1758–63), with its great arched facade and superb staircase, and Brocket Hall, Hertfordshire (1760s onward), where a dull exterior contains another remarkable staircase and a great saloon in which the painted historical and allegorical decoraration by John Hamilton Mortimer offers a substantial alternative to the lighter Adam style. At Wardour Castle, Wiltshire, Paine created, in the 1770s, his most breathtaking interior—a centrally placed pantheon containing a circular staircase.

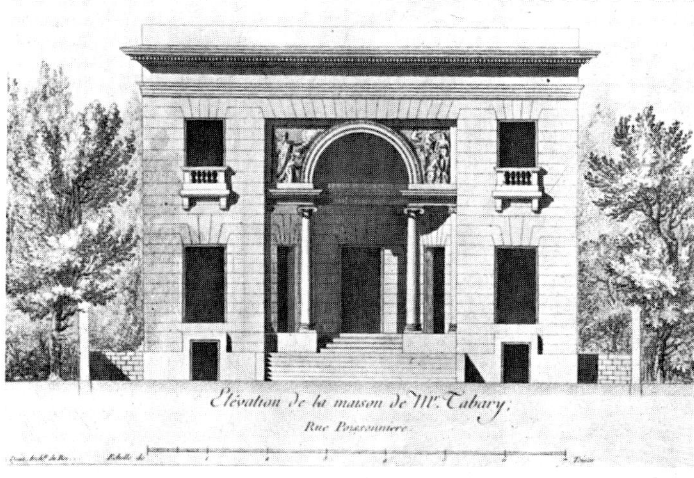

Sir Robert Taylor also created a pantheon at the Bank of England, in 1765, which he flanked by four identical transfer offices inspired by the Early Christian church of S. Costanza in Rome, believed in the eighteenth century to be an ancient Roman temple of Bacchus. In the late 1760s, at Purbrook, Hampshire, whose plan was similar to that of Paine's Kedleston Hall, Derbyshire (1757), he placed a Roman atrium in the center, perhaps the first reconstruction of its kind. But Taylor is particularly associated with the creation of a series of beautiful villas, of which the dramatically situated Sharpham, Devon (c. 1770), may stand as an example, where the Palladian tradition is enlivened by imaginative planning with interlocking rooms of contrasting shapes. Although Taylor had initiated this tradition at Harleyford Manor, Buckinghamshire, as early as 1755, it was not fully exploited until the end of the century by Sir John Soane, John Nash, and James Lewis.

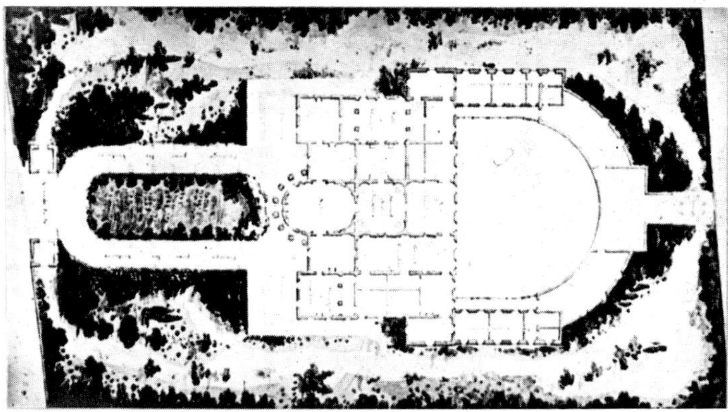

Paine and Taylor scarcely traveled abroad, but the career of Sir William Chambers (1723–1796) reveals the essentially cosmopolitan character of the style we call neoclassicism, which emerged in the 1740s and 1750s. As a pupil of J.-F. Blondel in Paris in 1749–50 he came into close contact with the brilliant group of designers who were developing a new Franco-Italian style, anti-rococo and neoclassical: men like L.-J. Le Lorrain and J.-L. Legeay, Charles de Wailly and M.-J. Peyre. From Paris Chambers moved naturally to Rome, where he spent the years 1750 to 1755, and learned much from Piranesi and Clérisseau. The outcome of all this learning and activity is clearly seen in the designs he made in Rome in 1751–52 for a mausoleum for Frederick, Prince of Wales. In some ways these designs, Chambers's first architectural production, constitute the beginnings of English neoclassical architecture, but they also represent a point from which Chambers subsequently retreated stylistically. Combining elements from such antique Roman buildings as the Tomb of Caecilia Metella and the Pantheon with features based on the Festa della Chinea designs of the 1740s by Frenchmen such as Le Lorrain and E.-A. Petitot, Chambers's mausoleum was too heady to be acceptable in England in the early 1750s. On his return from Rome in 1755 he prepared designs in an ill-digested Grand Prix manner for Harewood House, Yorkshire. When these were turned down by Edwin Lascelles in 1756 Chambers finally lost his nerve and retreated for the rest of his career into a safe, second-generation Palladianism inspired by Isaac Ware and enlivened with pretty motifs culled from the work of French

*233. Jacques Gondoin, project for a square in front of the École de Chirurgie, Paris, 1769. Important features for the plan included a new facade for the church of St.-Come and a fountain against the wall of the adjoining destined monastery*

*234. Jacques Gondoin, École de Chirurgie (now École de Médecine), Paris, anatomy theater, 1769–75*

*235. Jacques Gondoin, École de Chirurgie (now École de Médecine), Paris, plan, 1769–75*

*236. Jacques Gondoin, École de Chirurgie (now École de Médecine), Paris principal facade, 1769–75*

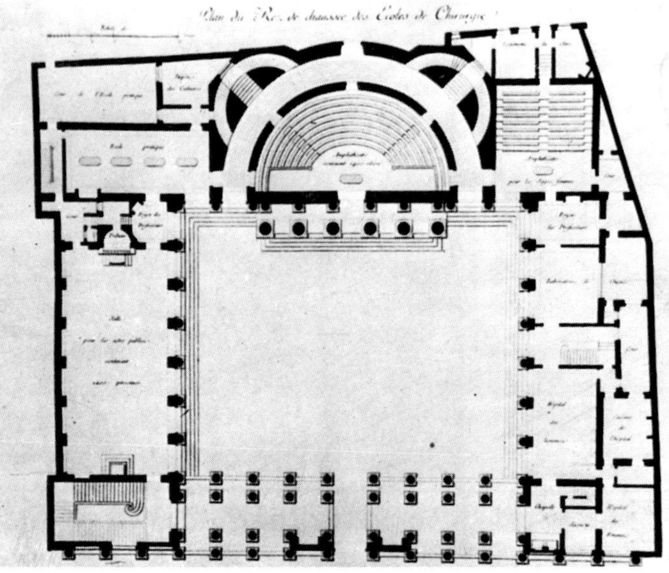

*237. Jacques Gondoin, École de Chirurgie (now École de Médecine), Paris, courtyard facade, detail, 1769–75*

*238. James Paine, Stockeld Park, Yorkshire, exterior, 1758–63*
*239. James Paine, Stockeld Park, Yorkshire, stair hall, 1758–63*

architects ranging from A.-J. Gabriel (born 1698) to J.-G. Soufflot (born 1713) and J.-D. Antoine (born 1733). On a small scale, as at the Casina at Marino near Dublin (begun 1758), this was enchanting, but it was quite inadequate for a major public building such as Somerset House, London (1776–96). Like a number of English eighteenth-century architects, Chambers was perhaps at his best with staircase design. His *Treatise on Civil Architecture* (1759), expanded in a third edition to *A Treatise on the Decorative Part of Civil Architecture* (1791), was widely influential in England and France as a scholarly and broadly based survey of the use of the orders in antique and Renaissance architecture. Chambers's pupil James Gandon (1743–1823) was in some ways more successful than his master in creating a monumental architecture inspired by French neoclassical precedent. At the Four Courts in Dublin, which he took over from Thomas Cooley (1740–1748) in 1785, Gandon produced a powerful building, which, if it has Peyre for a father, has Sir Christopher Wren for a grandfather. Cooley, an assistant of Robert Mylne, was also a better architect than Chambers. His masterly and original Dublin Exchange (1769–79) reveals a close knowledge of contemporary French work and is one of the finest buildings of its date in Europe.

Cooley and Gandon worked almost exclusively in Ireland, and their buildings had litle impact in England. But if Chambers lacked the flair to create a new language out of the architectural experiments he had witnessed in Paris and Rome, there was one architect who was determined to achieve that very synthesis, Robert Adam. In 1754 he left his native Scotland for France and Italy, where, like Chambers, he became intimate with Piranesi and Clérisseau. With the assistance of Clérisseau and two other draftsmen in 1757 he prepared measured drawings of the great late Roman palace at Split in Dalmatia, which he published in sumptuous form in 1764 as *Ruins of the Palace of the Emperor Diocletian at Spalato.* The speed with which Adam worked was characteristic of him—he spent only five weeks at Split—as also was an ability to rouse public interest in a Picturesque and arresting manner. The captivating engravings by Francesco Bartolozzi and others were in a rhetorical style inspired by Piranesi that Adam used again in the depiction of his own buildings, published in 1773 and 1779 as *The Works in Architecture of Robert and James Adam, Esquires.* This gift for self-advertisement, this determination to achieve success, explains much about his eye-catching, all-inclusive, yet individual style. He could not afford to be doctrinaire. Greek, Roman, Palladian, neo-Palladian, neoclassical, Picturesque, all were grist to his mill. He had a quick eye for everything that was going on around him and assimilated his observations into a style of unique loveliness, which matured rapidly from Harewood House, Yorkshire (begun 1759); Kedleston Hall, Derbyshire (1760 onward); Osterley Park, Middlesex (1761 onward); Syon House, Middlesex (1762–69); Luton Hoo, Bedfordshire (1766–70); Newby Hall, Yorkshire (1767–85); and Kenwood House, Hampstead (1767–69). The desire to please, which is so strong in the

*240. James Paine, Brocket Hall, Hertfordshire, staircase, 1760 onward*

*241. James Paine, Brocket Hall, Hertfordshire, saloon, 1760 onward*

*242. Sir Robert Taylor, Bank of England, London, rotunda, 1765*

*243. Sir Robert Taylor, Bank of England, London, Transfer Office, 1765*

*244. James Paine, Wardour Castle, Wiltshire, stair hall, 1770–76*

*245. Sir Robert Taylor, Harleyford Manor, Buckinghamshire, plan, 1755*

*246. Sir William Chambers, Casina, Marino, near Dublin, begun 1758*

enchanting series of rooms contained in these houses, is frankly not an ambition that one particularly associates with the neoclassical movement, although those in search of the characteristically neoclassical interest in archaeology will find many hints from the Roman Baths, particularly at Syon. The essential adaptability of the Adam style is clearly conveyed in the preface to Part 2 of his *Works in Architecture,* where he writes of the orders, for example, that the Tuscan is needlessly austere, the Composite needlessly elaborate, the "great size of the volute of the Grecian Ionic[is] much too heavy," while those used by the Romans "border on the other extreme." "We have therefore," he concluded, "generally taken a mean between them." So perhaps the English *via media,* the comfortable compromise, must be taken into account in considering Adam's success. From the Grecian Ionic he adopted what he called the "double fillet" in the volute, which "far exceeds in grace and beauty that used by the Romans." Indeed, he claimed that he favored Greek profiles because Roman moldings were "considerably less curvilineal than those of the ancient monuments of Greece." An example of his empirical approach is his refusal to fix a definite entablature for each order: "A latitude in this respect is often productive of great novelty, variety and beauty."

What this meant in practice can be well appreciated in the celebrated anteroom at Syon of the mid-1760s. The volutes and moldings of the capitals here were taken from the Erechtheum as illustrated in J.-D. Le Roy's pioneering publication of 1758, *Les ruines des plus beaux monuments de la Grèce.* However, for the necking of the capitals he drew on a purely Roman source, familiar from the Baths and subsequently illustrated in Charles Cameron's *Description of the Baths of the Romans* (1772). The decoration of the Erechtheum necking he daringly and attractively transposed to the frieze of the entablature. Elsewhere in the room the gilded martial trophies anticipatory of the Empire style are derived from Piranesi's illustrations of the trophies of Octavian Augustus on the Campidoglio in Rome, which had already been imitated at the Villa Madama. The ceiling design, on the other hand, looks back to an English Palladian precedent established at Houghton Hall, Norfolk, by Colen Campbell in the 1720s. But the room recalls yet another period, for the twelve superb blue verde columns were antique Roman ones, said to have been excavated from the bed of the Tiber, and were dispatched by James Adam in April 1765 from Civitavecchia. In this one room, then, all the known historical boundaries are transcended by Adam's brilliant classical synthesis. This synthesis is not intellectual in origin but scenic and Picturesque, as already shown in Chapter 2.

The immediately recognizable style that Adam established in the 1760s, when remodeling the great Whig country houses put up by the first- and second-generation Palladian architects, was transferred in the 1770s to London, where, on a smaller scale, he created some of the most refined if rather mannered interiors of the century: No. 20 St. James's Square (1771–74); Derby House, No. 23 Grosvenor Square (1773–74; demol-

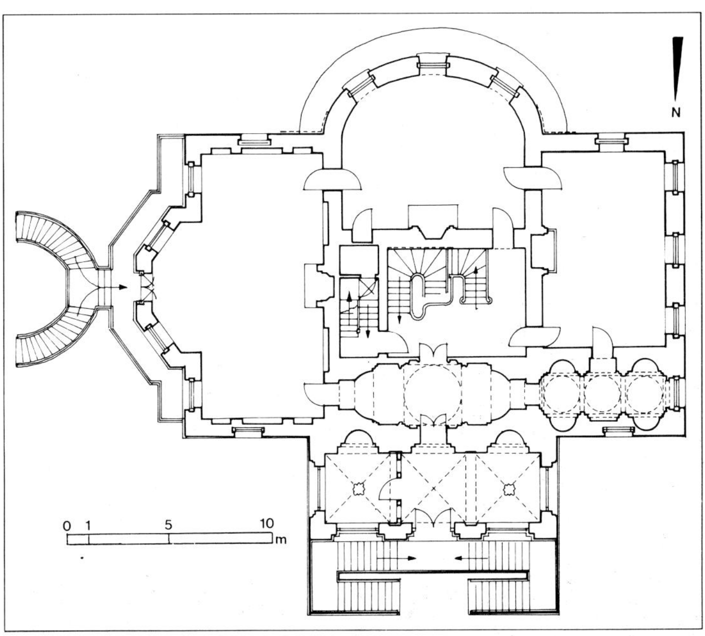

DRIVE
SLOWLY

*247. Sir William Chambers, Somerset House, London, vestibule, 1776–96*

*XIII. Claude-Nicolas Ledoux, room in the Hôtel d'Uzès, Paris, 1767–68. Paris, Musée Carnavalet.*

*XIV. Robert Adam, Kedleston Hall, Derbyshire, saloon, c. 1760–70*

*248. James Gandon, Four Courts, Dublin, 1786–1802*
*249. Thomas Cooley, Royal Exchange (now City Hall), Dublin, 1769–79*

*250. Robert Adam, harbor elevation of the palace of Diocletian at Split (Spalato), Dalmatia, 1757*

*251. Robert Adam, No. 20 St. James's Square, London, second drawing room, 1772*

*252. Robert Adam, Kedleston Hall, Derbyshire, south front, 1765–70*

*253. Robert Adam, Kedleston Hall, Derbyshire, saloon, c. 1760–70*

ished 1862); and No. 20 Portman Square (1775). This exquisite style was not transported to the Continent, perhaps because it depended on a highly trained group of craftsmen, led by the plasterer Joseph Rose, Jr., who moved from house to house.

It should not be thought, however, that Adam's genius was limited to the creation of these pastel boudoirs. His colonnaded Admiralty Screen in Whitehall, of 1759, points forward to the bolder open screens of Jacques Gondoin at the École de Chirurgie, Paris (1769–85); Holland at Carlton House, London (c. 1794); and Karl Friedrich Schinkel at the palace for Prince Albrecht, Berlin (1829–33). At Bowood, Wiltshire, in 1761–64, he erected a chaste Tuscan mausoleum, domed and barrel-vaulted, which an architect like Gondoin might have envied. There is a ruthless originality about his twin-towered church at Mistley, Essex (1776; partially demolished 1870), which may have inspired Soane's Dulwich Gallery (1812). The garden front of Adam's Kedleston Hall, Derbyshire, takes its place in the long line of applications of the Roman triumphal-arch motif from Alberti to C. R. Cockerell, while at the Register House (1774–92) and University (1789–93) at Edinburgh, he created some of the most successful monumental public buildings of the century.

Adam was rarely short of commissions or publicity, though the flashy innovatory aspect of his style made him unpopular with Sir William Chambers, pillar of the academic tradition, who acquired for himself many of the official appointments of the day and prevented Adam from being elected to the Royal Academy. Adam also had to face difficulties of a different kind—imitation—by an architect very different from Chambers, James Wyatt. Nearly twenty years younger than Adam, Wyatt rocketed to fame as a very young man with his Pantheon in Oxford Street, designed in 1769 and opened in January 1772 as an unprecedented setting for entertainment. The brilliant and wholly unexpected plan led from a fairly simple street front past elegant but small vestibules and card rooms into the breath-taking rotunda. The disposition should be compared and contrasted with Lord Burlington's Assembly Rooms at York. Whereas Burlington's main room was an austere archaeological reconstruction based on Vitruvius and Palladio, Wyatt's was essentially a scenic composition modeled not on the all-too-familiar Pantheon in Rome (from which the building took its name) but on the less familar and more exotic Hagia Sophia in Constantinople. This Byzantine source was somewhat unorthodox, but it lent itself to Picturesque adaptation that clearly caught the mood of the day. In any other country in Europe Burlington's Assembly Rooms would have been sufficiently novel if erected in 1769–72, but by then, England, having enjoyed a proto-neoclassicism during the Palladian Revival at the beginning of the century, needed something more hotly spiced to whet her jaded appetite. The feverishly excited reaction to Wyatt's display at the Pantheon is perfectly conveyed in Horace Walpole's account of his own impressions: "It amazed me myself. Imagine Balbec in all its glory! . . . There has been

*254. Robert Adam, mausoleum, Bowood, Wiltshire, 1761–64*

255. *Robert Adam, mausoleum, Bowood, Wiltshire, detail of the interior, 1761–64*

256. *Robert Adam, Syon House, London, anteroom, 1762–69*

257. *Robert Adam, Syon House, London, entrance hall, c. 1765*

258. *Robert Adam, Newby Hall, Yorkshire, sculpture gallery, begun 1767*

259. *Robert Adam, Register House, University, Edinburgh, 1774–92*

260. *Robert Adam, Culzean Castle, Ayrshire, stair hall, 1779–90*

a Masquerade at the Pantheon, which was so glorious a vision that I thought I was in the old Pantheon, or in the Temple of Delphi or Ephesus. . . . All the friezes and niches were edged with alternate lamps of green and purple glass, that shed a most heathen light. . . ."

With this one building Wyatt shot to the top of the architectural profession and thereafter never wanted for commissions. The first fruit of the Pantheon success was the commission in 1772 for Heaton Hall, near Manchester. That year, when he was twenty-six, Wyatt exhibited a drawing for the house at the Royal Academy; his client, Sir Thomas Egerton, later first earl of Wilton, was only twenty-three. Like many of Adam's commissions this was essentially the remodeling and extending of an earlier house. To each side of the existing house Wyatt added long, colonnaded, one-storied wings, terminating in canted bays so as to produce a chaste but varied composition: the kind of movement that Adam had tried but often failed to achieve. This sophisticated composition has led to speculation as to whether James may not have been assisted by his brother Samuel Wyatt (1737–1807), for the Heaton manner was subsequently developed by Samuel at Hurstmonceux Place, Sussex; Winnington Hall, Cheshire; Shugborough, Staffordshire; Belmont, Kent; and elsewhere. The elegant semicircular projection in the middle of the south front at Heaton is French in feeling, though one should remember that Adam had provided just such a feature exactly ten years earlier at Mersham-le-Hatch, in Kent. On the first floor, Wyatt's projection contains the Cupola Room in the so-called Etruscan style, which was used on five occasions by Robert Adam, most notably in the only surviving example, at Osterley Park, Middlesex (1775–79). Adam's is an ordinary rectangular room to which has been applied spidery decoration probably inspired by the plates in Piranesi's *Diverse maniere d'adornare i camini* (1769). Wyatt's room at Heaton, painted by Biagio Rebecca, is more imaginative in shape and the decoration more closely related to the structure. Another exquisite Etruscan room of the late 1770s is Thomas Leverton's at Woodhall Park, Hertfordshire. This style, which quickly found favor in France, was popular with those who, in the 1770s, had seen the arrival of Sir William Hamilton's first collection of Greek figured vases, then believed to be Etruscan.

Heaton was followed fairly quickly by Heveningham Hall, in Suffolk, where sometime between 1778 and 1784 Wyatt created a series of interiors that were probably the finest of his career. Just as Adam had been called to Kedleston to replace Paine, who was then regarded as old-fashioned, so Wyatt was called to Heveningham to replace Robert Taylor, who had designed the house in 1778 but was soon dismissed. Wyatt's patron, Sir Gerard Vanneck, was a merchant with no roots in the country. He wanted a house of display, a smart showpiece, and the result is, in a sense, a London mansion dropped down into remotest rural Suffolk. The entertaining rooms are one and a half stories high, so that, as in a London house of the period, there are few bedrooms and no state bedroom. Taylor had planned a large

*261. Robert Adam, University, Edinburgh, 1789–93; dome by Sir R. Anderson, 1887*

entrance hall with two tiers of columns, rather like his atrium at Purbrook, in Hampshire, but Wyatt decided that the height of the hall should speak for itself and allowed no columns to interfere with the flow upward into the wonderful barrel vault with its curious Gothic, concave fan vaults. It is instructive to compare the room with its ultimate source, Adam's library at Kenwood House, Hampstead, London (1767–69), whose plan and screen of columns based on the Roman Baths, and its remarkable curved vault decorated by the plasterer Joseph Rose, Jr., and the painter Antonio Zucchi, were revolutionary for their time. If anything, Wyatt's room is more of a unity. There is a logical relationship between the placing of the ribs of the vault, the pilasters on the wall, and the red and black marble bands across the floor. The foundation color of the walls and ceiling is apple green, with pilasters of yellow Siena scagliola, and capitals and enrichments in white. The seating furniture was also designed by Wyatt *en suite* with the whole room. Though this hall is the tour de force of the house, there are also an Etruscan room, library, and drawing room, all of high quality.

At Castle Coole, County Fermanagh, Wyatt was once more called in at the beginning to modernize and make fashionable what another architect had begun. The plans for the house are by Richard Johnston, dated Dublin, 1789, but before they could be executed Wyatt had waved the wand of London taste over them. On the facade, as executed by Wyatt, all superfluous ornament was eliminated, the unmolded window surrounds lack an entablature, and Johnston's Roman Doric was transformed into a bastardized Greek Doric of Wyatt's own invention. These Greek colonnades lead to pavilions inspired by Chambers's Casina at Marino. Inside Castle Coole, the two-storied entrance hall with its tiers of Doric columns was perhaps inspired by the interiors of Greek temples, but the most splendid interior is the great oval saloon in the middle of the garden front, with scagliola work by Domenico Bartoli and plasterwork by Joseph Rose, Jr. The whole production of the house was unusual, since it is doubtful that Wyatt ever saw it. His patron, Lord Belmore, was his own contractor and saw to it that Wyatt sent careful drawings for everything from ceilings to curtains and furniture. Once the joiners had finished the doors and windows they were set to work on Wyatt's furniture, which still survives in the rooms for which it was designed. The house cost more than double the original estimates, partly because of the decision to build it in Portland stone, necessarily imported from England. In June 1790 there was a total of sixty stonecutters and masons at work on the site. The whole house—design, materials, furniture, and plasterwork—is in every sense an importation from England. It was an extraordinary fantasy made reality, the quintessence of what one means by the Ascendancy in Ireland.

The Chambersian note, hinted at in Castle Coole and developed at Dodington Park, was frequently struck in Wyatt's works. In the mausoleum at Cobham Hall, Kent (1783), he was able to realize some of Chambers's early neoclassical ambitions. The canted corners with coupled columns are

*XV. Robert Adam, Syon House, London, Red Parlour. 1762–69*

*XVI. Robert Adam, Syon House, London, hall, c. 1765*

*262. James Wyatt, Heaton Hall, Lancashire, Cupola Room, 1772*

*263. Robert Adam, Osterley Park, Middlesex, dining room, 1775–79*

*264. Robert Adam, Kenwood House, Hampstead, London, library, 1767–69*

*265. James Wyatt, Castle Coole, County Fermanagh, saloon, 1790–97*

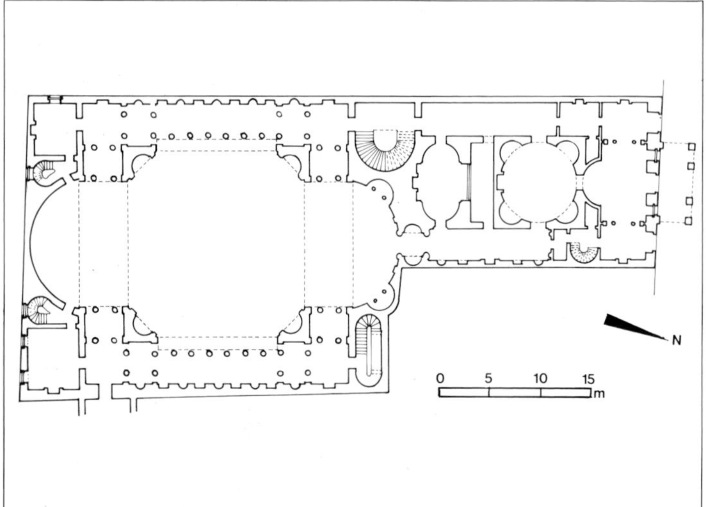


*266. James Wyatt, Pantheon, Oxford Street, London, plan, 1769*

*267. William Hodges,* Interior of the Pantheon in Oxford Street, *c. 1771. Leeds City Art Galleries, Temple Neusam House*

*268. James Wyatt, Heaton Hall, Lancashire, garden front, 1772*

*269. James Wyatt, Heveningham Hall, Suffolk, hall, 1778–84* ▷

*270. James Wyatt, mausoleum, Cobham Hall, Kent, 1783*
*271. James Wyat, mausoleum, Brocklesby Park, Lincolnshire, 1787*

echoes of Chambers's design for a temple for the earl of Tylney, while the pyramid on top reminds one of designs by Neufforge. Wyatt's even more sumptuous mausoleum at Brocklesby Park, Lincolnshire (1787), recalls Chambers's mausoleum for the Prince of Wales, and also, interestingly enough. Nicholas Hawksmoor's at Castle Howard, Yorkshire (1728). Both are based ultimately on the Tomb of Caecilia Metella on the Appian Way, but whereas Hawksmoor's columns are set closer together than classical precedent allows, and thus create a crowded, restless, Baroque effect, Wyatt's intercolumniation is the correct one for the Doric order. He has further enlivened the building with references to the Temple of Vesta in Rome and the temple to the same deity at Tivoli. Inside, Hawksmoor placed his order on a tall pedestal; Wyatt's rests directly on the floor.

Of Wyatt's many country houses, the last at which we shall look is Dodington Park, Gloucestershire, commissioned in 1796. By this date, however, he was far better known for his Gothic than his classical houses. He had made this style fashionable in the early 1780s with such buildings as Sheffield Place, Sussex; Sandleford Priory, Berkshire; Pishiobury Park, Hertfordshire; Lee Priory, Kent; and Slane Castle, County Meath. He continued to erect houses of this type right up until his death in 1813 but, with the exception of the astonishing Fonthill Abbey, Wiltshire, they do not rival in interest his classical work.

Dodington, designed after Adam's death, represents a new departure. Strikingly different from the tight symmetry of Castle Coole, the west front of Dodington is freely disposed like the elements in a Capability Brown landscape. The quadrant greenhouse, with a picture gallery following its curve behind it, stretches out lazily toward the remarkable domed cruciform church built by Wyatt on the site of the medieval church. In powerful contrast is the immense entrance portico on the west front of the house, Greek in spirit but Roman Corinthian in detail. Different again is the south front, which reverts to a Chambersian mode of composition, its pilasters and attic reminiscent of Somerset House. The east front is simple to the point of inadequacy, enlivened only by curved end bays. These three facades are completely different and unrelated; their seemingly casual asymmetry is continued on the east front by the office wing (demolished 1932), culminating in the elegant minor axis of the dairy with its Greek Doric tholos, or rotunda. Both the designing and the building of Dodington were slow processes. The plans were initiated in 1796 but the details of the facades were not settled until 1800 and building work was carried on until 1813. More than seven hundred drawings survive but few are signed or dated—this is typical of a certain slaphappy note about Wyatt's method of work.

The grandeur of the entrance portico is sustained by the scale of the interiors, particularly of the double-cube entrance hall, which runs its full length of twenty meters (sixty-five feet). In scale, originality, and quality this ranks with his hall at Heveningham as one of the best neoclassical

*272. James Wyatt, Dodington Park, Gloucestershire, stair hall, c. 1798*

*273. James Wyatt, Dodington Park, Gloucestershire, entrance hall, c. 1798*

274. *Lewis William Wyatt, Willey Park, Shropshire, entrance hall, 1812*

interiors in England. Wyatt had now moved away from the Adam-inspired interpretation of the antique that characterized Heveningham to a more sober version of the Roman atrium. The heavily gilded, coffered ceiling of the central space is reflected in the patterning of the floor in black marble, red Scottish stone, and cream Painswick stone enriched with thin strips of brass between the flagstones. Porphry scagliola columns, which have lighter lozenge-shaped coffering inspired by the Basilica of Maxentius in Rome, screen off raised areas at each end of the room. Visiting the house in the 1820s the young architect C. R. Cockerell could not help admiring the hall, but felt obliged to record in his diary: "I should say it is very injudicious to have scagliola oriental granite & gilt capital and ceilings in the Hall. If you begin thus, what can you end in? Nothing you can put in the drawing rooms & others can ever keep pace with such a commencement." In fact, Cockerell was too hard on Wyatt, for the staircase hall undoubtedly maintains the grandeur and drama of the entrance hall. In true Picturesque manner it is not approached axially but from one corner of the entrance hall, so that the first view of it is obliquely through the trio of arches in shadow. Behind them light flows down from the as-yet-concealed dome. The source for this magnificently architectural staircase hall and its arched colonnade is Chambers's staircase at Gower (sometimes called Carrington) House, Whitehall (1765–74; demolished 1886), itself inspired by Baldassare Longhena's staircase at S. Giorgio Maggiore, Venice (1643).

Dodington had a powerful influence on James Wyatt's nephew, Lewis William Wyatt (1777–1853), who was helping with the designs for it by 1801–2. In 1817 Lewis was called to Tatton Park, Cheshire, to complete the house begun about 1785 by another of his uncles, Samuel Wyatt. His proposals of 1807 included a giant, hexastyle, Corinthian portico identical to that at Dodington. This was not executed. The new entrance hall, carried out to Lewis Wyatt's designs with screens of porphyry Ionic columns carrying a segmental coffered vault, was also a variant of the hall at Dodington. The real fruit of Dodington, however, was not Tatton but Willey Park, Shropshire. Here in 1812 Lewis Wyatt produced the final synthesis of Burlingtonian Palladianism as successively developed by Paine and James Wyatt. As befits its late date, the house is both more Picturesque and more antique than would have been the case in the eighteenth century. It is superbly related to a Picturesque park and contains an interior more temple-like than that of any other English neoclassical house.

We should look finally at the work of an exact contemporary of James Wyatt's, Henry Holland (1745–1806). Though undoubtedly attracted stylistically to the Adam-Wyatt synthesis, which was the great achievement of the second half of the eighteenth century in England, he also pursued a calm, agreeable path, with one eye firmly fixed on the Louis XVI style in France, which gave most of his work a flavor of uncontroversial but elegant consistency unruffled by any real interest in the Greek Revival, the Picturesque, or antiquity.

*XVII. Robert Adam, Newby Hall, Yorkshire, Tapestry Room, begun 1767*

*XVIII. James Wyatt, Heaton Hall, Lancashire, Cupola Room, 1772*

*275. Henry Holland, Berrington Hall, Herefordshire, stair hall, 1778*

276. *Henry Holland, Carlton House, London, plan, 1783*

277. *Henry Holland, Carlton House, London, entrance portico and screen-wall, c. 1794*

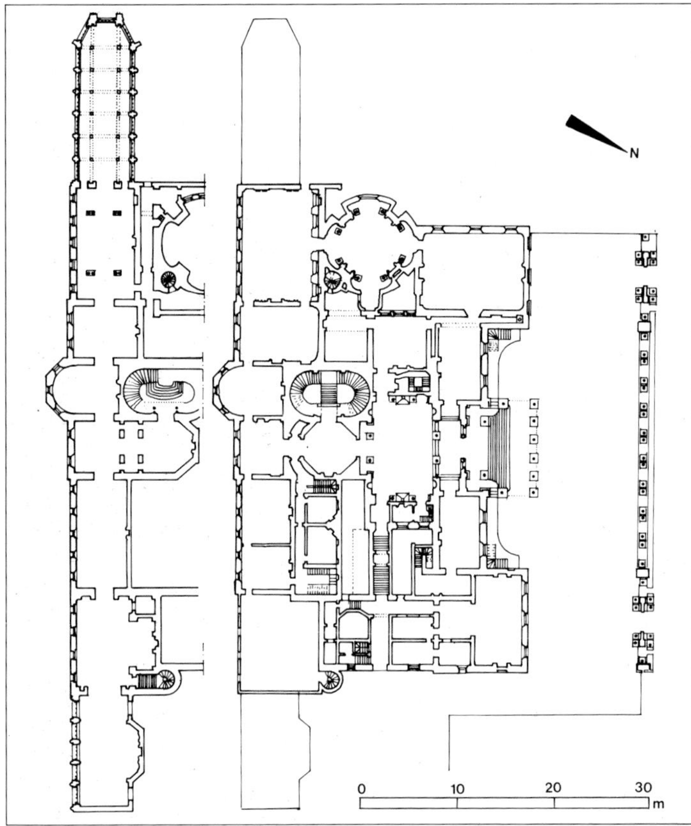

His first significant commission was for Brooks's Club in St. James's Street, London, in 1776. Behind a yellow brick facade of still basically Palladian disposition, on the first floor, lies the Subscription Room, in which Holland kept the Adam-like decoration to a minimum. The commission was one of extreme importance for Holland since the club was one of the most fashionable in London, patronized by the Prince of Wales and his intimate circle. The discreetly elegant interiors were popular with the club's members, so that not only was Holland commissioned to design Carlton House for the Prince of Wales, but other members followed the prince's example by patronizing Holland: notably the duke of Bedford at Woburn Abbey, Lord Spencer at Althorp, Samuel Whitbread at Southill House, and R. B. Sheridan at the Drury Lane and Covent Garden theaters.

In 1778 Holland began work on Berrington Hall, Herefordshire, where his partner from 1771, and father-in-law from 1773, the celebrated landscape designer Capability Brown, had been engaged from 1775. The exterior of Berrington is memorable, with its gaunt, emphatic portico and its monumental office courtyard laid out geometrically behind the house. The magnificent staircase hall is the richest surviving interior by Holland since the destruction of Carlton House. Its mood is not, perhaps, one we tend to associate with Holland, but it helps us to understand what it was that the Prince of Wales saw in him. The hall at Berrington has a dramatic double or ambiguous axis, with a coffered, arched recess which, in fact, leads only to the back staircase. Thus, as one enters from the entrance hall one has a dramatic view in perspective of the underbelly of the segmental arch. This painterly, Piranesian atmosphere, which is sustained as one mounts the cantilevered staircase beneath its glazed dome, had affinities with the staircase of a year or so later at Woodhall Park, Hertfordshire, by Thomas Leverton. Holland's drawing room, library, and boudoir at Berrington are also extremely fine, though their debt to Adam is clearer. The increasing richness in the decoration of these rooms reflects the marriage of Mr. Harley's daughter and co-heir to the son and heir of Admiral Lord Rodney in 1781.

The commission for Holland's most important work, Carlton House, came in 1783, the year in which the Prince of Wales, whose London residence it was to be, came of age. The site was occupied by a muddle of buildings put up in 1709 for Lord Carleton and partially remodeled in 1733 by Henry Flitcroft. Holland's extensive transformations were not completed until 1789, though the celebrated north front with its entrance portico and open screen-wall to Pall Mall were not ready until 1794. In 1785 Holland had visited Paris, where he would have seen such buildings as Rousseau's Hôtel de Salm, Ledoux's Hôtel de Thélusson, the Palais-Royal, the Hôtel de Condé, and Godoin's École de Chirurgie, which would have given him a number of ideas, particularly for the open Ionic screen along the road. The complex, interlocking plan of smallish rooms is probably French in origin, though the idea of the central octagonal tribune on which the whole

*278. Henry Holland, Carlton House, London, saloon, 1783–89*
*279. Henry Holland, Carlton House, London, entrance hall, 1783–89*

plan seems to pivot is perhaps derived from Adam—in particular, from his similarly placed circular tribune at Luton Hoo, Bedfordshire. To help him in the design of decoration and furniture, Holland employed a number of French craftsmen, of whom two are of special interest. They are Alexandre-Louis Delabrière and Dominique Daguerre, who in 1777 had been involved in the decoration of one of the most exquisite Parisian houses of the century, the Pavillon de Bagatelle in the Bois de Boulogne, designed for Louis XVI's brother, the Comte d'Artois, by F.-J. Bélanger. Contact between England and France reached a peak in exactly these years with the signing of the Anglo-French Treaty of Commerce in 1786. Moreover, after the Revolution many goods and much furniture were smuggled out of France and sold in England, with Daguerre acting as an important medium. The large scale of Carlton House and the enthusiasm of the Prince of Wales enabled Holland to develop a style of his own with the strong French influences that appealed to the Whig circle at the moment. We know the Carlton House interiors principally from the magnificent aquatints published in the second volume of William Henry Pyne's *Royal Residentes* (1819), though by that time they had been considerably enlivened by the architect John Nash and the decorator Walsh Porter with rather flashy draperies and seating furniture. The granite-green entrance hall seems to have remained much as Holland left it, as did the lovely lavender and blue circular saloon flanked by Greek Ionic columns with silvered capitals.

In 1794–96 Holland employed the architect Charles Heathcote Tatham (1772–1842) to make sketches in Italy of antique decorative fragments, including antique furniture, which Holland could use as a model. Tatham shipped back numerous antique ornamental and architectural fragments, which were subsequently bought (about 1821) by Sir John Soane, who utilized them in a characteristically claustrophobic way in the tiny study and dressing room leading from the dining room of his house-*cum*-museum in Lincoln's Inn Fields. In this way Holland exercised an important influence over the development of Regency furniture styles.

For the immediate influence of Carlton House in the late 1780s we need look no further than Dover House, Whitehall. When, in his early twenties, Prince Frederick, younger brother of the Prince of Wales, needed a London house, it was natural to look to Holland. The house chosen for him had been built in the 1750s by James Paine and stood some way back from Whitehall. Holland increased its accommodation and its privacy by filling in the courtyard with a beautiful domed circular vestibule inspired by French plans such as those in Neufforge's *Recueil élémentaire d'architecture* (9 vols., 1757–72). He further concealed the house from public view behind a blank rusticated screen-wall. This was punctuated by Greek Ionic columns with an order based on that of the Temple on the Ilissus, as illustrated in Stuart and Revett, but engaged against the wall in a manner inspired by a Hellenistic building also illustrated in Stuart and Revett, the so-called Library of Hadrian in Athens.

*XIX. Robert Adam, Osterly Park, Middlesex, dressing room in the Etruscan style, 1775–79*

*XX. Robert Adam, Kenwood House, Hampstead, London, library, 1767–69* ▷

In December 1786 Holland was called to Althorp, Northamptonshire, by the Whig grandee Lord Spencer. Holland's remodeling of this basically Elizabethan house resulted in one of the most convincing late Louis XVI interiors in England; the dressing room was painted in 1790–91 by the French artist T. H. Pernotin, whom Holland was at the time employing at Carlton House. Holland's work at Woburn Abbey, Bedfordshire, for the duke of Bedford, was more eclectic. Apart from some characteristically restrained interiors in his Anglo-Parisian manner, he provided a deep porte cochere in a style verging on the Greek Doric (demolished 1950); a Chinese dairy, after plates in Sir William Chambers's *Chinese Designs* (1757); and, in 1801, an exquisite little Temple of Liberty at one end of the sculpture gallery. Based on the Greek Ionic order of the Temple on the Ilissus, it was built to contain busts of the duke's favorite political heroes and was presided over by Joseph Nollekens's bust of the arch-Whig Charles James Fox, whose bust also presides over Brooks's Club.

Holland's last major commissions came in 1795 from the brewer Samuel Whitbread for the remodeling of his mid-eighteenth-century residence, Southill House, Bedfordshire. Mrs. Whitbread's drawing room and boudoir, painted by Delabrière with delicate white and gray coloring set off by a few chaste, Pompeian-style decorations, were finished by April 1800. The same artist painted some of the furniture, which still survives at Southill. The drawing room and dining room also contain furniture designed by Holland in a style moving away from Louis XVI to Regency. The large scale and rich gilding of this furniture create an opulent, almost royal, atmosphere, which contrasts with the refined and understated design of the rooms themselves. Holland's thoughtful Gallic manner separates him from his contemporaries, yet no one could deny that—like the better-known Adam and Wyatt—he formed a successful synthesis out of the myriad stylistic sources about which information had been accumulating so rapidly during the eighteenth century: Greek, Hellenistic, Roman, Renaissance, and neoclassical.

*280. Henry Holland, Southill House, Bedfordshire, drawing room, 1795*

*281. Henry Holland, Southill House, Bedfordshire, fireplace in the painted study, 1795*

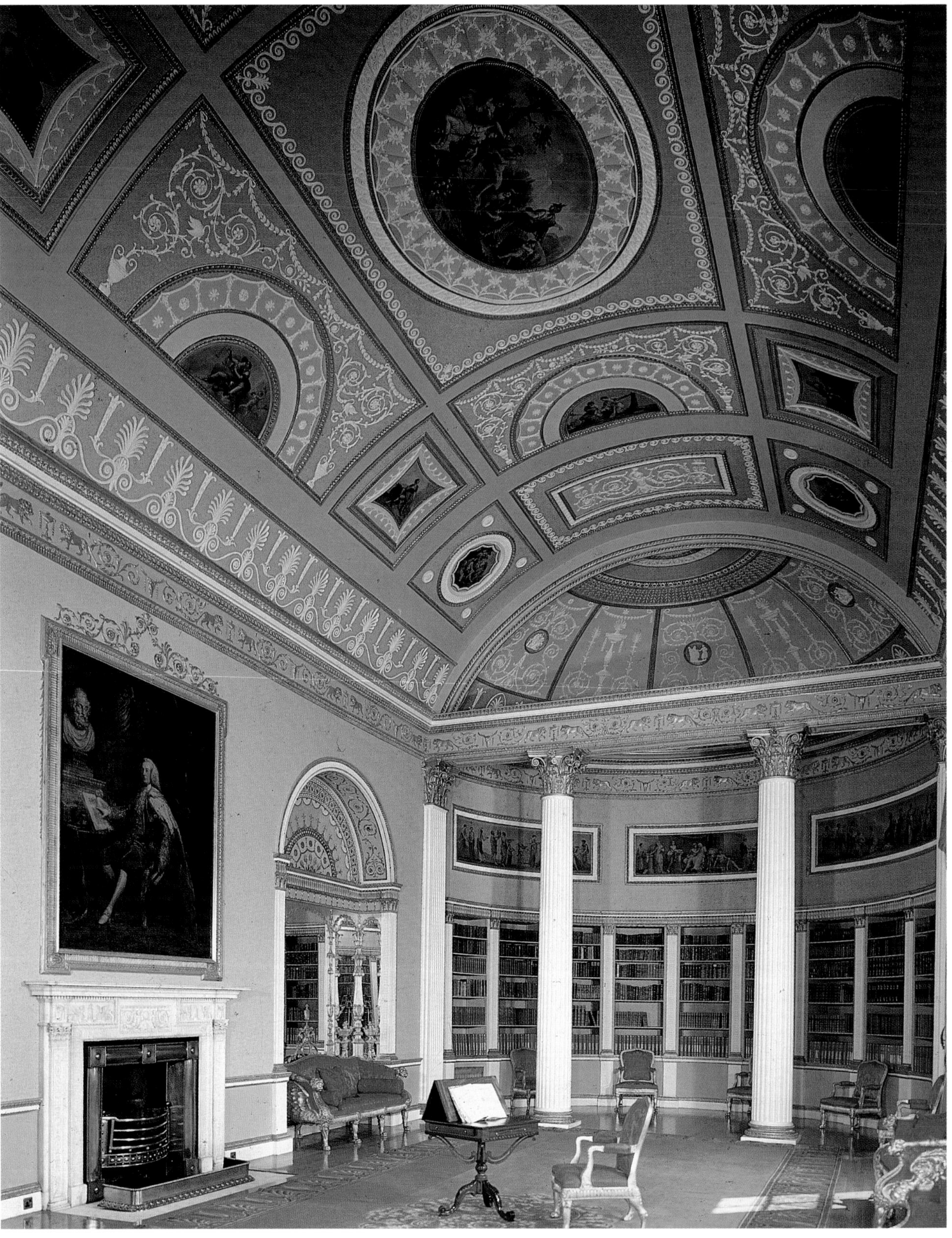

## Chapter Five
# VISIONARY ARCHITECTURE

### FRANCE: *Boullée and Ledoux*

The largeness of scale, the delight in formal geometry that are associated, as a rule, with the visionary architecture of the late eighteenth century are evident even in the earliest years of the century in the drawings, in particular, submitted to the Accademia di San Luca in Rome. The annual competitions organized there were a vital feature of architectural activity, even before G. P. Panini became *Principe* of the Accademia in 1754, serving to focus all aspiration and experiment in architecture, international rather than local. Many young architects visiting Rome thought to establish a reputation for themselves by winning one of its prizes. Marie-Joseph Peyre, as we have seen, started off with a grandiose cathedral (and two related palaces) and went on to design his equally vast *envoi de Rome,* an academic center, both of which he illustrated in 1765 in his *Oeuvres d'architecture.* The impetus that these gave to students in France was considerable. But, already, if we are to judge by the entries for the Prix de Rome dating from the 1750s, the overblown, intoxicating visions of the Accademia had become an established part of the French academic tradition. Blondel, as we know, did not approve. Whatever his reservations, they were not heeded by the students. The designs of the Prix de Rome winners of the late eighteenth century became consistently more and more grand. Even the members of the Académie grew alarmed. In August 1787, in a letter signed by de Wailly, Pâris, and Boullée, they complained to the director of the Académie de France à Rome, "Les projets envoyés à l'Académie ont très rarement répondu à son attente; la pluspart étoient plutôt des compositions gigantesques d'une éxécution impossible, que les productions d'architectes qui, mettant le dernier sceau à leur instruction, sont prêts à revenir dans leur patrie réclamer la confiance de leurs concitoyens" (*Correspondance des directeurs,* vol. 15, p. 161). Boullée himself, somewhat compromised by this pronouncement, later found it necessary to draw a distinction between "gigantesque" and "colossale." After the Revolution this largeness of vision was to be regarded as a positive need of resurgent citizens, a means of asserting their rights and their very existence. In his *Discours sur les monuments publics* addressed to the Conseil du Département de Paris in December 1791, Armand-Guy Kersaint declared, "Affermissons la liberté et tout deviendra facile; pour y parvenir joignons aux instructions de la parole le langage énergique des monuments: la confiance qu'il est nécessaire d'inspirer sur la stabilité de nos nouvelles lois, s'établira, par une sorte d'instinct, sur la solidité des édifices destinés à les conserver et à en perpétuer la durée." Architects in the years that followed were to produce an endless series of projects for vast public buildings, but the successive administrations of the Revolution were to leave nothing tangible—even their *fêtes* to the *Être suprême* were ephemeral manifestations.

A great many architects may be adduced to give evidence of the visionary splendor in late eighteenth-century France—Jean-Nicolas Sobre, J.-P. de Gisors (1755–1818), Pierre-Jules-Nicolas Delespine (1756–1825), Antoine-Laurent-Thomas Vaudoyer (1756–1846), J.-T. Thibault (1757–1826), J.-N.-L. Durand, and Jean-Jacques Tardieu (1762–1833) are some of them—but the two men who were most inspired and inspiring were Boullée and Ledoux. Their work was quite distinct, though there was clearly some interaction between them. Boullée seems to have been the first to break from the traditional bonds of architecture to produce a new visionary style, though it is just possible that Ledoux initiated the genre; both, however, grounded their first experiments on actual projects, even commissions.

The completion of the Hôtel de Brunoy in 1779 marks the vital change in Boullée's style; it became at once more solemn and splendid, and also more pretentious. In 1780 he prepared a series of designs for the rebuilding of Versailles of which only the last, the *grand projet,* survives. This shows a vastly extended building of dreadful uniformity and dullness. Boullée cannot have expected that it would be built. Gabriel's work at Versailles had been in abeyance for five years, finances were low, and the king was not greatly interested in large architectural projects. Similarly, the theater and church that Boullée designed immediately after, though ostensibly based on definite programs, were not in any sense realistic. They were *exercices de style.* His theater of 1781 for the Place du Carrousel, Paris, though related to an earlier project by Soufflot, is fitted unconvincingly into a vast colonnaded drum with a flattened dome above. The church (in a series of projects of the same year) was intended, he said, to stand on the foundations of Contant d'Ivry's unfinished Madeleine, but successive drawings show that he was slowly transforming Soufflot's Ste.-Geneviève rather into a building of unearthly grandeur. Absolutely it is beyond the bounds of eighteenth-century resources. The vaults are empyreal, the colonnades unending. Three thousand columns would have been required in the interior alone. Boullée's project of 1783 for a museum is an even grander and more purified variation on the columnar theme. But the innumerable columns, the interminable steps, and the great barrel vaults are on this occasion conspicuously and ostentatiously useless; the whole serves only a symbolic purpose. Even his projected library, which was formally commissioned in 1784—first for the site of the Couvent des Capucines, then, when that scheme was found to be too expensive, for the old Palais Mazarin—was grossly impractical.

There is no evidence that Boullée considered how a library might work. The limitations imposed by the site were no less willfully ignored. The celebrated perspective of the interior of the library can only with the greatest difficulty be related to the courtyard of the Palais Mazarin, which it was to enclose. The figures, moreover, were shown in togas, recalling, Boullée explained, Raphael's *School of Athens*—a conceit in which de Wailly had first indulged in his perspective of the foyer of the Théâtre-Français exhibited in 1771 (see illustration 166). The very meaning of the word *monument,* it is not surprising to find, was extended, at this time, from "a commemorative edifice" to a "public building of symbolic connotation." Boullée was, in effect, designing temples. His museum was manifestly inspired by

282. *Étienne-Louis Boullée, project for a theater for the Place du Carrousel, Paris, plan, 1781*

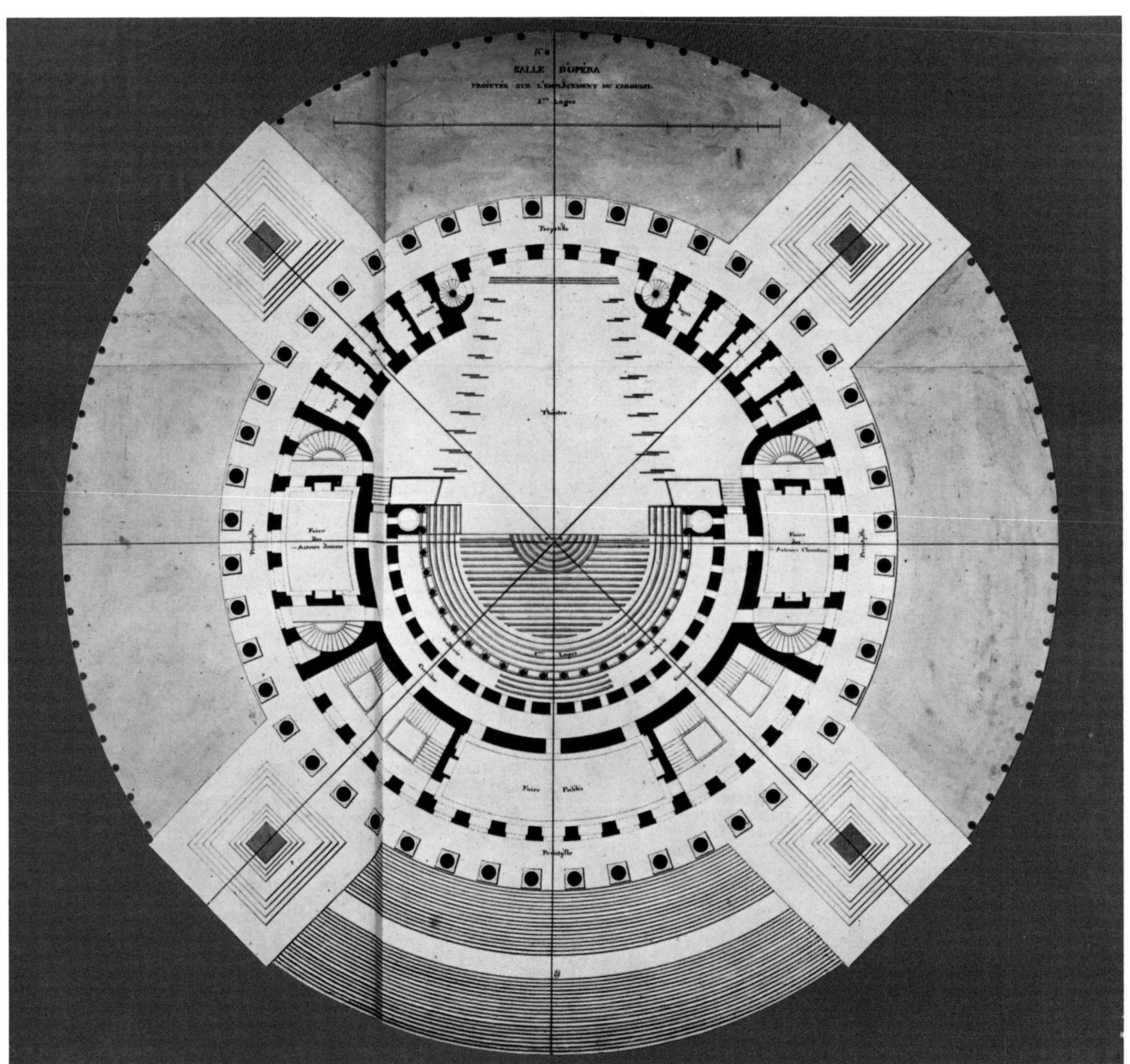

*283. Étienne-Louis Boullée, project for a theater for the Place du Carrousel, Paris, 1781*

*284. Étienne-Louis Boullée, project for a large church, perspective view, after 1781*

*285. Étienne-Louis Boullée, a large metropolitan church during Evensong, interior view, c. 1781*

*286. Étienne-Louis Boullée, project for the new hall of the Bibliothèque Nationale, Paris, 1784*

Alexander Pope's *Temple of Fame.* The dreadful pretension of his designs became more marked. Human conditions had ceased to be relevant. People were mere decorative adjuncts. "Jaloux enfin d'offrir le tableau le plus agréable," he wrote of his theater (or temple of pleasure), "j'ai cru y parvenir en disposant les spectateurs tellement que ce fussent eux qui décorassent ma salle et en formassent le principal ornement" (J. M. Pérouse de Montclos, ed., *E. L. Boullée: Architecture, Essai sur l'art,* 1968, p. 107). Human figures served only to increase the apparent size of his architecture. By 1784 he was able to epitomize his ideals in a great empty sphere designed as a cenotaph to Newton. "O Newton! Si par l'étendue de tes lumières et la sublimité de ton génie, tu as déterminé la figure de la terre, moi j'ai conçu le projet de t'envelopper de ta découverte" (ibid., p. 137). Boullée seems to have confused Newton and Galileo, but it scarcely mattered. His aim was to conjure up a vision of the immensity of the universe, to indulge celestial sensations. Thereafter, and particularly after the Revolution, his designs for even more magnificent public buildings, triumphal arches, gateways, towers of light, tombs, and pyramids pass into the realm of the truly sublime. He had sacrificed all reality and had determined to approach architecture as a painter; his motto, "Ed io anche sono pittore," was borrowed from Correggio, but he had reduced architecture to pictoral representation—little more. Drawing was all.

Boullée published nothing during his lifetime. However, his random notes and his *Essai sur l'art*—begun about 1780, but set down, for the most part, between 1790 and 1793 when he retired, ill, to the country—serve to illuminate his drawings and indicate something of his teachings. He had studied the works of Perrault—"Étant jeune, je partageais l'opinion publique; j'admirais la façade du péristyle du Louvre et regardais cette production comme tout ce qu'il y avait de plus beau en architecture" (ibid., p. 154)—but he found, in time, that he could not accept Perrault's contention that architecture was based, even in part, on an arbitrary system of rules. Boullée wanted an absolute, fixed and all-embracing. He sought to find it in nature: "Je ne saurais trop le répéter, l'architecte doit être le metteur en oeuvre de la nature" (ibid., p. 73). Nature was not to be too clearly defined, but he saw at once that forms and shapes served to conjure up thoughts and ideas.

"C'est par les effets que produisent leurs masses sur nos sens que nous distinguons les corps légers des corps massifs et c'est par une juste application, qui ne peut provenir que de l'étude des corps, que l'artiste parvient à donner à ses productions le caractère qui leur est propre. Les corps circulaires nous sont agréables par la douceur de leurs contours; les corps anguleux nous sont désagréables par la dureté de leurs formes; les corps qui rampent sur la terre nous attristent; ceux qui s'élévent dans les cieux nous ravissent et ceux qui s'étendent sur l'horizon sont nobles et majestueux" (ibid., p. 35).

There was thus a direct relationship between forms and the sensation they

*287. Étienne-Louis Boullée, project for a large museum, 1783*

288. *Étienne-Louis Boullée, project for a funerary monument*
289. *Étienne-Louis Boullée, project for a monument to Newton, 1784*

290. *Étienne-Louis Boullée, project for a monument in the form of a truncated Egyptian pyramid*

aroused. This was the basis of his theory—*la théorie des corps.* He chose for study the regular solids, for the despised irregularity in all things. He sought order desperately—not to be wondered at in the years of the Terror. Symmetry, his very image of order, was the inviolable rule. He built up his designs with cubes, cylinders, pyramids, and cones (always shown truncated, it should be remarked), but his ideal was the sphere, for not only was it the most regular of figures but, under the effects of light, it was capable of exhibiting the most infinite variety, from the darkest of shades to the sharpest brilliance. Light was an essential component in Boullée's ideal architecture.

"Le corps sphérique," he wrote, "sous tous les rapports, est l'image de la perfection. Il réunit l'exacte symétrie, la régularité la plus parfaite, la variété la plus grande; il a le plus grand développement; sa forme est la plus simple, sa figure est dessinée par le contour le plus agréable; enfin ce corps est favorisé par les effets de la lumière qui sont tels qu'il n'est pas possible que la dégradation en soit plus douce, plus agréable et plus variée. Voilà des avantages uniques qu'il tient de la nature et qui ont sur nos sens un pouvoir illimité" (ibid., p. 64).

In his design for a theater Boullée was already attempting to give form to this idea; in his monument to Newton he might be said to have achieved it. Ledoux, it is worth noting, was to outdo him in sheer boldness of conception in his shepherds' house for the park at Maupertuis, as was his pupil Sobre—using the device of a reflecting pool—in his Temple of Immortality. But Boullée was concerned not only with the finite beauty of forms; he saw that their effects might change under different conditions, at different times of the year, at different times of the day, in sunlight or in moonlight, and even in relation to the spectator's mood.

"Toutes nos idées, toutes nos perceptions," he remarked, quoting John Locke or his French disciple Étienne Bonnot de Condillac," ne nous viennent que par les objets extérieurs. Le objets extérieurs font sur nous différentes impressions par le plus ou le moins d'analogie qu'ils ont avec notre organisation" (ibid., p. 61).

Symbolism was thus of the highest importance in suggesting the character of each of Boullée's monuments: Certainly it was more important than practical considerations. The techiques of fortification were irrelevant to military architecture, Boullée said; the aim was "l'image de la force." Often his symbolism was overt, as with his trophies and shields applied to town gateways, or the text of the Constitution chiseled into the walls of his Palais National; more often it was obscure. For though his architecture might seem bland and formal, it was a distillation of a teeming esoteric knowledge. Like most French architects of the period, he was a Freemason. He was also an avid reader of travelers' tales. In his library he had James Bruce's account of the search for the source of the Nile, William Patterson on the Kaffirs and Hottentots, William Robertson's stories of the ancient American civilizations, and other tales of journeys to Siberia, China, and the South

*291. François Barbier, house for Racine de Monville, Désert de Retz, near Chambourcy, section, 1774–84*

*292. François Barbier, house and garden for Racine de Monville, Désert de Retz, near Chambourcy, 1774–84*

*293. Louis Carrogis de Carmontelle, Jardin de Monceau, Paris, plan 1773–78*

*294. Louis Carrogis de Carmontelle, Jardin de Monceau, Paris, the Tartar tent and the dromedary with its two keepers, 1773–78*

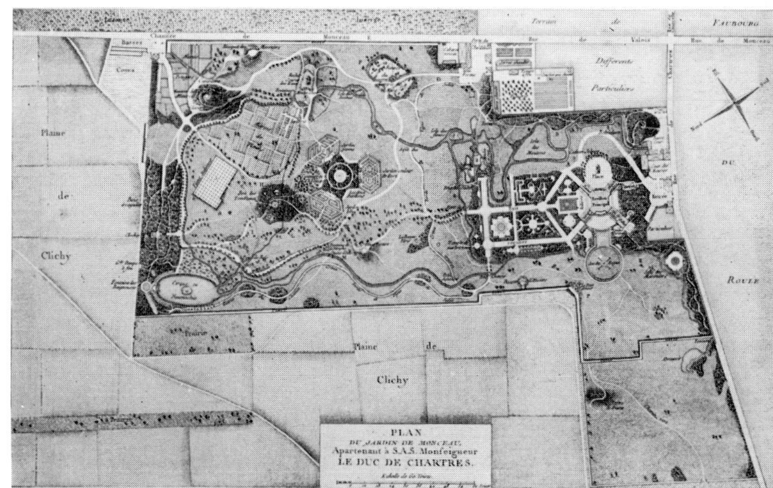

Seas. He himself scarcely moved out of Paris. This taste for the exotic was not to be overtly displayed in his designs. Everything was sublimated and given its purest form, for he aspired to the poetry of architecture. He aimed to elevate it above mere building (he despised Vitruvius for his humdrum mechanical interests) to a point beyond even the bounds of reason. His architecture was to be that of the sublime.

"La seule manière dont les artistes doivent s'entretenir entre eux," he wrote, "c'est de rappeler avec force et énergie ce qui excite leur sensibilité; c'est par cet attrait qui leur est propre qu'ils peuvent se stimuler et échauffer leur génie. Qu'ils se gardent bien d'entrer dans des explications qui tiennent trop au raisonnement, car l'impression d'une image sur nos sens s'attiédit quand nous nous appesantissons sur la cause que produit son effet. Commenter sur ses plaisirs, c'est cesser de vivre sous leur empire, c'est cesser

295. *Richard Mique,* hameau, *Petit Trianon, Versailles, 1778–82*

296. *Richard Mique,* hameau, *Petit Trianon, Versailles, the mill, 1778–82*

297. *François-Joseph Bélanger and Hubert Robert, the park at Méréville, near Étampes, 1784 onward*

298. *Painting by Hubert Robert of the park and the château at Méréville by François-Joseph Bélanger and Hubert Robert (Sceaux, Musée de l'Ile de France)*

d'en jouir, c'est cesser d'exister" (ibid., p. 164).

Boullée was no unbridled enthusiast. He founded his vision on study and careful thought. He worked beneath portraits of Copernicus and Newton. He possessed books on physics and astronomy. He read Francis Bacon and the Comte de Buffon and had clearly studied to advantage Condillac's *Traité des systèmes et des sensations* (1754). There are close links between his theory of forms and Jean-Baptiste-Louis Romé de l'Isle's *Cristallographie; ou, description des formes propres à tous le corps du regne minéral* (1738). Knowledge is at the root of his activities. Identifiable prototypes may be adduced for each of his visionary projects, giving evidence of a wide erudition. The most obvious are the buildings of the ancient Romans—the Colosseum, the Pantheon, the Pyramid of Cestius, the Tomb of Caecilia Metella, the mausoleums of Hadrian and Augustus, and that at Halicarnassus—all of which he stripped bare and rendered more noble and ethereal. He borrowed from Athanasius Kircher, from Fischer von Erlach, and even from Hubert Robert.

The liberating stimulus for Boullée's excursus, as for many of his contemporaries, was Jean-Jacques Rousseau and even his disciple Jacques-Henri Bernardin de Saint-Pierre, but the specific factor that served to alter the pattern of thinking on architecture was the introduction into France of the *jardin anglais.* Boullée himself was among the first to design one of these, possibly at the Château de Chaville, in 1765, certainly at Issy-les-Moulineaux a few years later. But the frenzied fashion for Picturesque gardening in France dates rather from the 1770s, when a spate of wonderfully resourceful but largely frivolous gardens was designed in something of an English manner: Simon-Charles Boutin's Tivoli at Montmartre (completed by

*299. François-Joseph Bélanger, the dairy at Méréville, now in the park of the Château de Jeurre*

*300. Chinese pavilion, Parc de Cassan, near L'Isle Adam*

*301. Chinese pavilion, Parc de Cassan, near L'Isle Adam*

302. *René de Girardin, the gardens at Ermenonville, with the tomb of Jean-Jacques Rousseau. Engraving by Merigot*

303. *René de Girardin, Temple of Fame, pavilion in the gardens at Ermenonville*

1771); L. Carrogis de Carmontelle's Monceau (1773–78); François Barbier's Désert de Retz (1774–84), for Boullée's own client Racine de Monville, where for the first time the house itself became a garden ornament—a simulacrum of a ruined column; then the *hameau* at Chantilly (1775) by Jean-François Leroy, and that at the Petit Trianon (1778–82) by Richard Mique (1728–1794); and also F.-J. Bélanger's gardens at Bagatelle (1780), the Folie Saint-James (1778–84), and Méréville (1784), this last finished off by Hubert Robert, who worked also at Betz with the Duc d'Harcourt and at Rambouillet, after 1783. The success of these, from an English point of view, varied greatly. "There are three or four very high hills," Horace Walpole wrote to his friend John Chute about Tivoli, on August 5, 1771, "almost as high as, and exactly in the shape of a tansy pudding. You squeeze between these and a river, that is conducted at obtuse angles in a stone channel, and supplied by a pump; and when walnuts come in, I suppose it will be navigable" (*Letters,* vol. 8, p. 64). Carmontelle's garden at Monceau was so flagrantly frivolous—a succession of *tableaux vivants* designed to ensure a maximum of conversational stimulus with a minimum of fatigue—that even its designer sought to distinguish it from the more serious English attempts to give order to nature: "Ceci," he wrote on the wall, "n'est point un jardin anglais" (F. A. de Frémilly, *Souvenirs,* 1909, p. 7).

But there were, of course, many gardens in which noble aims were pursued, moral and uplifting aims. The finest of these were the gardens at Ermenonville, belonging to the Marquis René de Girardin. The hermit here was no less a man than Rousseau. And it was from Girardin that one of the most important theoretical studies was to come, *De la composition des paysages,* of 1777. "Ce n'est donc ni en architecte ni en jardinier, c'est en poète ou en peintre qu'il faut composer des paysages," he counseled (p. 8). Within six years this work had been translated into English. However, the first book of this sort to appear in France was, as one might expect, English—Thomas Whately's pioneering study on the theory of the Picturesque garden, *Observations on Modern Gardening,* of 1770, which F.-P. de Latapie translated into French the following year. Walpole was quick to notice this, too: "They have translated Mr. Whateley's book," he told Chute in his same letter, "and lord knows what barbarism is to laid at our door." This was followed by two French works, C.-H. Watelet's *Essai sur les jardins,* of 1774, and Jean-Marie Morel's *Théorie des jardins,* issued two years later. Walpole's own study, *The History of the Modern Taste in Gardening,* first printed in 1771, was translated into French in 1785 by the Duc de Nivernois.

Morel had worked with Girardin at Ermenonville as early as 1766, but they had quarreled furiously as to the propriety of littering a landscape garden with buildings. He departed, piqued, to design no fewer than forty other gardens to his own liking. His writings make it clear that he did not object to building as such; cottages and barns or sheds that served a useful purpose and were designed in the traditional manner were altogether

*304. Pierre-François-Léonard Fontaine, funerary monument for the ruler of a great empire, Grand Prix design, 1785*

*305. Antoine-Laurent-Thomas Vaudoyer, house for a cosmopolitan, 1785*

*306. Jean-Nicolas Sobre, project for a Temple of Immortality*

acceptable, as were old and rambling manor houses, but he wanted nothing new, nothing that might obtrude in the landscape. He liked best nature unadorned, and he described at great length the way in which he composed by natural means, making open expanses or enclosures, solids and voids. There should be no great insistence on logic, he explained, for the aim was poetry. His raw materials were grass and trees, rock, and water—still or running; he was alilve to the effects of running water, the rustle of wind, and, of course, the play of light. Four successive chapters in his book were devoted to the changing effects of the four seasons. His interests, it is evident, are much the same as Boullée's, though Morel, it must be stressed, unlike Boullée, did not care much for symmetry. The transposition of these ideas into architectural theory, however, was probably not made by Boullée himself. His *Essai* was preceded by Le Camus de Mézières's *Le génie de l'architecture; ou, l'analogie de cet art avec nos sensations,* issued in 1780. Le Camus was spurred on by the landscape gardeners; indeed, he dedicated his book to Watelet. "Mon zèlè," he wrote, " s'est soutenu en fixant mon attention sur les ouvrages de la nature. Plus j'ai examiné, plus j'ai reconnu que chaque objet possède un caractère qui lui est propre, et que souvent une seule ligne, un simple contour suffisent pour l'exprimer" (p. 3). Le Camus's ideas are less well developed than those of Boullée, the language certainly less elevated; his dogged insistence on indicating at length how his analogies might be incorporated into the routines of planning and detail design serve to set his book in an altogether different category from that of the *Essai.* But throughout there are parallels and similarities, for the preoccupations of both men were the same: "Un édifice très éclairé," Le Camus writes, "bien aeré, lorsque tout le reste est parfaitement traité, devient agréable et riant. Moins ouvert, plus abrité, il offre un caractère sérieux: la lumière encore plus interceptée, il est mystérieux ou triste" (p. 43). It is scarcely necessary to trace at further length the connection between the ideas of Boullée and ideas regarding composition introduced into France by gardening theorists in the 1770s.

Even at the most humdrum level one can note his borrowings from gardeners: His biographer Jean-Marie Pérouse de Montclos has suggested that his great theater is no more than an enlarged Temple of Love, while the monument to Newton itself, though it accords with a description in Pope's *Temple of Fame,* may equally be an illustration of the Miau Ting, or the Halls of the Moon, described in Sir William Chambers's *Dissertation on Oriental Gardening* (1772), available in French by 1773. The French, inspired by the visions of Panini and Piranesi and then the English, were learning to accept visual criteria alone.

The authority of the Picturesque theorists and of such men as Boullée was enormous. For though Boullée published nothing, he was active as a teacher. Indeed, many of his designs seem to have been prepared as a direct result of his teaching; they are based on the Grand Prix programs and incorporate, moreover, ideas that appear first in his students' submissions: magisterial corrections, as it were, to their hesitant essays. Not that they were slow to learn. Even outside Boullée's classes his works must have been known. Antoine-Laurent-Thomas Vaudoyer, a pupil of A.-F. Peyre, claimed to have produced his design for a *maison d'un cosmopolite,* a house in the form of a globe, in 1785, the year after Boullée designed his monument to Newton. And Pierre-François-Léonard Fontaine, a student of Jean-François Heurtier and A.-F. Peyre, who was awarded the second Grand Prix in 1785—but only after the students rioted when they heard that he had failed to win because the Académie feared to recompense so fine a draftsman—showed in his proposed "Monument sépulcral pour les souverains d'un grand empire" that he was in all things a true follower of Boullée. Boullée's influence was paramount.

Ledoux's impact as a visionary architect was not, at first, made through the mediums of teaching, drawing, and writing. He had very few students, but he liked to build. The forty *barrières* encircling Paris that he began in 1785, when he was already fifty, and built rapidly during the following four years—in part, under the supervision of J.-D. Antoine and Jean-Arnaud Raymond—showed that by changing the scale and measures of traditional

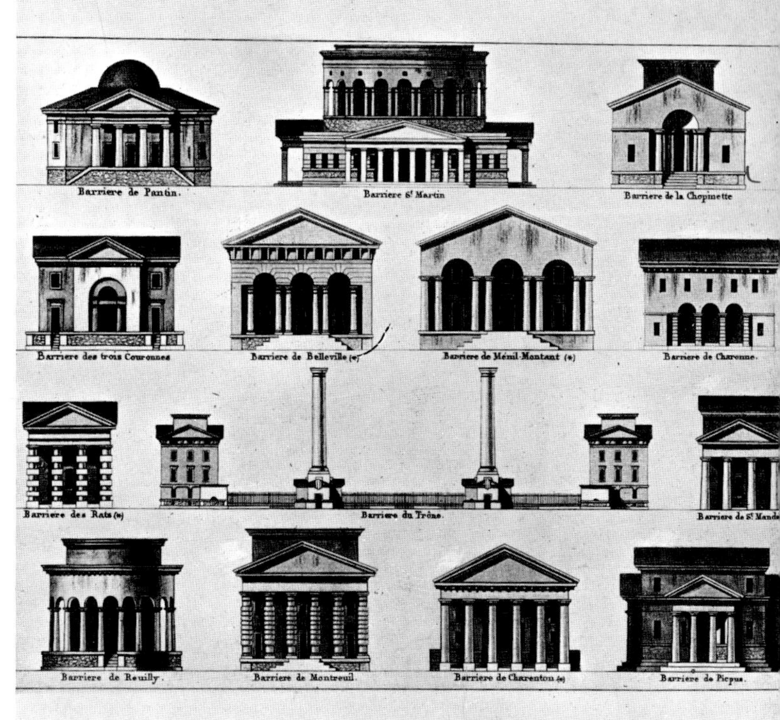


*307. Claude-Nicolas Ledoux, projects for* barrières, *Paris, 1785–89*

forms, and by assembling these simplified geometrical forms in a bolder, if more complex, arrangement than usual, applying ornament only sparingly and then in a new relation to the surface or mass, an architecture of extraordinary novelty and power could be fashioned. Ledoux was a potent innovator. Most of the *barrières,* which continued to be built even after the Revolution, were torn down in the mid-nineteenth century, but four remain—the Barrière d'Enfer, Place Denfert-Rochereau; the Barrière du Trône, Place de la Nation; the Rotonde de la Villette, Place de Stalingrad; and the Rotonde de Monceau, Place de la République Dominicaine. The last shows Ledoux at his least adventurous, but the monumental building at the head of the Bassin de la Villette embodies his boldest aspirations. A giant arcaded drum is placed four-square on a solid, rectangular mass. At the core is a circular court. The silhouette is hard and sharp; and, though the detailing is strong, it is totally subservient to the geometry of the whole. Its air of primordial splendor is overwhelmingly impressive.

The extraordinary projects for which Ledoux is famous were not published as a group until 1804, two years before his death, when the first volume of *L'architecture considérée sous le rapport de l'art, des moeurs et de la législation* was issued. This contained his writings and one hundred and twenty-five plates illustrating the extant buildings and his project for an ideal city centered on the saltworks at Arc-et-Senans, on the edge of the forest of Chaux. Not until 1847 did his supposed son, Daniel Ramée, issue the second edition, containing two hundred and thirty extra plates, relating to Ledoux's realized work and unfulfilled commissions. Other isolated engravings exist—many of the plates included in the published volumes may have been distributed separately. The earliest dates from 1771, but this is unremarkable. Some of the designs for the buildings erected at Arc-et-Senans are dated 1776, just after the work there had begun; others are from 1780; but the first dated engraving for a design that is odd and altogether unconformable by contemporary standards is that of 1778 for an imagined hunting lodge for the Prince de Bauffremont. Later commissions—the Château de Maupertuis (c. 1780); the house for M. de Witt (1781); the Bishop's Palace at Sisteron (c. 1781); the Château d'Éguière, which must also be contemporary; and even that remarkable group of fifteen houses in the Rue St.-Georges, Paris, for M. Hosten (four were built from 1792 until 1795, just after Ledoux was released from prison)—are all unusual enough, but are not really so extraordinary. They are lacking in the brutal harshness of composition that makes so startling the prince's lodge, and, especially, the other famous designs for the Utopian city of Chaux—among them the Maison d'Éducation; the Cénobie (or commune) for sixteen families; the Panaréthéon (or Temple of Virtue); the Oikema (or Temple of Love); and the cemetery. The last, not unlike Boullée's monument to Newton, may date from the late 1770s, though this seems unlikely; all were probably designed and engraved only after Catherine the Great's son, in the guise of the Comte du Nord, visited Paris in 1782 and accepted the dedication of the book (it was to be dedicated, in the end, to his son, Alexander I). Ledoux was probably most active designing in the idle years that followed his release from prison in 1795. He built nothing then. From this period, also, must date the revisions to the works built early in his career, which make his engravings such telling evidence of his activity as an architect. The prospectus for his book did not come out until 1803.

For all the arbitrary nature of his refashioning, Ledoux's executed buildings from the late 1770s onward, and all his subsequent projects, reveal him as a designer of unparalleled power and vision, although his vision was less elevated than that of Boullée. He had a livelier imagination, clearly well-stimulated by knowledge of the odd and curious in architecture—and inspired also by the curious in literature, if we are to judge by a comparison of his account of a traveler to his ideal city with that of the hero in Tiphaigne de la Roche's *Giphantie* (1760), who discovers a new land where nature continues still to create new plant and animal species. Boullée, of course, responded also to the exotic, but he was careful always to distill such interests.

Ledoux introduced minarets into the design of a country house without

308. Claude-Nicolas Ledoux, *Barrière du Trône, Paris, 1785–89*

309. Claude-Nicolas Ledoux, *Rotonde de la Villette, Paris, 1785–89*

qualm. Like Boullée, he was intrigued by symbolism and mystery. He was, not surprisingly, a Freemason and seems so have been involved in an abortive initiation ceremony with William Beckford, possibly at Maupertuis. But whereas Boullée subordinated such rich and varied interests to a consistent and completely coherent vision of architecture, Ledoux was altogether erratic. He evolved no sustained or sustaining theory. His writings reveal him at his most wayward: He offered notions, not a philosophy. His style is rhapsodic and hortatory. Often, when his ideas can be connected to known facts or realities, he is revealed as commonplace enough, but his overblown language serves to distort and confuse. His text is a farrago. There is no clear organization, no argument, and much is already familiar. "Vous qui voulez devenir architecte," he wrote, "commencez par être peintre" (*L'architecture,* 1804, p. 113). His criteria throughout are not unlike those of Boullée: For example, his overwhelming responsiveness to nature, evident, in particular, in the natural and pleasant settings in which he placed his designs; his insistence on symmetry; his feeling for the qualities of solid geometry, light and shade, and poetry in architecture. "L'architecture," he wrote, "est à la maçonnerie ce que la poésie est aux belles-lettres: c'est l'enthousiasme dramatique du métier, ne peut en parler qu'avec exaltation" (ibid., pp. 15-16). He was fearful also of too much reason or knowledge: "L'érudition," he warned, "cette souveraine empesée, conduit rarement à l'heureux délire" (ibid.).

He aimed to be an inspired genius, and consciously thought of himself as the revolutionary prophet, both the architectural and moral kind. There is more social concern evident in his writings than in Boullée's. Indeed, he is often regarded as an early socialist, but most of his exhortations belong to the realm of post-Revolutionary cant. There is little evidence of sustained thinking. He dedicated his book to the czar of Russia, sent two hundred and thirty-seven of his drawings to the czar just before the Revolution, and was proud to recount his dealings with the king: "De tous temps," he wrote, "les souverains ont donné le ton" (ibid., p. 26). His hints as to the organization of the ideal city indicate that he envisaged an authoritarian regime, while his paean to the riches of nature as sufficient unto the needs of the poor, though it may recall Rousseau and Bernardin de Saint-Pierre, makes embarrassing reading. One may doubt at times that Ledoux was even a humanitarian. Yet he did design and build the saltworks at Arc-et-Senans as a noble architectural enterprise, which was unusual enough at the time, and in his visionary designs showed that canon forges could be conceived as elevating works of art; even the humblest dwellings, shepherds', coopers', and woodmen's houses, are of no less exalted an architecture than the house of the *Directeurs de la Loue,* or even the house of the *Directeur de la Saline* itself. This last had an altar in the center, dramatically lit, approached from a giant flight of steps. Everything was grist to Ledoux's creative mill and could be endowed with greatness and nobility. God, of course, was the supreme architect.

*310. Claude-Nicolas Lecoux, projects for* barrières, *Paris, 1785–89*

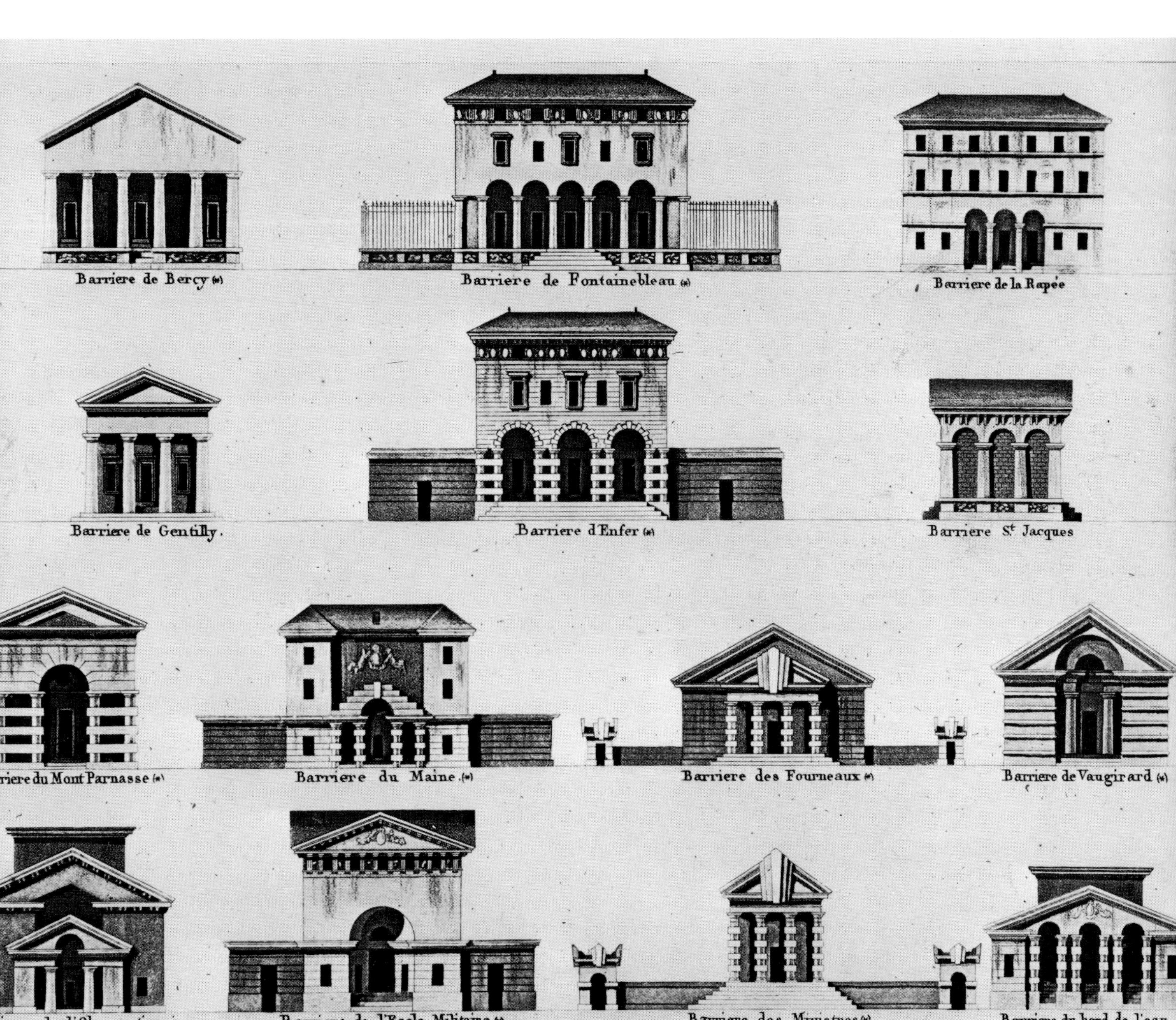

*311. Claude-Nicolas Ledoux, Barrière d'Enfer, Paris, 1785–89*

*312. Claude-Nicolas Ledoux, Barrière d'Enfer, Paris, detail, 1785–89*

*313. Claude-Nicolas Ledoux, project for* barrières, *Paris, 1785–89*

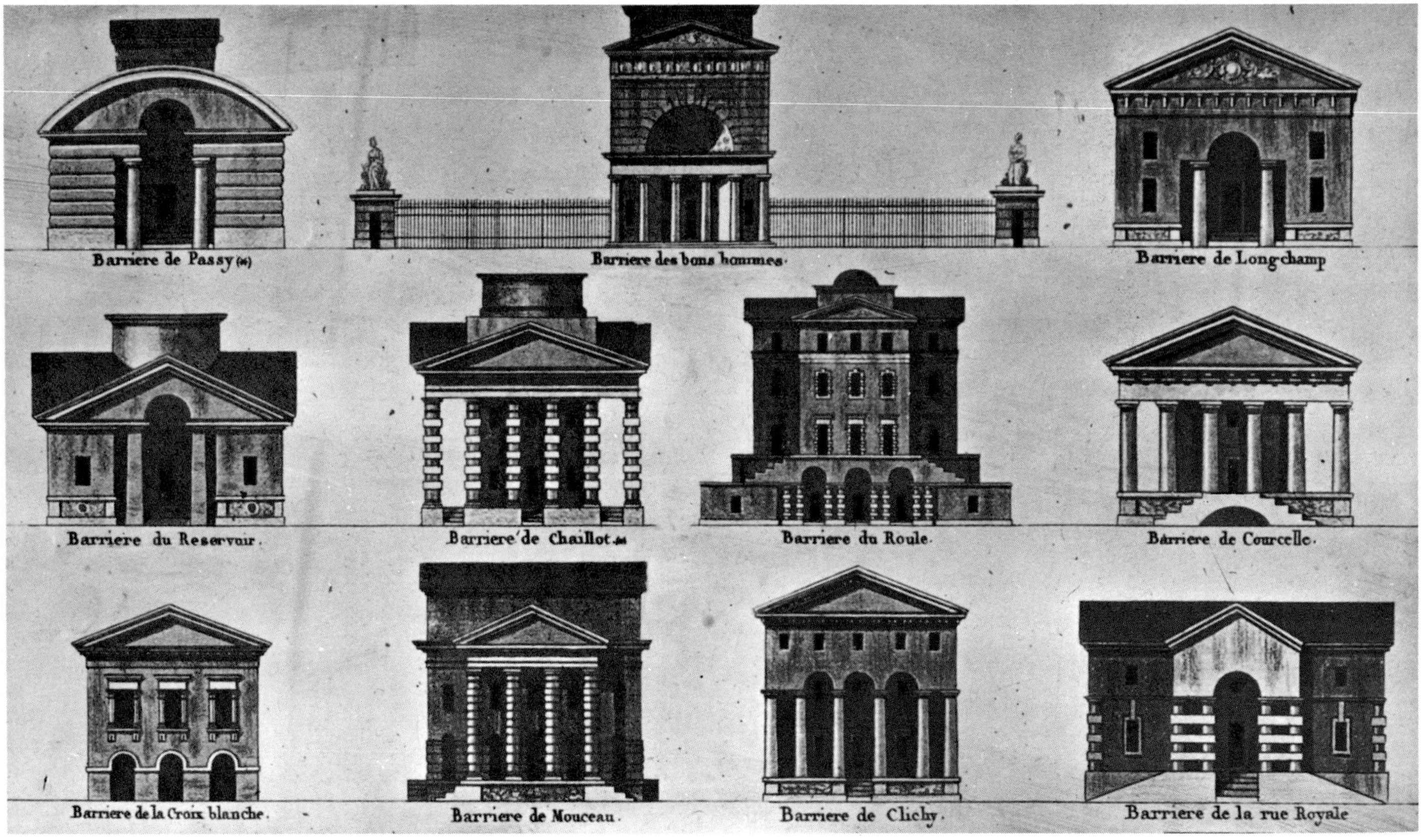

*XXI. James Wyatt, Heveningham Hall, Suffolk, hall, 1778–84*

*XXII. Claude-Nicolas Ledoux, Saline de Chaux, Arc-et-Senans, exterior, 1775-79*

*314. Claude-Nicolas Lecoux, house of the director of the Saline de Chaux, Arc-et-Senans, elevation, 1775–79*

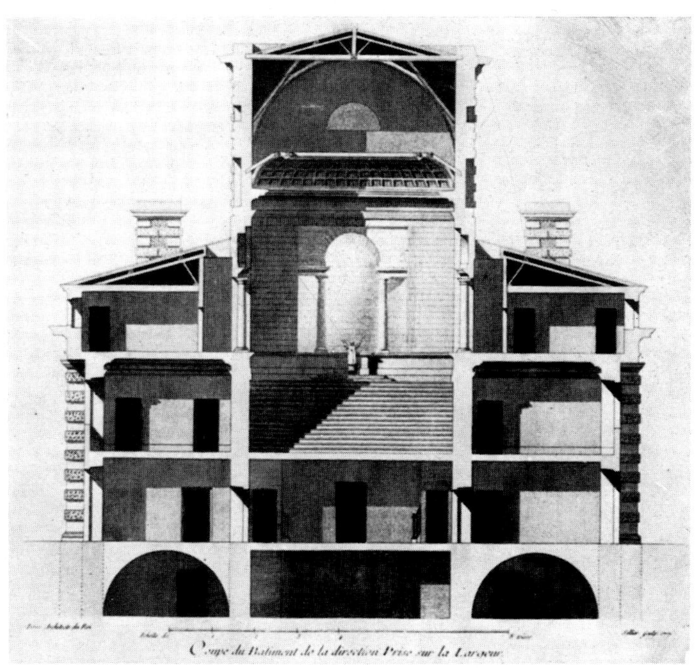

*315. Claude-Nicolas Ledoux, house of the director of the Saline de Chaux, Arc-et-Senans, section, 1775–79*

Ledoux, though, was infinitely less solemn than Boullée; he was livelier and less gloomy. "L'art sans éloquence," he wrote, "est comme l'amour sans virilité" (ibid., p. 16). Boullée produced endless projects for cenotaphs and cemeteries; indeed, most of his visionary designs have sepulchral overtones. All have a funerary ostentation and are set in desert landscapes. Ledoux concentrated rather on communal buildings and houses in attractive surroundings. His designs are undoubtedly more engaging than Boullée's, and all his works offered more possibilities for adaptation, but Ledoux was not often imitated. His architecture was thought to be undisciplined. Yet, much as Piranesi had set the tone and style that inspired Ledoux, so Ledoux suggested to architects how they might break from the classical norms to produce a new and radical architecture. Boullée provided the highest ideal; Ledoux offered a practical model. Together they were responsible for the profound change in architecture that is characterized as Revolutionary.

### ENGLAND: *Dance and Soane*

In his *Description of the House and Museum on the North Side of Lincoln's Inn Fields,* of 1835–36, Sir John Soane wrote of the Breakfast Parlour in his house: "The view from this room into the Monument Court and into the Museum, the mirrors in the ceiling, and the looking-glasses, combined with the variety of outline and general arrangement in the design and decoration of this limited space, present a succession of those fanciful effects which constitute the poetry of architecture."

The same sentiments and the same language occur, as we have seen, in Boullée's *Architecture, Essai sur l'art,* written in the 1780s and 1790s as part of his bizarre retreat from reality. In these years his long-suppressed ambition to be a painter finally surfaced in the form of demands for a poetic architecture of a vague ennobling symbolism, recalling the immutability of death, light, dark, and the stark geometry of the sphere, cube, and pyramid: "Nos édifices," he declared, "surtout les édifices publics, devroient être, en quelque façon, des poèmes. Les images, qu'ils offrent à nos sens, devroient exciter en nous des sentiments analogues à l'usage, auquel ces édifices sont consacrés" (see H. Rosenau, *Boullée and Visionary Architecture,* 1976, p. 118). But the buildings he most enjoyed designing were, ironically, the most functionless, as is the horrifying empty sphere of the celebrated Newton cenotaph. It is interesting to speculate to what extent Soane may have been aware of Boullée's obsession with "the poetry of architecture." Although Boullée's *Essai sur l'art* was not published until 1953, he was an energetic teacher of architecture, and through his pupils Soane may have learned of Boullée's ideas. In his Royal Academy lectures, first delivered in 1809, Soane observed: "The 'lumière mystérieuse,' so successfully practised by the French Artist, is a most powerful agent in the hands of a man of genius, and its power cannot be too fully understood, nor too highly appreciated. It is, however, little attended to in our Architecture, and for

*316. Claude-Nicolas Ledoux, Saline de Chaux, Arc-et-Senans, principal gate, 1775–79*

*317. Claude-Nicolas Ledoux, ideal city of Chaux, Arc-et-Senans, aerial view, from his* Architecture, *1804*

*318. Claude-Nicolas Ledoux, ideal city of Chaux, Arc-et-Senans, perspective view, from his* Architecture, *1804*

this obvious reason, that we do not sufficiently feel the importance of Character in our buildings, to which the mode of admitting light contributes in no small degree."

It is from Le Camus de Mézières's book *Le génie de l'architecture,* of 1780, that Boullée and Soane derived their belief in the creation of architectural character by means of the mysterious effect of light that creates an architecture "mystérieux ou triste," and Boullée observed: "C'est la lumière qui produit les effets. Ceux-ci nous causent des sensations diverses et contraires, suivant qu'ils sont brillans ou sombres. . . . Si je peux éviter que la lumière arrive directement, et la faire pénétrer sans que le spectateur aperçoive d'où elle part, les effets résultans d'un jour mystérieux produiront des effets inconcevables, et en qualque façon, une espèce de magie vraiment enchanteresse" (see H. Rosenau, *Boullée and Visionary Architecture,* p. 126).

This could surely stand as an evocation of the effects aimed at and achieved by Soane in such interiors as the Breakfast Parlour at Lincoln's Inn Fields, the Bank of England, and the Law Courts. Soane, indeed, was able, as Boullée was not, to forge within the classical tradition a personal style that was both poetic and practical. As Sir John Summerson has observed (*Sir John Soane,* 1952, p. 15): "In 1792, when [Soane's] style arrives suddenly at maturity, there was not, anywhere in Europe, an architecture as unconstrained by classical loyalties, as free in the handling of proportions and as adventurous in structure and lighting as that which Soane introduced at the Bank of England in that year." The sources of this style are to be found both in France and in England. Soane had been profoundly influenced by the Abbé Laugier's demand for a new architecture that would reconstitute the lightness and grace of Gothic structure in a purified and reformed version of the classical language. We know that Soane possessed eleven copies of Laugier's *Essai sur l'architecture.* What is less well known is that a manuscript survives of Soane's translation of the book from which many of Laugier's ideas were taken, Cordemoy's *Nouveau traité de toute l'architecture.* But Soane's sources were also English. He had worshiped at the shrine of his old master, George Dance, the younger (1741–1825), to whose work we now give our attention.

Adam, Chambers, and Mylne all arrived in Rome, the melting pot of early neoclassicism, in 1754–55, and the eighteen-year-old George Dance followed in 1759. He had been sent there by his architect father in order to join his brother Nathaniel, a painter, who had arrived four years earlier. Soon George Dance met Piranesi, and together they made the first accurate measured drawings of the Temple of Castor and Pollux in the Forum. In 1762 he entered the competition for a design for a public gallery for statues and pictures organized by the Accademia at Parma. The design with which he won the Gold Medal in 1763, characterized by stone domes and bleak rusticated walls, shows how much he had absorbed of the emergent neoclassicism of the French Grand Prix projects. This was the style of heroic grimness that M.-J. Peyre was to encapsulate in his *Oeuvres d'architecture,* of

*319. Claude-Nicolas Ledoux, project for a hunting lodge for the Prince de Bauffremont, 1778*

*320. Claude-Nicolas Ledoux, project for the shepherds' house in the park at Maupertuis, 1780*

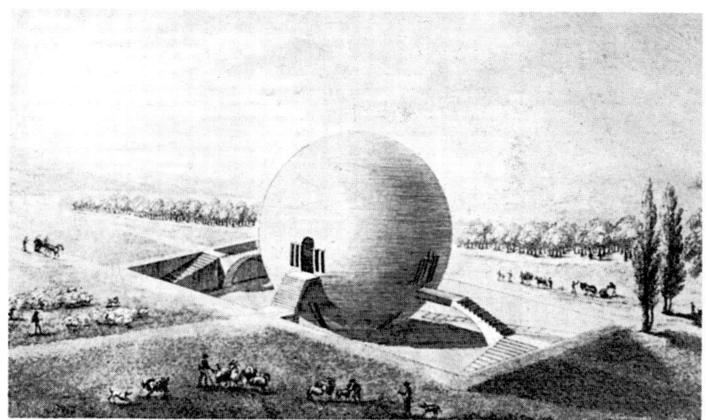

*321. Claude-Nicolas Ledoux, Château d'Éguière, c. 1780*

*322. Claude-Nicolas Ledoux, Hosten Houses, Rue St.-Georges, Paris, elevation, 1792–95*

*323. Claude-Nicolas Ledoux, Hosten Houses, Paris, elevation, section*

*324. Claude-Nicolas Ledoux, the Cénobie, ideal city of Chaux, Arc-et-Senans, from his* Architecture, *1804*

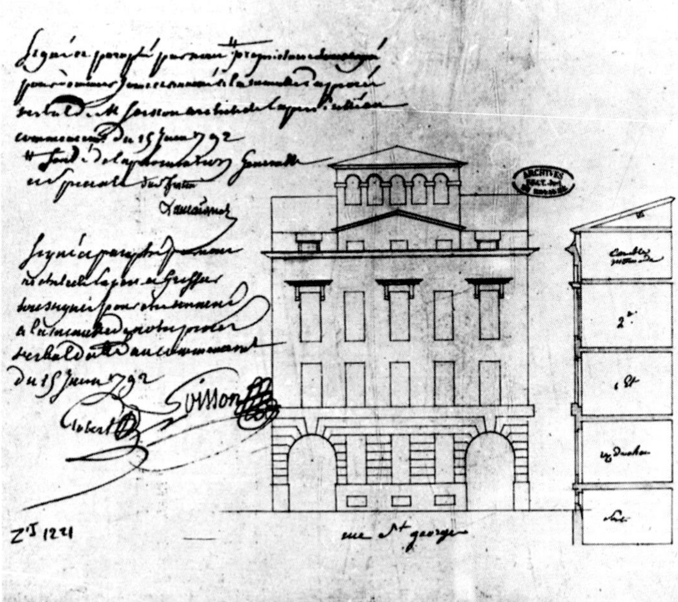

1765, and that also inspired the dreams of the young Soane, Dance's junior by twelve years.

Dance returned to England late in 1764 and by the following spring was at work on his first commission, the church of All Hallows, London Wall, in the City of London. Inspired by the Roman Baths, and roofed with a barrel vault—not the coffered ellipse used by Inigo Jones and James Gibbs—the church has an internal Ionic order that lacks a full entablature and has instead a highly enriched frieze. This not very daring novelty, which was due to Dance's reading of Laugier's *Essai sur l'architecture,* we know shocked Soane when he first saw it. Dance's next building was Newgate Gaol (designed in 1768–69), which combines themes derived from Peyre with a Mannerist handling of rustication inspired by Giulio Romano. Elements from the powerful style of Vanbrugh also appear in the centrally placed Keeper's House, where they help reinforce the dramatic "narrative" content of the building, which was evidently intended to be expressive of its grim function. In the *Cours d'architecture,* which J.-F. Blondel began delivering to his students in 1743 (it was not published until 1771), the prison was upheld as the sole permanent building type for the style later described as "architecture parlante." This seems to relate not only to Newgate Gaol but also to Burke's category of the Sublime, of which he wrote: "Whatever is fitted in any sort to excite the ideas of pain and anger . . . whatever is in any sort terrible . . . is a source of the sublime."

In the late 1770s Dance remodeled a country house, Cranbury Park, in Hampshire, for a family friend, providing a top-lit ballroom that contains the seeds of the mature Dance-Soane style. This vast room has semi-domes to east and west derived from the Roman Baths, but in the center is a beautiful, shallow cross vault in a starfish pattern that was adapted from a

*XXIII. George Dance, design for the library of Lansdowne House, London, 1788–91*

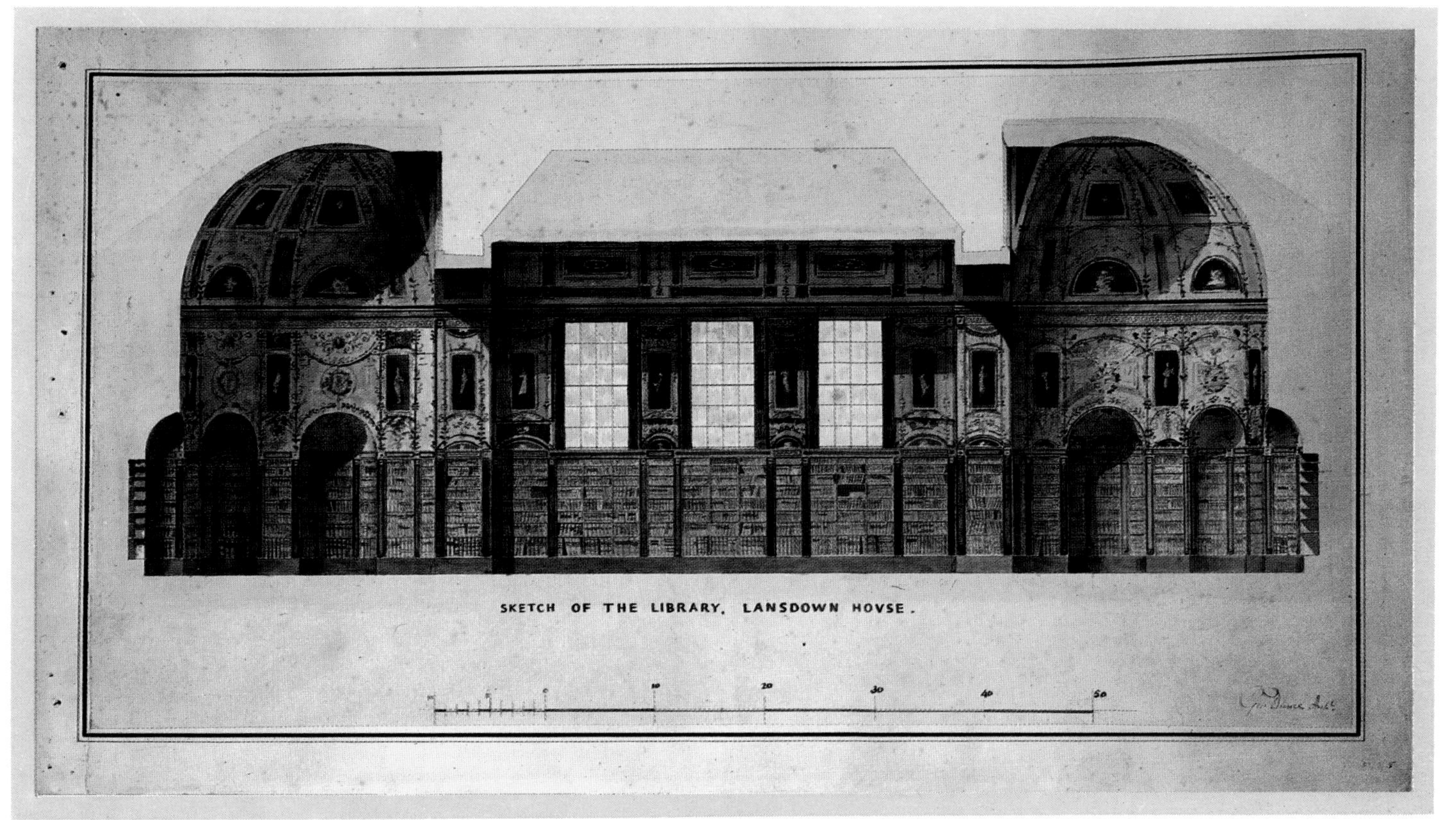

*XXIV. Sir John Soane, No. 13 Lincoln's Inn Fields (Sir John Soane's Museum), London, Breakfast Parlour 1812*

*325. Claude-Nicolas Ledoux, cemetery, ideal city of Chaux, Arc-et-Senans, section, from his* Architecture, *1804*

*326. Claude-Nicolas Ledoux, project for a cooper's house, ideal city of Chaux, Arc-et-Senans, from his* Architecture, *1804*

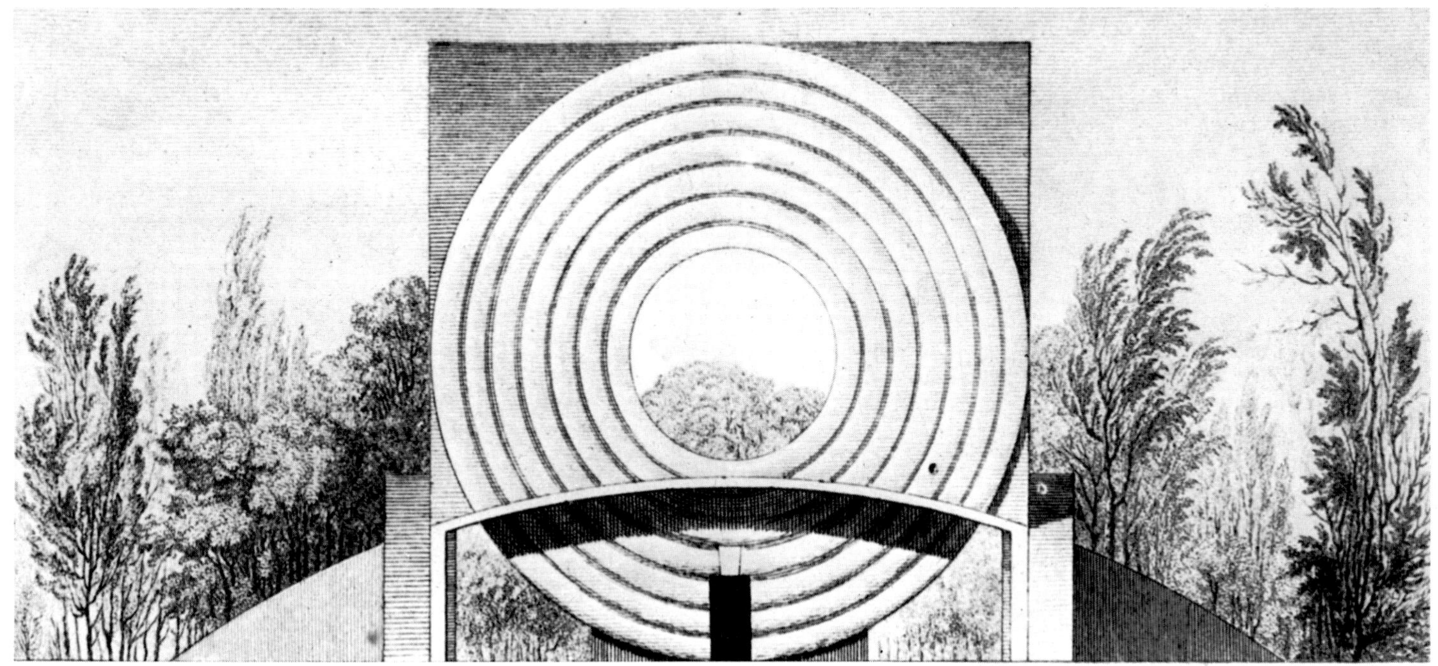

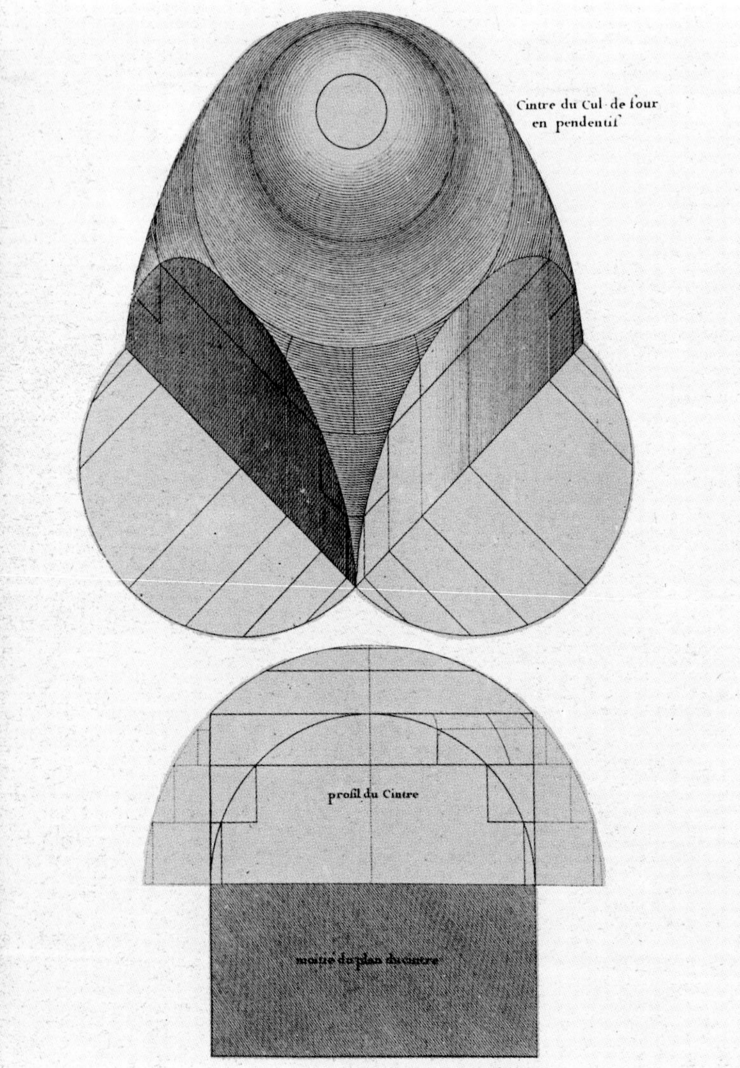


*327. Plate from Jean-Baptiste de La Rue's* Traité de la coupe des pierres, *1728*

*328. George Dance, Cranbury Park, Hampshire, detail of the ballroom ceiling, c. 1778*

*329. George Dance, Newgate Goal, London, 1768–80*

330. *George Dance, Guildhall, London, Common Council Chamber, 1777–79*

plate in Pietro Santi Bartoli's *Gli antichi sepolcri ovvero mausolei romani* (1697; new edition 1757). This important book, which was almost certainly known to Adam and was later owned by Soane, played a decisive role in disseminating knowledge of ancient Roman interior decoration. The groin vault in a starfish pattern, first imitated by Dance at Cranbury, became the hallmark of Soane's interiors, beginning with the study of his first house at Lincoln's Inn Fields, begun in 1792. The influence on Dance and Soane of this "sepulchral" architecture is particularly interesting in light of Boullée's obsession with the romantic effects of "buried architecture."

Dance developed the Cranbury theme in two interiors at the Guildhall in London, from 1777 to 1779. In the Common Council Chamber the dome and its pendentives are all parts of the same sphere, a device that may have been inspired by Jean-Baptiste de la Rue's *Traité de la coupe des pierres* (1728): Plate XXXIV shows the construction of a "cul-de-four en pendentifs sur un quarré." This is an attack on the Renaissance and Baroque conception of a domed space in which the dome is a separate handsome entity resting on clearly defined piers. At the Guildhall the dome is reduced to its essence. The whole room becomes a kind of dome, a basic tent or covering. This primitivist tent- or umbrella-like aspect is emphasized by the scalloped curves of decorative and nonstructural origin. The fluting applied to the dome is perhaps derived from the ruin of the Serapeum at Hadrian's Villa, which Dance may have seen and which was illustrated in the 1760s by Piranesi in *Vedute di Roma.* This type of fluting also became a feature of Grand Prix designs as, for example, in Sobre's Maison de Plaisance (1782). Another novelty of the Council Chamber was the space at the east and west ends that rose higher than that in the center, thus enabling the western end to be illuminated by two largely invisible windows casting light from a hidden source. This "lumière mystérieuse" was also a characteristic of the library that Dance designed within an uncompleted shell constructed by Adam at Lansdowne House, London, at the end of the 1780s. Dance remodeled Adam's vaults, creating semi-domes at each end of the long central space. The overall form of these domed spaces may derive from the Temple of Minerva Medica in Rome, but the sliced-off semi-domes, with their concealed Diocletian windows, were inspired by a French Grand Prix precedent. We find them in Pierre-Nicolas Bernard's project for a *palais de justice,* of 1782, and in Sobre's *hôtel de ville,* of five years later.

A related obsession of Dance's was top-lit octagonal halls in a stripped Gothic style, such as those at St.-Bartholomew-the-Less, London (1789); at St. Mary, Micheldever, Hampshire (1808); and at the house he built for the great patron and collector Sir George Beaumont at Coleorton, Leicestershire (1804). The combination of a kind of reductionist Gothic with Romantic toplighting echoes the ambitions of both Laugier and Boullée. In a very different interior at a London lunatic asylum, St. Luke's Hospital, Old Street (1781), Dance provided a nightmare-like, seemingly endless repetition of arches that anticipated the extreme shrill attenuation,

*331. George Dance, St. Luke's Hospital, London, interior, 1781*

*332. George Dance, project for No. 6 St. James's Square, London, after 1815*

both horizontal and vertical, of Bernard Poyet's Rue des Colonnes, Paris (1798), and Friedrich Weinbrenner's Kaiserstrasse, Karlsruhe (1808). Again we are reminded of Burke, who, in defining the delightful horrors of the Sublime, analyzed the effect of "infinity and things multiplied without end."

The abstraction and linearity that we also find in Dance's work make him an architectural counterpart to John Flaxman. Dance reduced both Gothic and classical styles to a strange disembodied synthesis that recalls Flaxman's depiction of the Greek world in his illustrations of Homer and Aeschylus, and of medieval Catholicism in his illustrations of Dante. But before we consign Dance to that chill vacuum let us recall what C. R. Cockerell said of him in his Royal Academy lectures in the 1840s: "Dance showed himself the most complete Poet Architect of his day—no one can doubt that Newgate is a prison, that St. Luke's is an asylum, prison or place of milder confinement for the unhappy and bewildered in mind, or that the front of the Guildhall, though anything but Gothic, is still the metropolitan and magnificent place of Government and civil authority."

What we have said of Dance is, in general, true of Soane, for never were two artists more mutually dependent on each other in the development of a common style. Dance, as the older man, often provided the motifs first, although the last design by him—of which we have a record—shows a definite dependence on Soane. This is his unexecuted project, dating from some time after 1815, for a house for Lord Bristol at No. 6 St. James's Square, London. It is basically a kind of warehouse, a three-storied glass box that was inspired by Soane's ruthlessly novel Loggia in the Waiting Room Courtyard at the Bank of England, of 1804–5. Soane was appointed Surveyor to the bank in 1788, succeeding Sir Robert Taylor. His extensive additions to and remodelings of Taylor's work occupied him on and off for the next thirty-six years and undoubtedly represent the apotheosis of his unique architectural style. His first task was to rebuild completely Taylor's Stock Office immediately north of the Bartholomew Lane vestibule. Rain had seeped in through Taylor's lead roof and had decayed the principal roof timbers. Soane therefore concentrated his attention on a new roof set on stone piers with brick arches springing from them, replacing Taylor's interiors of lath and plaster and timber, which had been susceptible to both fire and water. Soane's vault was constructed of what he called cones—tapering hollow blocks of terra-cotta based on those used in the Byzantine buildings of Ravenna. He chose them for their fireproof qualities as well as for their lightness. Soane's floating, disembodied space—marked by sharply incised lines, ribs, and grooves—owes something, as Summerson has shown, to the Baths of Diocletian, Dance's Common Council Chamber at the Guildhall, Taylor's Reduced Annuities Office (1782–88) at the Bank of England, Piranesi's engravings, and to Laugier's emphasis on considerations of structure and utility through analogy to the primitive hut. As an indication of the daring step Soane took at the Bank Stock Office we may

*333. George Dance, design for the library, Landsdowne House, London, 1788–91*

compare it with a related interior of 1791–93, his Yellow Drawing Room at Wimpole Hall, Cambridgeshire. In this extraordinary, domed, T-shaped room Soane evidently went as far as he dared in adapting to domestic purposes the radical novelties pioneered by Dance at the Common Council Chamber, in 1777. At the bank he allowed himself more freedom. When he turned his attention, in 1794, to Taylor's Rotunda, also in need of repair, it emerged wondrously transformed. Where Taylor's space (see illustration 242) had been a pale echo of the Pantheon, Soane's is an imaginative re-creation of the spirit—not the letter—of an antique domed space. With Dance's help he provided an abstract synthesis in which the classical orders were reduced schematically to geometrical incised lines, the whole saved from totally chill austerity by the romantic lighting effects, the "lumière mystérieuse" of Le Camus de Mézières.

In the same style as the Bank Stock Office and Rotunda, Soane went on to turn Taylor's Transfer Office immediately north of the Rotunda into the Old Shutting Room. This dates from 1794–96, and was followed, in 1797–99, by the adjacent Consols Office, with its startling ring of caryatids, which, according to the original design, was to have been decorated even more richly. The development south of the Rotunda came much later, in 1812–23, but the stylistic consistency was remarkable. The caryatids of the Consols Office, greatly increased in height, turn up in the lantern of the Old Dividend or Four Percent Office, and are replaced by a noble Ionic colonnade in the Old Colonial or Five Percent Office, both completed in 1818. From 1804 to 1805 Soane provided a new western entrance to the bank in the newly realigned Prince's Street. The Picturesque vista from the barrel-vaulted Greek Doric entrance vestibule toward the dramatic open Loggia along the north side of the Waiting Room Courtyard is one of the most brilliant realizations of Soane's belief in the "poetry of architecture." Indeed, the whole bank could be seen as an embodiment of that belief. The way in which it grew slowly and haphazardly, with Soane obliged to combine and retain all manner of heterogeneous fragments of earlier buildings, and even to remodel his own, meant that the planning was empirical and not neoclassical. None of the grand gateways really led anywhere; nothing was related to anything else in a way that an ancient Roman or a modern Frenchman would have understood. In its piecemeal, haphazard growth and plan it was thoroughly English and thoroughly Picturesque, yet in actual design no building in Europe was more neoclassical. Its poetry has never been better captured than by Sir Osbert Sitwell in his autobiographical volume *Great Morning* (1948), where he describes how in the evening "this one-storey building emptied altogether of life, and with its garden-courts and cloisters, resembled a monastery or a deserted temple rather than the most famous financial institution in the world. By one of the passionate paradoxes of its creator—surely the most original of all English architects—it seemed to offer a quiet, leafy, well-kept retreat from the world."

*334. Sir John Soane, Bank of England, London, Lothbury Court, 1797*

*335. Sir John Soane, Bank of England, London, Lothbury Court, detail of the colonnade, 1797*

*336. Sir John Soane, Bank of England, London, entrance vestibule to the Waiting Room Courtyard, 1804–05*

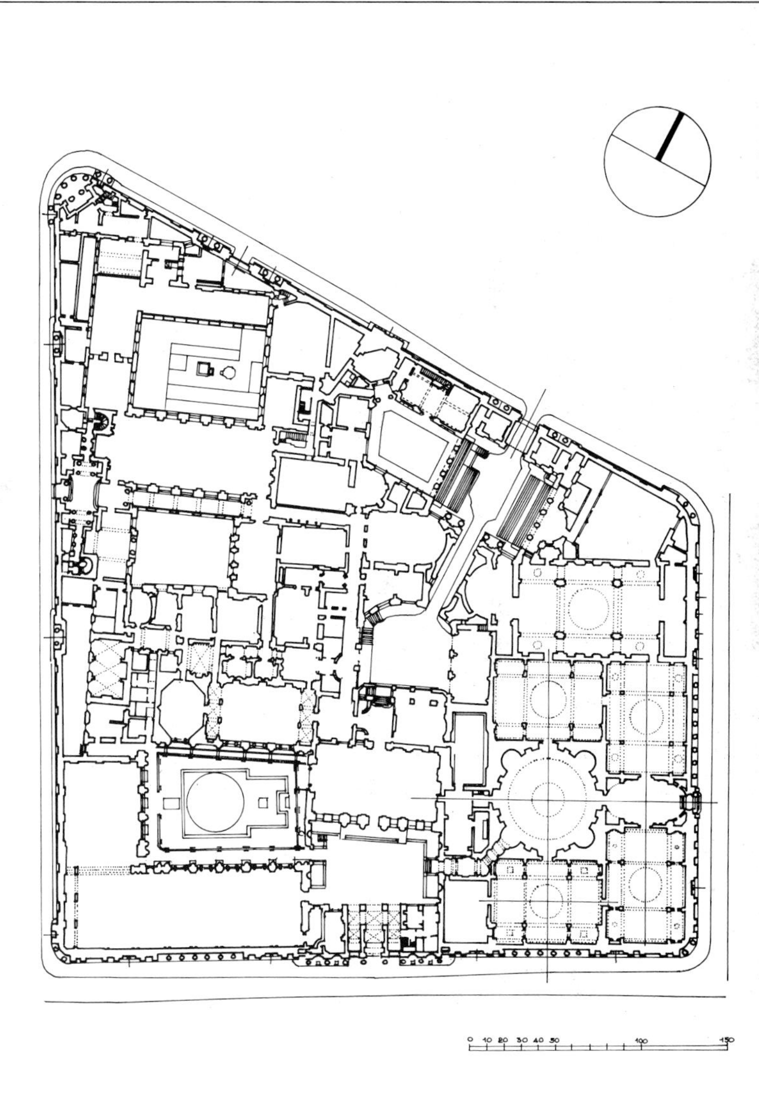


*337. Sir John Soane, Bank of England, London, 1788–1833, ground-floor plan as in 1924*

*338. Sir John Soane, Bank of England, London, Stock Office, 1792*

*339. Sir John Soane, Bank of England, London, Old Colonial Office, 1818*

*340. Sir John Soane, Pitzhanger Manor, Ealing, near London, Front Parlour, 1800–02*

*341. Sir John Soane, No. 13 Lincoln's Inn Fields (Sir John Soane's Museum). London, Dome Room, 1808–9, 1712*

One type of interior not fully exploited at the Bank of England, but particularly associated with Soane's mature style, is that dominated by a kind of hanging ceiling or domed canopy. Its first tentative appearance is in the Front Parlour of Soane's own house, Pitzhanger Manor (1800–1802), at Ealing, near London. Of markedly funereal appearance, with sarcophagi in tomblike recesses and much other antique sculpture, this room must originally have been close in spirit to Thomas Hope's contemporary house-*cum*-museum in Duchess Street, London. The shadowy and funereal overtones of Soane's room were certainly not accidental and forcibly recall Boullée's ambition to create an "architecture ensevelie." Indeed, Boullée declared in his *Essai sur l'art* that the "Temple of Death" was the type of building that, more than any other, calls for the "poésie de l'architecture," so as to convey "l'image de l'architecture ensevelie, en n'employant que des proportions basses et affaissées et enfouies dans la terre, former enfin par les matières absorbant la lumière, le noir tableau de l'architecture des ombres dessiné par l'effet d'ombres encore plus noires. Ce genre d'architecture formé par des ombres," he proudly added, "est une découverte d'art qui m'appartient. C'est une carrière nouvelle que j'ai ouverte" (see H. Rosenau, *Boullée and Visionary Architecture,* pp. 124, 135). However, in such interiors as the Breakfast Parlour (1812) at Lincoln's Inn Fields, the National Debt Redemption Office, Old Jewry, City of London (1817), the Privy Council Chamber, Downing Street (1824), the Freemasons' Hall, Great Queen Street (1828), and the Law Courts at Westminster (1820s), Soane's obsession with toplighting and with high side lighting creates an eerie and mysteriously subterranean effect—occasionally inspired by Gothic vaulting and lighting arrangements—that represents the final and uniquely personal synthesis of the "lumière mystérieuse" of the visionary architecture of France and the Picturesque tradition of eighteenth-century England.

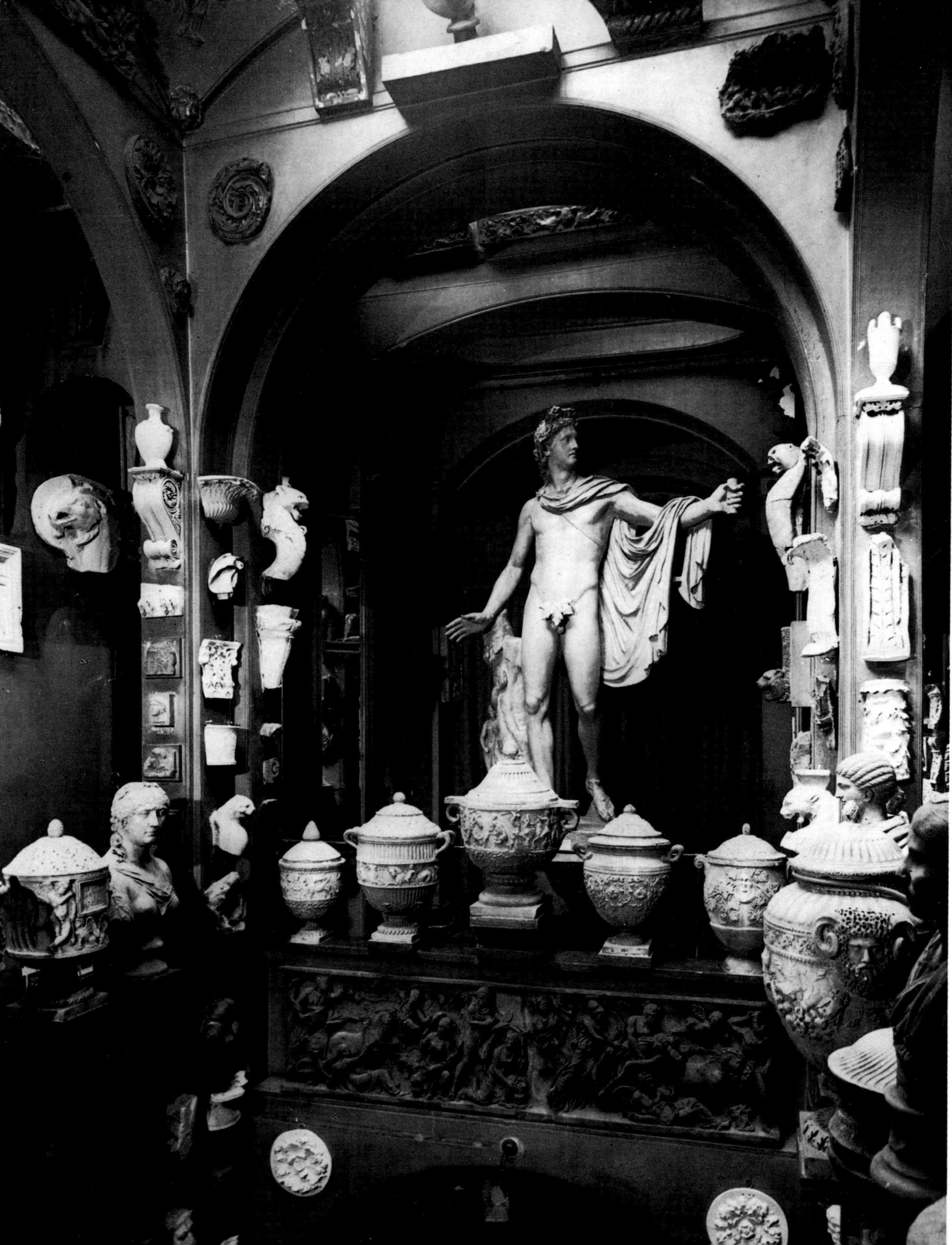

*342. Sir John Soane, No. 13 Lincoln's Inn Fields (Sir John Soane's Museum). London, Breakfast Parlour, 1812*

*343. Sir John Soane, Privy Council Chamber, London, 1824*